Social Work and Service Learning

Social Work and Service Learning

Partnerships for Social Justice

Edited by Meryl Nadel, Virginia Majewski, and Marilyn Sullivan-Cosetti

ROWMAN & LITTLEFIELD PUBLISHERS, INC.
Lanham • Boulder • New York • Toronto • Plymouth, UK

ROWMAN & LITTLEFIELD PUBLISHERS, INC.

Published in the United States of America
by Rowman & Littlefield Publishers, Inc.
A wholly owned subsidary of The Rowman & Littlefield Publishing Group, Inc.
4501 Forbes Boulevard, Suite 200, Lanham, Maryland 20706
www.rowmanlittlefield.com

Estover Road
Plymouth PL6 7PY
United Kingdom

British Library Cataloguing in Publication Information Available

Library of Congress Cataloging-in-Publication Data

Social work and service learning : partnerships for social justice / edited by Meryl
Nadel, Virginia Majewski, and Marilyn Sullivan-Cosetti.
    p. cm.
  Includes index.
  ISBN-13: 978-0-7425-5945-5 (cloth : alk. paper)
  ISBN-10: 0-7425-5945-9 (cloth : alk. paper)
  ISBN-13: 978-0-7425-5946-2 (pbk. : alk. paper)
  ISBN-10: 0-7425-5946-7 (pbk. : alk. paper)
 1. Social work education. 2. Service learning. I. Nadel, Meryl, 1947– II. Majewski,
Virginia, 1948– III. Sullivan-Cosetti, Marilyn, 1943–

HV11.S5864 2007
361.3071'55—dc22
                                            2007003742

Printed in the United States of America

♾ ^TM The paper used in this publication meets the minimum requirements of American
National Standard for Information Sciences—Permanence of Paper for Printed Library
Materials, ANSI/NISO Z39.48-1992.

Contents

Contents

PART III—ASSESSING OUTCOMES OF SERVICE-LEARNING EXPERIENCES

PART IV—THE BIGGER PICTURE: CIVIC ENGAGEMENT ON CAMPUS

List of Figures

List of Tables

Preface

We are pleased to offer the social work and service-learning communities this unique volume focusing on service learning in social work. Our goal is to provide a readable and comprehensive introduction to service learning as a social work education modality by bringing together theoretical background, practical on-the-ground experience, and research-based outcomes data. With authors from programs across the United States (from Hawaii to Nebraska and West Virginia to New York), programs that are rural, urban, and suburban, public and private, large and small, undergraduate and graduate, we demonstrate that service learning is a viable and productive option for human service agencies and students at both the graduate and undergraduate levels. The service-learning approach can be applied across the curriculum: it is particularly effective in encouraging critical thinking, active learning, and student empowerment and in increasing students' grasp of social justice issues, as our authors illustrate. It can also serve as preparation for the field practicum.

The origins of this book date to May 2003 and to the Invitational Conference on Service Learning in Social Work Education, sponsored by the University of Nebraska at Omaha. Three social work faculty engaged in service learning, Paul Sather, Patricia Carlson, and Barbara Weitz (chapter 6), were motivated to organize the conference by concerns in two areas. First, they had experienced a paucity of stimulating workshops on service learning at the national conferences. Second, when interesting, innovative approaches were presented, little time was provided to evaluate and consider the implications raised by the presentations. As Paul Sather, a conference organizer, stated, "We concluded that there needed to be some kind of forum where those engaged in the work could discuss issues related to definitions of the work and cutting-edge approaches to incorporating service learning in social work education" (personal communication, 2006).

The resulting small, highly interactive, energizing, two-day meeting offered ample opportunity to hear from experts, reflect on the wide variety of presentations, and brainstorm future directions. Outcomes included the establishment of a social work service-learning listserv, a workshop at the 2003 Association of Baccalaureate Social Work Program Directors (BPD) conference, and the decision to publish a monograph on social work service learning. The monograph was originally conceived as one of a series of discipline-specific service-learning volumes published under the auspices of the American Association for Higher Education (AAHE). Upon discovering that no further monographs were planned, the editors identified Rowman & Littlefield as an excellent publishing match for what has become a book rather than a monograph. About half of the chapters herein originated as presentations at the Omaha conference.

We view this volume as filling a gap for two particular populations, although it may well be useful to others. We anticipate that social work educators will make use of the book to familiarize themselves with service learning as a pedagogical approach. In addition to chapters providing theoretical background and outcomes assessment data, we include chapters describing model courses to encourage faculty and invite both replication and innovation. We hope that all chapters will excite and inspire faculty to experiment with this creative and stimulating teaching method. Faculty members may want to read the entire book to gain a thorough grounding in the service-learning perspective or may focus on the areas of greatest interest to them. However, readers will find that even chapters that may seem tangential to their interests contain ideas that can spark the development of creative service-learning projects. Please note that this book does not include discussion of the field practicum.

It is our intent that the book be useful to social work practitioners and human services administrators in addition to educators. Service learning provides agencies, communities, and practitioners with a different opportunity than the typical field placement. Service learning is often conceptualized as located at the midpoint on a continuum from volunteer work to internship, combining the opportunity to serve with the opportunity to learn. It is community focused, offering agencies a chance to collaborate with academic colleagues to meet identified community needs. We expect that administrators and practitioners will glean new ideas for solving problems or implementing needed services by means of service-learning projects. Throughout their chapters, our authors demonstrate the genuine community collaboration and increased appreciation for community social justice issues generated by service-learning projects.

We have divided the content into four sections. We think this organization makes the volume useful and accessible to those who already utilize service learning, as well as to those new to the approach. However, please note that chapters often cross these boundaries. For example, program chapters utilize evaluation, while evaluation chapters also describe their programs. Part I offers an overview of theories and concepts crucial to an understanding of service-learning pedagogy. In chapter 1, Amy Phillips provides an overview of the service-learning approach, including historical and definitional issues, as well as notes the importance of maintaining a social change/social justice focus. Service learning is situated within the higher education civic engagement movement. Chapter 2, by Sharlene Furuto, examines the components of service-learning pedagogy, emphasizing its theoretical underpinnings and comparing traditional and service-learning structures. In chapter 3, Virginia Majewski takes the reader from the theoretical to the practical, considering strategies for infusing service-learning activities into social work courses across the curriculum using the Council on Social Work Education's *Educational Policy and Accreditation Standards (EPAS)* (2001) as a guide.

Part II offers models for incorporating service learning into a wide variety of courses in all curriculum areas. Its authors share their own experiences with the goal of inspiring others. David Droppa, author of chapter 4, illustrates how service learning may be used in a social welfare policy and services course to give students real-life policy experience. Marie Watkins, Leanne Charlesworth, and Annemarie House, in chapter 5, show how service learning in youth development agencies can benefit students in a beginning practice course. Chapter 6, by Paul Sather, Patricia Carlson, and Barbara Weitz, focuses on the research course component of a more comprehensive service-learning infusion sequence. This chapter describes the creative integration of multicourse service learning with a long-term commitment to two local communities of color. Chapter 7's authors, Natalie Ames and Stephene Diepstra, employ an engaging oral history project to facilitate students' learning of human behavior and the social environment concepts. In chapter 8, John Yoakam and Patricia Bolaños depict how four courses utilized service-learning projects to deepen students' understanding of human diversity. Meryl Nadel, in chapter 9, writes about a service-learning immersion experience at a summer camp for HIV-infected and -affected families that gives students the opportunity to learn about populations-at-risk through working directly with one such group. To conclude this section of the book, Robin Allen, William Rainford, Roy Rodenhiser, and Kara Brascia discuss the integration of a service-learning activity into a large general education (core) course (chapter 10).

Part III explores outcomes assessment of service-learning experiences. Chapter 11, by Rose Malinowski, depicts an assessment process that evaluates a complex, four-semester, service-learning project. Chapter 12's authors,

Virginia Majewski and Allan Turner, present the results of a long-term follow-up study of participants in a service-learning immersion course on an American Indian reservation. Marilyn Sullivan-Cosetti, in chapter 13, describes the analysis of a comprehensive, three-year, undergraduate, service-learning sequence.

Our final section, Part IV, positions social work service learning for future involvement within the broader context of the civic engagement movement. The authors of chapter 14, Mary Campbell and Nancy Bragg, urge social work educators to play major leadership roles in this important educational arena. The book concludes with descriptions of the contributors. Most have provided e-mail addresses and are open to contact from interested readers.

The language of service learning bears mention as it reflects this particular modality. Social justice is a frequent theme in these chapters, indicating the ability of service learning to allow students to experience both injustice and resilience. The reader will also notice that the term *client* is not used. *Community partner*, *participant*, and other terms indicating the reciprocal nature of the work are explained as they appear. Finally, a note on the hyphen. In accord with Campus Compact usage, *service learning* is not hyphenated as a noun but is hyphenated as an adjective (i.e., service-learning course).

This volume has truly been a collaborative effort. While the editors thank our publisher, all the contributors, and their respective programs, this book could not have come to fruition without the participation of students and community partners. It is our fondest hope that this book will succeed in conveying some of the excitement and mutual learning that occurs when service-learning projects are effectively implemented. Please use it as an aid to create your own versions of active, reflective, experiential service and learning for social justice.

REFERENCE

Council on Social Work Education. (2001). *Educational policy and accreditation standards*. Alexandria, VA: Author.

Part I

DEFINING THE FIT:
THEORY AND CONCEPTS

Chapter One

Service Learning and Social Work Education: A Natural but Tenuous Connection

Amy Phillips

OVERVIEW OF SERVICE LEARNING

For the past two decades, service learning has gained attention and increased implementation as a mode of experiential education in primary, secondary, and postsecondary environments.[1] The 1980s saw the creation of Campus Outreach Opportunity League (1984) and Campus Compact (1985), both of which promoted civic engagement and learning through service in higher education. The National and Community Service Act of 1990 provided, among other authorizations, grants to public schools to support service learning, and the National and Community Service Trust Act of 1993 established the Corporation for National and Community Service, which encourages service activities through its three major programs: Senior Corps, AmeriCorps, and Learn and Serve America. These pieces of national legislation, plus independent institutional- and community-based initiatives, have together ensured the growing utilization of service learning at all educational levels. Campus Compact reports that its membership grew from 4 member institutions in 1985 to 975 member institutions in 2005 with a total of 12,480 service-learning courses offered at these institutions during the 2004–2005 academic year.[2] In the context of K–12 education, the National Youth Leadership Council in its third annual service-learning research compendium, *Growing to Greatness 2006,* reports that 28 percent of "public schools engaged in service-learning which is curriculum-based, has clear learning objectives, and meets community needs" (Scales and Roehlkepartain's study, as cited in National Youth Leadership Council 2006, vi).

Sometimes referenced as a synonym for generic volunteer and practica experiences, service learning is actually an intentional, structured tool for social

3

change rooted in a "philosophy of reciprocity, which implies a concerted effort to move from charity to justice" (Jacoby and Associates 1996, 9). Service learning not only enhances students' knowledge in a particular discipline but also requires that they apply that knowledge to the practice of addressing social problems in collaboration with community partners who define and direct the community-based service-learning experience. Students also engage in structured reflection on the connections between theory and practice, thereby increasing their critical-thinking skills. While various interpretations and definitions of service learning abound, service learning is generally seen as "a set of pedagogical practices that attempts to synthesize and connect service experiences to specific spheres of knowledge for the dual purposes of mastering that knowledge and developing citizen skills that support one's active participation in democratic processes" (Koliba 2000, 825).

With service learning gaining in popularity in communities, K–12 schools, and universities, numerous resources have become available to assist educators and community members interested in starting, improving, and discussing service-learning endeavors. Examples of such resources include the National Service-Learning Clearinghouse (www.servicelearning.org, a project of Learn and Serve America) with its website and listservs, Campus Compact (www.compact.org), the University of California, Berkeley, Service-Learning Research and Development Center (http://gse.berkeley.edu/research/slc), the *Michigan Journal of Community Service Learning* (www.umich.edu/~mjcsl), the American Association for Higher Education's series on service learning in the disciplines, the National Service-Learning Partnership (http://nslp.convio.net/site/PageServer?page name=ABT_index), the Center for Information Research on Civic Learning and Engagement (CIRCLE, www.civicyouth.org), and numerous national and regional conferences.

SERVICE LEARNING AND THE HIGHER EDUCATION CIVIC ENGAGEMENT MOVEMENT

In the arena of higher education, service learning has been a strong component of the higher education civic engagement (HECE) movement, a movement often acknowledged to have been prompted by Ernest L. Boyer's 1990 publication, *Scholarship Reconsidered: Priorities of the Professoriate*. In this influential work, Boyer called upon the academy to redefine the meaning of scholarship and suggested that social problems should inform scholarly investigation through a "scholarship of application" (21). As Boyer put it, "To sustain the vitality of higher education in our time, a new vision of scholarship is required, one dedicated not only to the renewal of the academy but, ultimately, to the renewal of society itself" (81).

The HECE movement prompted the *Journal of Public Affairs* to devote its first special issue in 2002 to civic engagement and higher education, with John Saltmarsh of national Campus Compact serving as the issue's guest editor. Saltmarsh explained the publication of this supplemental issue by noting the ongoing effort of institutions of higher education to reclaim their own civic identity in the face of "corporatization":

> A civic vision of higher education's role and responsibility in democratic renewal is a much needed counterweight to the corporatization of higher education. Higher education has been led down the path of corporate restructuring and management, instilling a privatized, consumerist vision of the academy. While there has been an equilibrium that historically defined the purpose of education in the United States, with preparation for democratic citizenship balanced by job preparation, the dominance of the corporate model has created a pervasive imbalance. Reclaiming the civic mission of higher education redresses that imbalance. The pedagogical corollary to the corporate model is the commodification of education, turning students into consumers, knowledge into a consumer good, and citizens into spectators. Redressing the pedagogical imbalance means shifting from a "banking" model of teaching and learning to adopting a "dialogic" model where students, teachers, and community members are participants in an educational process where knowledge is collectively created. (Saltmarsh 2002, vi–vii)

In the context of Saltmarsh's introductory statements, the issue's articles proceed to contribute to the civic engagement and higher education conversation by discussing the institutionalization of service learning, campus-community partnerships, community-based research, and other civic engagement issues and methods.

From the standpoint of the HECE movement, service learning is a form of civic engagement, and Saltmarsh's definition of civic engagement as "community-based public problem solving that not only generates new knowledge and higher order cognitive outcomes, but develops the civic skills of critical thinking, public deliberation, collective action, and social ethics" (Saltmarsh 2002, viii) might easily apply to service learning as well.

As a result of the pedagogy's increasing application in higher education, the academic literature is rich with numerous definitions of service learning (National Service-Learning Clearinghouse, n.d.; Olney and Grande 1995), principles and paradigms of practice (Gronski and Pigg 2000; Jacoby and Associates 1996; Wright 2000), and articulations of its anecdotal and empirical outcomes (e.g., Astin et al. 2000; Everett 1998; Eyler and Giles 1999; Eyler et al. 2001; Hironimus-Wendt and Lovell-Troy 1999; Knee 2002; Koliba 2000; Pascarella and Terenzini 2005; Rocha 2000; Roschelle, Turpin, and Elias, 2000. See also the *Michigan Journal of Service Learning, Special Issue*, 2000). Service-learning outcome studies have shown results ranging from "reductions in modern racism" (Myers-Lipton 1996, as cited in Hironimus-Wendt and Lovell-Troy 1999, 362), to "more sophisticated analyses and solutions for social problems and issues" (Batchelder and Root 1994, as cited in Everett 1998, 300), to "[better] ability to apply concepts beyond the classroom" (Miller 1994 and Rocha 2000, as cited in Knee 2002, 215), to commitment to social activism (Pascarella and Terenzini 2005). There is some, but far less, discussion regarding the impact of service learning on community partners (Bringle and Hatcher 1996, as cited in Williams, King, and Koob 2002; Bushouse 2005; Cruz and Giles 2000; Jorge 2003; Kozeracki 2000; Roschelle, Turpin, and Elias 2000; Schmidt and Robly 2002; Ward and Wolf-Wendel 2000), on classroom faculty (Bringle et al. 2000; Driscoll 2000; Lowe and Reisch 1998; Pribbenow 2005; Wallace 2000), on student academic learning (Eyler 2000), and on the university environment and structure (Holland 2000). In general, however, there is widespread agreement that service learning, with its praxis of study-action-reflection, has the potential in higher education to enhance student classroom learning, critical awareness, and civic participation, as well as to build university and community partnerships for addressing community needs.

SERVICE LEARNING, CIVIC ENGAGEMENT, AND SOCIAL WORK EDUCATION

Since its core curriculum includes values/ethics, diversity, social and economic justice, and social welfare policy and services, one would expect social work to be a foundational discipline of the HECE movement and at the forefront of service-learning methodological development. But the relationship between the three has been tenuous, at best. It is true that Barry Checkoway, professor of social work and urban planning at the University of Michigan, was a coordinator of and participant in the Wingspread Conferences in 1998 and 1999[3] and he is an influential voice in the HECE conversation; however, with the exception of Checkoway (who is actually a historian by training, not a social worker), the twenty-three contributors to the *Journal of Public Affairs* issue discussed above were from disciplines such as communications, anthropology, history, sociology, education, political science, American studies, public health/services/government, economics, and English. In addition, as A. K. Johnson Butterfield and T. M. Soska reported in a 2004 issue of the *Journal of Community Practice* on universities and civic engagement, social work has been virtually absent from federally sponsored projects and conferences related to community-university partnerships for community building.

A review of titles and abstracts from articles published over the last ten years in social work education journals indicates that the disciplinary dialogue about civic engagement has been sporadic but present, with various pedagogical approaches to a civically engaged curriculum finding their way into publication. In the *Journal of Social Work Education*, eleven articles discussed pedagogical frameworks or methods related to political participation, participatory action research, service learning, community-based learning, and policy practice (Anderson and Harris 2005; Forte 1997; Hamilton and Fauri 2001; Ishisaka et al. 2004; McNicoll 1999; Poulin, Kauffman, and Silver 2006; Rocha 2000; Rocha and Johnson 1997; Sanfort 2000; Wells 2006; Wolk et al. 1996). The *Journal of Baccalaureate Social Work* published four articles related to service learning (Bordelon 2003; King 2003; Lucas 2000; Sanders, McFarland, and Sunday Bartolli 2003), and the *Journal of Teaching in Social Work* produced seven articles regarding social change interventions, "hands-on learning," policy practice, participatory action research, and service learning (Butler and Coleman 1997; Hayashi and Favuzzi 2001; Juliá and Kondrat 2000; Knee 2002; Raber and Richter 1999; Saulnier 2000; Williams, King, and Koob 2002). It is a tribute to these educators that this conversation has taken place in the literature, given that the dialogue has largely occurred outside the context of a common language for discussing service learning and civic engagement, without routine use of the "service learning" label for many of the methods mentioned above, and without disciplinary recognition that service learning helps support social work education's standing as a civically engaged discipline.

As can be seen from the publication dates of many of the articles referenced above, social work education is a relative latecomer to service-learning methodology. A. George (1982, as cited in Knee 2002) and N. Kropf and M. Tracey (2000, as cited in Williams, King, and Koob 2002) speculate that this is due to the discipline's view of, and reliance on, the field practicum as the social work program's service-learning component. This reliance, however, overlooks a primary function of service learning, which is to enable the student to engage in service "as a community member, not as a service provider" (Williams, King, and Koob 2002, 58). Also, it is this educator's experience that students in social work practica are more engrossed in learning the specific knowledge and skills relevant to their particular placements than in embodying the service-learning hallmark principles of critical reflection and reciprocity (Jacoby and Associates 1996).

Nevertheless, service learning as a defined methodology is increasingly finding its way into the social work classroom and academic literature (Anderson and Harris 2005; Bordelon 2003; King 2003; Knee 2002; Lucas 2000; Pierpont, Pozzuto, and Powell 2001; Poulin, Kauffman, and Silver 2006; Rocha 2000; Timmermans and Bouman 2004; Wells 2006; Williams, King, and Koob 2002). As R. Hayashi and T. Favuzzi (2001) have pointed out, service-learning activities and structures may easily be incorporated into social work courses since the absence of accreditation guidelines allows for substantial flexibility and creativity. (There is no mention of service learning in the Council on Social Work Education's *Educational Policy and Accreditation Standards*.)

Social work's sluggishness in adopting service learning as a training tool is unfortunate since, as mentioned above, service learning's beneficial outcomes are well noted, it is a methodology consistent with social work's history of experiential education, and it may be uniquely suited to addressing some of social work's educational difficulties. The latter include field supervisors' concerns about student preparedness for field placements (DeWeaver and Kropf 1995 and Koerin and Miller 1995, as cited in Williams, King, and Koob 2002), the shortage of macro practice field placements (Butler and Coleman 1997), and student struggles to reflect critically on the theory/practice connection in field placements (Coates and McKay 1995). N. Kropf and M. Tracey (2002) have suggested that classroom service-learning projects could address field placement issues by serving as a "bridge" to field placements. S. S. Butler and P. A. Coleman (1997) advocate for service learning as an opportunity for students to gain much-needed macro practice experience, and the reflective aspect of service learning could further bolster students' ability to think critically about theory and experience.

More significantly, however, service learning represents an opportunity for social work to reinforce its mission to "promote social justice and social change with and on behalf of clients" (National Association of Social Workers 1999, 1). This author suggests that just as "social justice"[4] is one of the foundational values inherent in social work's purpose, so should "social change for social justice" emerge as a primary purpose of social work service learning. Actually, all six core values[5] of social work are appropriate for informing the purpose of social work service learning,[6] but as numerous social workers and others have pointed out, social work is a frequent supporter of the societal status quo. Without a firm grounding in a justice orientation as reflected in progressive, critical perspectives and practices, the profession is at continual risk of forsaking its social change mission (Finn and Jacobson 2003; Chambon, Irving, and Epstein 1999; Pease and Fook 1999; Margolin

1997; Coates and McKay 1995; Fisher 1995; Specht and Courtney 1994; Coates 1992; Abramovitz 1993; Freire and Moch 1990).

Service-learning theorists and practitioners in various disciplines, including social work, have been discussing service learning for the purpose of promoting social change for social justice. Some of their ideas, reviewed below, may inform social work's intradisciplinary discussion about the purpose and use of service learning.

SERVICE LEARNING FOR SOCIAL CHANGE AND SOCIAL JUSTICE

In the May 1996 issue of the *Phi Delta Kappan*, Joseph Kahne and Joel Westheimer raised the question "In the Service of What?" in regard to service learning. Speaking in the context of the 1990 national service legislation and primarily of public school projects (though their thinking is applicable at the postsecondary level), they proposed that "little attention has been given to sorting out the goals and motivations that underlie the spectrum of service learning projects" (598). They stated that the then current focus of service learning was charity, not change, suggesting that "while requiring students to 'serve America' . . . might produce George Bush's 'thousand points of light,' it might also promote a thousand points of the status quo" (596). To sort out what service-learning projects are in the service of, Kahne and Westheimer proposed a conceptual "change versus charity" matrix for examining service-learning curricula (see table 1.1) (595). These authors posit that examining the moral, political, and intellectual dimensions of service-learning projects will help identify the underlying purpose of a service-learning program.

Catherine Ludlum Foos (1998), a philosophy professor, took issue with the growing charity-versus-change question regarding service learning. Her discussion was grounded in a juxtaposition of C. Gilligan's (1977, 1982) moral development theory with K. Morton's 1995 essay validating various approaches to service. For Foos, preferencing social change orientations over other models could be equivalent to valuing male over female moral

Table 1.1. Service-Learning Goals

	Moral	*Political*	*Intellectual*
Charity	Giving	Civic Duty	Additive Experience
Change	Caring	Social Reconstruction	Transformative Experience

Source: Kahne and Westheimer (1996).

reasoning, and she argued against "'a single mode of social experience and interpretation'" (20), advocating instead for moving students toward "mature service," whether in the context of a charity approach or a social change approach.

Sociologists Robert Hironimus-Wendt and Larry Lovell-Troy in their 1999 essay, "Grounding Service Learning in Social Theory," discussed the praxis (reflection plus action) components of service learning and deemed service-learning pedagogy particularly attractive to sociologists because of its fit with "activist community sociology," its validation of "experience as one among many sources of knowledge," and its potential to further "the goals of social justice and the development of our students into citizen-scholars, consistent with the critical sociology paradigm" (Hironimus-Wendt and Lovell-Troy 361; see chapter 3 for more information on praxis). They acknowledged that their approach to service learning was grounded in critical education theory along the lines of Paulo Freire and Henry Giroux. In deference, however, to some educators less "critical in their theoretical orientations" (363), Hironimus-Wendt and Lovell-Troy proposed grounding service learning in the philosophies of John Dewey and C. Wright Mills. Such grounding "[conceptualizes] education as an active process requiring reflective thinking about experience . . . [links] school and community . . . [and embeds] educational ideas in a larger hope for social melioration" (366). The authors hoped to attract additional colleagues to service learning through this particular theoretical grounding.

Ward and Wolf-Wendel (2000), from the field of education, used the service mission of special-focus colleges and universities (SFCUs)—tribal colleges, historically black colleges and universities, and Hispanic-serving institutions—to highlight the "doing for" orientation of service learning at predominantly white institutions, as opposed to the "doing with" service orientation at SFCUs. "Doing for" service learning "emphasizes service that is centered on the campus—that is, service that is focused on doing for the community" and benefits campus constituents (768). The authors identified this as the charity approach, as opposed to the social change, critical community-service approach (Rhoads 1997)[7] more prevalent at SFCUs. Basing their discussion in social change and critical community-service frameworks, Ward and Wolf-Wendel provide ideas for how campuses can move away from a privileged "doing for" approach to a more community-centered "doing with" approach.

A. R. Roschelle, J. Turpin, and R. Elias (2000) offered a service-learning case study from the peace and justice studies program at the University of San Francisco. Viewing service learning as praxis, through their qualitative study, these authors demonstrated that a new "sociological imagination" developed in students through the reflection/action process of service learning and that it "foster[ed] a lasting commitment to social justice" (840).

Ryan Tolleson Knee (2002) used service learning in an undergraduate social work research course to counter conventional pedagogy, which Knee saw as alienating students from research and from an examination of real-life social problems. While students in his traditional courses struggled to comprehend the connection between research and social justice, Knee found that, as a result of the service-learning course, students "understood how the [service-learning project] helped to promote citizen participation, and in particular how it empowered oppressed citizens by actively seeking their input and by using their contributions to effect positive change, thereby solidifying a stronger correlation between core social work values and research" (221).

Marullo and Edwards (2000) adopted the charity versus social justice paradigm as a way of synthesizing the work of contributors to their edited, two-issue series of *American Behavioral Scientist* on "universities' responses to troubled times" [volumes 42(5) and 43(5)]. The authors were straightforward about their intention not only to showcase community-service activities grounded in a social justice approach but to offer these efforts as examples of programs that can help make higher education "a vehicle for transforming society to make it more just" (897). Marullo and Edwards clearly view service learning as "justice work," as long as service learning (1) involves a politicization process for students and (2) emerges from and simultaneously reinforces an institutional transformation process. The authors posed a set of six questions designed to promote reflection on how service learning can reflect both processes:

1. Does the community-service work undertaken by students in their service-learning classes empower the recipients?
2. Are students required to examine whether and how their service work helps to address the root causes of the problem?
3. Does the service learning encourage students to see that the shortcomings of individuals in need are not the sole cause of the problems that service-learning activities attempt to address?
4. Are the institutional operations of the university-community partnerships organized in a way to support and sustain the collaborative efforts of faculty, students, and community members?
5. Does the university-community collaboration build community, increase social capital, and enhance diversity?
6. Do educational institutions operate their community partnership programs in accord with social justice principles?

Amy Phillips

PROMOTING SERVICE LEARNING
IN SOCIAL WORK EDUCATION

Obviously, service-learning educators from a variety of disciplines have been engaged in conversation for some time about the nature of service learning — its purposes, paradigms, and principles. Social work needs only to continue to add its voice to the discussion, and, in fact, the School of Social Work at the University of Nebraska at Omaha has encouraged this process through its 2003 Invitational Conference on Service Learning in Social Work Education and its sponsorship of the 2004 Midwest Biennial Social Work Education Conference on Civic Education and Social Work Education. But to strengthen the relationship between service learning and social work education, and to do justice to service learning as methodology and philosophy, it seems that social work educators must formally and collectively engage in a developmental process steeped in reflection, collaboration, reciprocity, and commitment to social change for social justice. This author would offer the following "generative praxis" as a potential process:

1. Small groups (possibly under the sponsorship of the Council on Social Work Education) of social work educators, their community partners, students, and relevant campus staff meet across the country for a designated period, studying the service-learning literature, engaging in service learning, and reflecting on their experiences in order to develop articulations about the purpose(s) of service learning in social work education. It may be true, as this and other authors have pointed out, that social work education has been slow to adopt service-learning pedagogy, but this hesitation may well work to the advantage of social work. Given the breadth and depth of the literature about service learning already available, it is highly beneficial to have that information at our disposal and to use it in this generative praxis, regardless of the discipline from which it emerges. These service-learning praxis groups also draw on social work values, ethics, and theories for assistance in articulating the purposes of social work service learning and ensure that group methodology is consistent with service learning and social work principles.
2. As articulations of purposes begin to emerge, groups move toward identifying the components of social work service learning needed to reflect and carry out its purposes.
3. Throughout the process, groups are free to be in conversation with each other and with the larger social work community (possibly facilitated by the Council on Social Work Education) for feedback, input, output, and any other generative activity.

4. From the above service-learning praxis (perhaps the first for any field) emerges a critical and creative paradigm for service learning in social work education that can be replicated as needed on the macro (national) or micro (campus/community) level. It would be this educator's preference that such a paradigm not become an institutionalized or accreditation standard as such a designation often leads to a decidedly non-critical perspective and often-lengthy shelf life.

5. With a disciplinary definition and understanding of service learning, social work could add further substantive research to the body of literature attempting to demonstrate the impacts of service learning on campus and community participants.

It would also be this educator's preference that "social change for social justice" act as a strong frame of reference for the above praxis. With this frame of reference, a language of service learning as "justice learning" might emerge, thereby reflecting and promoting all core values of the social work profession and encouraging more extensive and critical civic engagement on the part of both students and the discipline at large.

NOTES

1. For an overview of the history of service learning in the United States, see Peter Titlebaum, Gabrielle Williamson, Corine Daprano, Janine Baer, and Jayne Brahler, *Annotated History of Service Learning, 1862–2002*, on the National Service-Learning Clearinghouse website. Retrieved September 3, 2006, from www.servicelearning.org/welcome_to_service-learning/history/index.php.

2. Campus Compact, *2005 Annual Service Statistics*. Retrieved September 3, 2006, from www.compact.org/about/statistics/2005.

3. The conferences, held at the Wingspread Conference Center in Racine, Wisconsin, brought together university administrators, faculty, and representatives from foundations and civic organizations to "formulate strategies for renewing the civic mission of the research university" (see the *Wingspread Declaration on Renewing the Civic Mission of the American Research University* by Harry Boyte and Elizabeth Hollander. Retrieved September 3, 2006, from http://iche.sas.upenn.edu/overview/wingspread.htm).

4. In the book presentation of their Just Practice Framework, J. L. Finn and M. Jacobson (2003) discuss various definitions of social justice. They draw on D. Saleebey (1990) to provide a social justice definition for social work:

 a) Social resources are distributed on the principle of need with the clear understanding that such resources underlie the development of personal resources, with the proviso that entitlement to such resources is one of the gifts of citizenship.

b) Opportunity for personal and social development is open to all with the understanding that those who have been unfairly hampered through no fault of their own will be appropriately compensated.

c) The establishment, at all levels of a society, of agendas and policies that have human development and the enriching of human experience as their essential goal and are understood to take precedence over other agendas and policies is essential.

d) The arbitrary exercise of social and political power is forsaken.

e) Oppression as a means for establishing priorities, for developing social and natural resources and distributing them, and resolving social problems is forsworn. [Saleebey, D. (1990). Philosophical disputes in social work: social justice denied. *Journal of Sociology and Social Welfare, 17*(2), 29–40.]

5. The National Association of Social Workers Code of Ethics lists social work's core values as service, social justice, the dignity and worth of the person, the importance of human relationships, integrity, and competence.

6. Michael King provides a nice discussion of the link between service learning and key social work values in his 2003 article in the *Journal of Baccalaureate Social Work*.

7. R. A. Rhoads (1997) offers eight "guiding principles for structuring critical community service activities." They are reproduced here in the hope that they may be useful to social work discussions regarding service learning in social work education.

1. Critical community service calls attention to the notion that a commitment to working with others is fundamentally tied to an individual's sense of self and vision of others.

2. Critical community service demands that mutuality undergird all service activities and projects.

3. Community building must be recognized as a central objective to critical community service.

4. Critical community service seeks to build multicultural service communities and this ought to involve a wide range of diverse students in community service work.

5. Critical community service must include reflective action linked to broader social concerns, with the goal being to foster a critical consciousness among students.

6. Critical community service seeks to link traditional classroom learning (academic or theoretical knowledge) with the experiential learning that often accompanies service.

7. Critical community service is intended to create social change, and therefore it is expected that participants engage in the larger struggle to improve social conditions.

8. Critical community service must be thought of as part of the larger struggle to create a more liberatory form of education.

REFERENCES

Abramovitz, M. (1993). Should all social work students be educated for social change? *Journal of Social Work Education, 29*(1), 6–11, 17–18.

Anderson, D. K., and Harris, B. M. (2005). Teaching social welfare policy: A comparison of two pedagogical approaches. *Journal of Social Work Education, 41*(3), 511–26.

Astin, A., Vogelgesang, L., Ikeda, E., and Yee, J. (2000). *How service learning affects students*. Los Angeles: University of California, Higher Education Research Institute.

Batchelder, T. H., and Root, S. (1994). Effects of an undergraduate program to integrate academic learning and service: Cognitive, prosocial, and identified outcomes. *Journal of Adolescence, 17*(4), 341–56.

Bordelon, T. D. (2003). People first: A case study in partnering with the community. *Journal of Baccalaureate Social Work, 8*(2), 147–61.

Boyer, E. L. (1990). *Scholarship reconsidered: Priorities of the professoriate*. Princeton, NJ: Carnegie Foundation for the Advancement of Teaching.

Bringle, R. G., Games, R., Foos, C. L., Osgood, R., and Osborne, R. (2000). Faculty fellows program: Enhancing integrated professional development through community service. *American Behavioral Scientist, 43*(5), 882–94.

Bringle, R. G., and Hatcher, J. A. (1996). Implementing service learning in higher education. *Journal of Higher Education, 67*(2), 221–39.

Bushouse, B. K. (2005). Community nonprofit organizations and service-learning: Resource constraints to building partnerships with universities. *Michigan Journal of Community Service Learning, 12*(1), 32–40.

Butler, S. S., and Coleman, P. A. (1997). Raising our voices: A macro practice assignment. *Journal of Teaching in Social Work, 15*(1/2), 63–80.

Chambon, A. S., Irving, A., and Epstein, L. (Eds.). (1999). *Reading Foucault for social work*. New York: Columbia University Press.

Coates, J. (1992). Ideology and education for social work practice. *Journal of Progressive Human Services, 3*(2), 15–30.

Coates, J., and McKay, M. (1995). Toward a new pedagogy for social transformation. *Journal of Progressive Human Services, 6*(1), 27–43.

Council on Social Work Education. (2001). *Educational Policy and Accreditation Standards*. Retrieved September 3, 2006, from www.cswe.org.

Cruz, N. I., and Giles, D. W., Jr. (2000). Where's the community in service-learning research? *Michigan Journal of Community Service Learning, Special Issue*, 28–34.

DeWeaver, K., and Kropf, N. (1995). *Gatekeeping in baccalaureate social work education*. San Diego, CA: Council on Social Work Education.

Driscoll, A. (2000). Studying faculty and service-learning: Directions for inquiry and development. *Michigan Journal of Community Service Learning, Special Issue*, 35–41.

Everett, K. D. (1998). Understanding social inequality through service learning. *Teaching Sociology, 26*(4), 299–309.

Eyler, J. (2000). What do we most need to know about the impact of service-learning on student learning? *Michigan Journal of Community Service Learning, Special Issue*, 11–17.

Eyler, J., and Giles, D. E., Jr. (1999). *Where's the learning in service-learning?* San Francisco, CA: Jossey-Bass.

Eyler, J., Giles, D. E., Jr., Stenson, C., and Gray, C. (2001). *At a glance: What we know about the effects of service-learning on college students, faculty institutions and communities, 1993–2000* (3rd ed.). Nashville, TN: Vanderbilt University and the Corporation for National Service.

Finn, J. L., and Jacobson, M. (2003). *Just practice: A social justice approach to social work*. Peosta, IA: Eddie Bowers Publishing.

Fisher, R. (1995). Political social work. *Journal of Social Work Education, 31*(2), 194–203.

Foos, C. L. (1998). The "different voice" of service. *Michigan Journal of Community Service Learning, 5,* 14–21.

Forte, J. (1997). Calling students to serve the homeless: A project to promote altruism and community service. *Journal of Social Work Education, 33*(1), 151–66.

Freire, P., and Moch, M. (Trans.). (1990). A critical understanding of social work. *Journal of Progressive Human Services, 1*(1), 3–9.

George, A. (1982). A history of social work field instruction. In B. W. Sheafor and L. E. Jenkins (Eds.), *Quality field instruction in social work* (37–59). New York: Longman.

Gilligan, C. (1977). In a different voice: Women's conceptions of self and morality. *Harvard Educational Review, 47*(4), 481–517.

———. (1982). *In a different voice: Psychological theory and women's development*. Cambridge, MA: Harvard University Press.

Gronski, R., and Pigg, K. (2000). University and community collaboration: Experiential learning in human services. *American Behavioral Scientist, 43*(5), 781–92.

Hamilton, D., and Fauri, D. (2001). Social workers' political participation: Strengthening the political confidence of social work students. *Journal of Social Work Education, 37*(2), 321–32.

Hayashi, R., and Favuzzi, T. (2001). A course on disability advocacy combining distance education, community-service learning, and on-campus seminars. *Journal of Teaching in Social Work, 21*(3), 111–29.

Hironimus-Wendt, R. J., and Lovell-Troy, L. (1999). Grounding service learning in social theory. *Teaching Sociology, 27*(4), 360–72.

Holland, B. (2000). Institutional impacts and organizational issues related to service-learning. *Michigan Journal of Community Service Learning, Special Issue*, 52–60.

Ishisaka, H. A., Sohng, S. S. L., Farwell, N., and Uehara, E. S. (2004). Teaching notes: Partnership for integrated community-based learning: A social work community-campus collaboration. *Journal of Social Work Education, 40*(2), 321–36.

Jacoby, B., and Associates. (1996). Service-learning in today's higher education. In B. Jacoby and Associates, *Service-learning in higher education: Concepts and practices* (3–25). San Francisco, CA: Jossey-Bass.

Johnson Butterfield, A. K., and Soska, T. M. (2004). University-community partnerships: An introduction. *Journal of Community Practice, 12*(3/4), 1–11.

Jorge, E. (2003). Outcomes for community partners in an unmediated service-learning program. *Michigan Journal of Community Service Learning, 10*(1), 28–38.

Juliá, M., and Kondrat, M. E. (2000). Participatory action research and MSW curricula. *Journal of Teaching in Social Work, 20*(3), 101–24.

Kahne, J., and Westheimer, J. (1996). In the service of what? The politics of service learning. *Phi Delta Kappan, 77*(9), 592–99.

King, M. E. (2003). Social work education and service learning. *Journal of Baccalaureate Social Work, 8*(2), 37–48.

Knee, R. T. (2002). Can service learning enhance student understanding of social work research? *Journal of Teaching in Social Work, 22*(1/2), 213–25.

Koerin, B., and Miller, J. (1995). Gatekeeping policies: Terminating students for nonacademic reasons. *Journal of Social Work Education, 31*(2), 247–60.

Koliba, C. J. (2000). Moral language and networks of engagement: Service learning and civic education. *American Behavioral Scientist, 43*(5), 825–38.

Kozeracki, C. A. (2000). ERIC Review: Service learning in the community college. *Community College Review, 27*(4), 54–71.

Kropf, N., and Tracey, M. (2000). *Service learning as a transition into foundation field.* Paper presented at the Annual Program Meeting of the Council on Social Work Education, February.

———. (2002). Service learning as a transition into foundation field. *Advances in Social Work, 3*(1), 60–71.

Lowe, J. I., and Reisch, M. (1998). Bringing the community into the classroom: Applying the experiences of social work education to service-learning courses in sociology. *Teaching Sociology, 26*(4), 292–98.

Lucas, E. T. (2000). Linking social work and service learning. *Journal of Baccalaureate Social Work, 5*(2), 167–78.

Margolin, L. (1997). *Under the cover of kindness: The invention of social work.* Charlottesville: University Press of Virginia.

Marullo, S., and Edwards, B. (2000). The potential of university-community collaboration for social change. *American Behavioral Scientist, 43*(5), 895–912.

McNicoll, P. (1999). Issues in teaching participatory action research. *Journal of Social Work Education, 35*(1), 51–62.

Miller, J. (1994). Linking traditional and service-learning courses: Outcome evaluations utilizing two pedagogically distinct models. *Michigan Journal of Community Service Learning, 1*, 29–36.

Morton, K. (1995). The irony of service: Charity, project and social change in service-learning. *Michigan Journal of Community Service Learning, 2*, 19–32.

Myers-Lipton, S. (1996). Effect of a comprehensive service-learning program on college students' level of modern racism. *Michigan Journal of Community Service Learning, 3*, 44–54.

———. (1998). Effect of a comprehensive service-learning program on college students' civic responsibility. *Teaching Sociology, 26*(4), 243–58.

National Association of Social Workers. (1999). *Code of ethics.* Washington, DC: Author.

National Service-Learning Clearinghouse. (n.d.). "Service-Learning Is . . ." Retrieved on September 3, 2006, from www.servicelearning.org/article/archive/35.

National Youth Leadership Council. (2006). *Growing to greatness 2006: The state of service-learning project.* St. Paul, MN: Author.

Olney, C., and Grande, S. (1995). Validation of a scale to measure development of social responsibility. *Michigan Journal of Community Service Learning, 2*, 43–53.

Pascarella, E. T., and Terenzini, P. T. (2005). *How college affects students: A third decade of research*, vol. 2. San Francisco, CA: Jossey-Bass.

Pease, B., and Fook, J. (Eds.). (1999). *Transforming social work practice: Postmodern critical perspectives.* London: Routledge.

Pierpont, J. H., Pozzuto, R., and Powell, J. Y. (2001). Service learning and systems of care: Teaching students to learn from clients. *Journal of Family Social Work, 5*(3), 79–93.

Poulin, J., Kauffman, S., and Silver, P. (2006). Field notes: Serving the community and training social workers: Service outputs and students outcomes. *Journal of Social Work Education, 42*(1), 171–84.

Pribbenow, D. A. (2005). The impact of service-learning pedagogy on faculty teaching and learning. *Michigan Journal of Community Service Learning, 11*(2), 25–38.

Raber, M., and Richter, J. (1999). Bringing social action back into the social work curriculum: A model for "hands-on" learning. *Journal of Teaching in Social Work, 19*(1), 77–91.

Rhoads, R. A. (1997). *Community service and higher learning: Explorations of the caring self.* Albany: State University of New York.

Rocha, C. J. (2000). Evaluating experiential teaching methods in a policy practice course: The case for service learning to increase political participation. *Journal of Social Work Education, 36*(1), 53–63.

Rocha, C. J., and Johnson, A. K. (1997). Teaching family policy through a policy practice framework. *Journal of Social Work Education, 33*(3), 433–44.

Roschelle, A. R., Turpin, J., and Elias, R. (2000). Who learns from service learning? *American Behavioral Scientist, 43*(5), 839–47.

Saleebey, D. (1990). Philosophical disputes in social work: Social justice denied. *Journal of Sociology and Social Welfare, 17*(2), 29–40.

Saltmarsh, J. (2002). Introduction. *Journal of Public Affairs, 6, Supplemental Issue 1,* v–ix.

Sanders, S., McFarland, P., and Sunday Bartolli, J. (2003). The impact of cross culture service-learning on undergraduate social work students' perceptions of culture, race, and economic justice. *Journal of Baccalaureate Social Work, 9*(1), 19–40.

Sanfort, J. (2000). Developing new skills for community practice in an era of policy devolution. *Journal of Social Work Education, 36*(2), 183–86.

Saulnier, C. F. (2000). Policy practice: Training direct service social workers to get involved. *Journal of Teaching in Social Work, 20*(1), 121–44.

Scales, P. C., and Roehlkepartain, E. C. (2006). Community service and service-learning in U.S. public schools, 2004. In James C. Kielsmeier, Marybeth Neal, and Alison Crossley, *Growing to Greatness 2006: The State of Service-Learning Project* (vi). St. Paul, MN: National Youth Leadership Council.

Schmidt, A., and Robly, M. A. (2002). What's the value of service-learning to the community? *Michigan Journal of Community Service Learning, 9*(1), 27–33.

Specht, H., and Courtney, M. E. (1994). *Unfaithful angels: How social work has abandoned its mission.* New York: Free Press.

Timmermans, S. R., and Bouman, J. (2004). Seven ways of teaching and learning: University-community partnerships at baccalaureate institutions. *Journal of Community Practice, 12*(3/4), 89–101.

Wallace, J. (2000). The problem of time: Enabling students to make long-term commitments to community-based learning. *Michigan Journal of Community Service Learning, 7,* 133–41.

Ward, K., and Wolf-Wendel, L. (2000). Community-centered service learning: Moving from doing for to doing with. *American Behavioral Scientist, 43*(5), 767–80.

Wells, M. (2006). Teaching notes: Making statistics "real" for social work students. *Journal of Social Work Education, 42*(2), 397–404.

Williams, N., King, M., and Koob, J. J. (2002). Social work students go to camp: The effects of service learning on perceived self-efficacy. *Journal of Teaching in Social Work, 22*(3/4), 55–70.

Wolk, J. L., Pray, J. E., Weismiller, T., and Dempsey, D. (1996). Political practica: Educating social work students for policymaking. *Journal of Social Work Education, 32*(1), 91–100.

Wright, M. D. G. M. (2000). A critical-holistic paradigm for an interdependent world. *American Behavioral Scientist, 43*(5), 808–24.

Chapter Two

The Components of Service Learning as Pedagogy in Social Work Education

Sharlene Furuto

The preceding chapter discussed the historical background of service learning and its connection to the higher education civic engagement movement and reviewed the relevant literature. This chapter will look at several definitions of service learning, the theoretical underpinnings of service learning from a social work perspective, and the components of service learning. In addition, the author proposes a model for service learning integrated into a micro practice course.

DEFINITIONS OF SERVICE LEARNING

A commonly cited definition of *service learning* is that of R. Bringle and J. Hatcher: "a course-based, credit-bearing, educational experience in which students (1) participate in an organized service activity that meets identified community needs and (2) reflect on the service activity in such a way as to gain further understanding of course content, a broader appreciation of the discipline, and an enhanced sense of civic responsibility" (1995, 112). Another scholastic definition offered by J. P. F. Howard states, "Academic service learning is a pedagogical model that intentionally integrates academic learning and relevant community service" (1998, 22). The emphasis is on a pedagogical, rather than a values, leadership development, or social responsibility model; an intentional effort is made to use community-based learning in support of academic learning and to use academic learning to inform the community; there is an integration of experiential and academic learning; and the service-learning experience must be relevant to the particular academic course content.

Service learning has also been defined as a method of teaching that emphasizes the integration of community service with academic coursework, curricula, or graduation requirements in schools, colleges, and universities (Serow et al. 1996; Chapin 1998; Peterson and McCook 2003). Course goals and objectives are enhanced by thoughtfully organized service that the community identifies. Students spend a sufficient amount of time engaged in providing service alongside community members. A reflection time during which students can think, talk, and write about what was done and seen during the actual service activity is integral to service learning (Chapin 1998; Feinberg 2002).

Furthermore, R. C. Wade and D. W. Saxe (1996) indicate that service learning should have a social action perspective. Service-learning experiences are frequently directed toward questioning the status quo, responding through compassionate service, and promoting social justice for those in need. Change, care, social reconstruction, and a transformative experience are characteristics of service-learning goals (Chapin 1998).

Operationalizing the foregoing definitions through engaging in service and learning provides students the opportunity to encounter competing perceptions of the common good, to grapple with diverse viewpoints on the root causes of social problems, and to question whom and what knowledge is for. Service learning not only helps students master the content of the course but also asks students to consider the social work context and how that knowledge base is used in practice (Enos and Troppe 1996). Service learning, in essence, complements the theoretical base of social work practice.

THEORETICAL UNDERPINNINGS OF SOCIAL WORK THAT SUPPORT SERVICE LEARNING

Theories related to the functioning of and interrelationships between social systems, the strengths perspective in practice, and empowerment all support service learning as part of the social work curriculum. This section briefly reviews these theoretical underpinnings of social work and illustrates how they support the use of service-learning pedagogy in social work education.

Systems Theory in Social Work Education

Systems theory, or the systems approach, with its attention to the person-in-environment as an interrelated whole rather than to linear cause-and-effect relationships, provides the foundation for social work practice (Dale et al. 2006; Rogers 2006; Zastrow and Kirst-Ashman 2001) and may well apply to service learning in social work education. The person-in-environment represents an integral whole in which the person and the situation are both cause and effect in a complex set of relationships. The focus of systems theory is on the processes or the interactions occurring within the person-in-environment.

When conducting assessments, for example, students need to understand the complex interactions between the recipient of service and other social systems; that is, they must study the whole system rather than just its parts. Social systems theory enables them to identify problems in the dynamics, processes, and transactions within the system as a whole rather than focusing only on the person or only on the environment, or on a linearly defined cause-effect relationship.

Systems theory concepts, such as systems of concern, boundaries, purpose, development, organizational structure, roles, rules, communications, incentives, and power (Compton, Galaway, and Cournoyer 2005), can well be applied to service-learning projects in many courses across the social work curriculum. During project implementation, students become part of a dynamic system, which they learn to analyze and appreciate.

The Strengths Perspective

The strengths perspective represents a widely accepted approach to social work practice that focuses on the strengths, rather than the weaknesses or problems, of the client, family, group, organization, or community. D. Saleebey posits that "everything you do as a social worker will be predicated, in some way, on helping to discover and embellish, explore and exploit clients' strengths and resources in the service of assisting them to achieve their goals, realize their dreams, and shed the irons of their own inhibitions and misgivings, and society's domination" (2006, 1).

This collaborative approach depends greatly on the social worker's continuously looking for strengths in the client system and for opportunities in the environment to advance the problem-solving process. Furthermore, the recipient of service must be encouraged not only to believe in him- or herself but also to use these strengths to become empowered and liberated from the problem situation.

Essential to the strengths perspective is the triadic relationship of three groups of three components: competence, capacities, and courage; promise, possibility, and positive expectations; and resilience, reserves, and resources (Saleebey 2006). Also important are the concepts of empowerment, membership, resilience, healing and wholeness, dialogue and collaboration, and suspension of disbelief (Saleebey 2006).

The strengths perspective comprises several principles: (1) every individual, group, family, organization, and community has strengths; (2) trauma and abuse, illness and struggle may be injurious, but they may also be sources of challenge and opportunity; (3) the upper limits of the capacity to grow and change are assumed to be unknown, and the social worker must take individual, group, and community aspirations seriously; (4) clients are best served by the social worker's collaborating with them; (5) every environment is full of resources; and (6) caring, caretaking, and context are central themes (Saleebey 2006).

Four subsidiary principles of the strengths perspective advise the social worker (1) not to take no for an answer, (2) to help correct the effects of being labeled, (3) to take advantage of the considerable resources of culture and ethnicity, and (4) to normalize (to turn from dwelling on problems to focusing on what the client wants and the possibilities for getting where he or she wants to be) and to externalize (to get people's stories out to those individuals, associations, agencies, and institutions that need to hear them) (Compton, Galaway, and Cournoyer 2005).

In the service-learning context, as in the broader social work practice context, it is plausible to expect that students should apply, in a conscious manner, the strengths approach with community members. Instructors might also model this approach by identifying strengths in the students themselves and pointing out how students apply them during the service-learning experience.

Empowerment

The philosophy of empowerment practice requires attention to the redistribution of power, resources, and decision making so that stakeholders can decide on goals and actions for themselves (Staples 1999). A partnership or empowerment approach to planning, implementation, and evaluation involves community members and constituencies, processes that may result in relevant, respectful, and effective programs (Poindexter, Saunders Lane, and Capobianco Boyer 2002).

Empowerment is a complex concept that has both personal and political implications, according to K. K. Miley, M. O'Melia, and B. DuBois (2004). At the personal level, empowerment refers to a subjective state of mind— feeling competent and experiencing a sense of control. At the political level, it refers to the objective reality of opportunities in societal structures and the reallocation of power through a modification of social structures (Swift and Levin 1987). "Empowerment involves the process of increasing personal, interpersonal, or political power so that individuals, families, and communities can take action to improve their situations," according to L. M. Gutierrez

(1994, 202). Empowerment emphasizes strengths and creating solutions that incorporate elements of social action.

Social workers engaged in empowerment-focused practice seek to develop the capacity of individuals to understand their environment, make choices, take responsibility for their choices, and influence their life situations through organization and advocacy. Empowerment-focused social workers also seek to gain a more equitable distribution of resources and power among different groups in society. This concentration on developing the capacity of individuals to understand and influence their environment for equity and social justice is key to acquiring more equitable resource distribution in a democratic society (Gamble and Weil 1995).

The principles of an empowerment approach include the following, according to J. A. B. Lee (1994):

1. All oppression is destructive of life and should be challenged by social workers and clients.
2. The social worker should maintain a holistic vision in situations of oppression.
3. People empower themselves, and social workers should assist.
4. People who share common ground need each other to attain empowerment.
5. Social workers should establish an "I and I" relationship with clients.
6. Social workers should encourage the client to speak for him- or herself.
7. The social worker should maintain a focus on the person as victor.
8. The social worker should maintain a social change focus.

Social work students learn about systems theory, the strengths approach, and empowerment throughout the social work curriculum, more specifically in their required courses on human behavior in the social environment (HBSE). This knowledge can be applied throughout the social work curriculum as it provides the theoretical underpinnings for all of practice. Students familiar with this theoretical base who apply it in their service learning gain a deeper knowledge and understanding of what the theoretical concepts mean and how they are manifest in reality. Students who apply this theoretical knowledge in the micro, mezzo, and macro practice courses, as well as in policy, research, and courses on substance abuse, domestic violence, child welfare, and the like, will also gain a deeper and richer understanding of the social work course content.

Social work educators, as role models in the professional use of self, apply systems theory, the strengths perspective, and empowerment as they develop and nurture the service-learning experience. For example, they assess and

identify students' strengths for the implementation of service-learning projects. They help students become empowered with respect to their own skill
development when they inject students into an already existing dynamic system to carry out a service-learning experience. Applying and modeling this
knowledge can itself be a learning experience for their students.

With this brief overview of how students and educators can benefit from
the application of systems theory, the strengths approach, and empowerment,
the next section addresses the essential components of service learning.

THE COMPONENTS OF SERVICE LEARNING AS PEDAGOGY

A growing literature describes the introduction of service learning in higher education pedagogy (Woolcock 1997; Heffernan 2001; Jacoby and Thomas
1996). J. Saltmarsh and K. Heffernan (2000) cite the common principles of accepted academic practice in community-service learning: (1) establish that academic credit is for learning and not for service, (2) do not compromise academic rigor, (3) set learning goals for students, (4) establish criteria for the
selection of community-service placements, (5) provide educationally sound
mechanisms to harvest the community learning, (6) provide supports for students to learn how to harvest the community learning, (7) minimize the distinction between the student's community-learning role and classroom-learning
role, (8) rethink the faculty instructional role, (9) be prepared for uncertainty
and variation in student learning outcomes, and (10) maximize the community-
responsibility orientation of the course.

Several other authors have described the components of service learning
(Cohen and Kinsey 1994; Hollis 2002; Butin 2003; Weigert 1998), echoing
the following four criteria established by the National and Community Service Act of 1990 (as cited in Cohen and Kinsey 1994):

1. Students participate in and learn through organized service experiences
   that meet community needs and are coordinated in collaboration with the
   school and community.
2. The service-learning experience is integrated into the academic curriculum, specifically providing structured time to ponder, discuss, or write
   about actual service activities.
3. The service-learning experience affords students the opportunity to use
   newly acquired skills and knowledge in real-life situations in their own
   communities.
4. The service-learning experience and related activities enhance what is
   taught in school by extending student learning beyond the classroom and

into the community, even helping the student develop a sense of caring for others.

S. A. Hollis (2002) cites nine components when using service learning as a form of pedagogy: (1) preliminary planning, goal setting, and administrative techniques involving close coordination with the community organization and its staff; (2) student participation in a formal orientation and review of the community organization's structure, goals, and terms of service; (3) consideration of students' interests in making work assignments; (4) student involvement in meaningful and socially beneficial work assignments; (5) inclusion of focused reading and research assignments that relate directly to the conditions they encounter in their service work; (6) incorporation of critical reflection journals designed to encourage students to focus on social conditions and use sociological principles to frame their observations; (7) focused in-class discussions and reflection; (8) reflective evaluation, which encourages students to synthesize their understandings, reflect on how their own powers of observation developed over the course of the experience, and arrive at new and better-informed conclusions about their experiences and observations; and (9) evaluation incorporating feedback from the faculty, the served community, and the host community organization.

Additionally, D. W. Butin (2003) claims that four criteria are necessary for service learning to be legitimate, ethical, and useful: respect, reciprocity, relevance, and reflection. First, it is important that students always be respectful of the circumstances, outlooks, and ways of life of those being served. The server is a human being who must respect the situation he or she is entering. Second, the service should be meaningful and relevant and benefit both the server (often the white, middle-class student) and the served (often the underprivileged population). In fact, the community should not only identify the particular need for the service but also work alongside the students. There needs to be a reciprocal relationship between the student and the community whereby both learn from and serve each other, perhaps in different ways.

Third, the service must be relevant to the academic content of the course. The service should be a central component of a course and help students engage with, reinforce, extend, or question the course content. Students should be encouraged to see inequities in the community and bring these observations into the classroom. Last, service learning does not provide transparent experiences. Reflection is required to provide context and meaning. Students need to have sufficient contact with the community to appreciate not only the ambiguity and complexity of the service-learning experience but also the results of meaningful research, discussion, and reflection. Reflection helps students draw upon their observations and experiences to understand the "real" world and barriers social workers face when advocating for change.

K. M. Weigert (1998) discusses service learning in contrast to other forms of experiential learning. She proposes six key elements to differentiate effective service learning from voluntarism, community service, and other forms of experiential learning: (1) the student provides meaningful service that is useful or helpful and makes a contribution, (2) the service that the student provides meets a need or goal, (3) members of the community collaborate with the faculty to define the need or service, (4) the service provided by the students is a manifestation of one or more course objectives, (5) service is integrated into the course through one or more assignments that require some form of reflection on the service in the context of course objectives, and (6) assignments grounded in service are evaluated or graded based on the learning rather than merely the service, and the community has a role in the assessment.

Common to the above service-learning components espoused by the National Community Service Act as cited in J. Cohen and D. Kinsey (1994), Hollis (2002), Butin (2003), and Weigert (1998) are the student, the community, and the university in partnership. The following section provides an example of service learning in a micro social work practice course designed and implemented by the author. This example illustrates the significance of each partner in the learning process.

INTEGRATION OF SERVICE LEARNING INTO A MICRO SOCIAL WORK PRACTICE COURSE

This educational model of service learning in a social work micro practice course emphasizes the importance of three partners: the student, the community, and the university. All partners are active collaborators in the service-learning experience, as each is central to the success of student learning, community enhancement, and social work education. Regular and frequent contact among all three partners promotes an ideal experience from which all partners benefit.

Student Roles and Responsibilities

The student has several crucial responsibilities when engaged in the service-learning project. First, the student becomes familiar with the concept of service learning, what it is, what it is not, and how it is connected not only to the course objectives and assignments but also to the real world. This is important whether the service-learning assignment is optional or mandatory.

Second, the student is responsible not only for learning the concepts and skills from the textbook and classroom lectures and activities but also for applying these while working with community members. For example, in the micro practice course, students use their knowledge of the planned change process and basic interviewing skills in their interactions with community members. Oftentimes, agency staff members quiz students about the latest theory being used in multilevel social work practice, giving students the opportunity to be major contributors in sharing knowledge.

Third, the student participates fully in meaningful community service within the realm of micro social work practice that community members themselves have identified. In doing so, students need to be dependable, trustworthy, confidential, and honest while interacting with community members and agency staff.

Fourth, the student needs to stop, focus, and reflect upon what is happening periodically. Reflection is the tool students use to process and synthesize observations, information, and ideas gained through the service experience and in the classroom. Here, students can analyze concepts, evaluate their experiences, and form opinions in the context of the micro social work practice course, advocacy, civic responsibility, and social justice. Oftentimes, students keep a reflection journal or write a reflection paper.

Fifth, to extend individual learning to class learning, students share their service-learning experience and reflections in small or large group discussions. Students may be required to acknowledge their learning in actual case presentations, class discussions, or class presentations. Some common reflection themes students have discovered when doing micro service learning include the following: everyone needs help at some time or other, civic responsibility is important, dependability and reliability are critical when working with others, and sometimes theory and practice are not congruent. In addition, the student further enhances learning by reflecting on the application and critique of assigned readings, class lectures, and exercises; gaining deeper understanding of inequity and organizing for economic justice; and growing and developing personally, professionally, or both while serving individuals.

Likewise, to extend individual learning to enhance the community, the student may be required to share information gathered and analyzed from the community. For example, students who conduct life-reflection oral history interviews with seniors may produce a book of remembrance for the senior.

Finally, students sometimes discover when reflecting that they have learned lessons and gained life experiences that were available only in the community. Having an actual service recipient with whom to talk, rather than a classmate with whom to role-play, can be a powerful learning experience for undergraduate and graduate students. Learning outside the classroom sometimes goes beyond theories and skills to answering ultimate questions such as, What happened? What can be done? and What can I and others do?

Community Roles and Responsibilities

The second partner in service learning is the community. A professional community-university partnership or reciprocal relationship, in which both the human service organization and university are actively engaged, is critical for student learning, community enhancement, and the implementation of service-learning pedagogy. Preliminary preparation often occurs with the collaboration of the faculty member and community leader or agency director prior to the start of the academic term. The key role of the community members or service providers in identifying service needs in response to the university's request cannot be overstated.

First, the community takes responsibility for identifying the service the students will perform. The community knows its needs best and is in a prime position to define this service. The service component of one course in Missouri (Heffernan 2001) sought to acquaint students with problem solving and the needs of people with disabilities. Students were required to assist individuals with physical impairments in a variety of tasks, such as reading and writing letters. Students kept a weekly reflective journal and made a final presentation of an accessory product designed for their client. The client came to class to contribute to the discussion of the feasibility of the use of the product.

Second, it is the community that provides the service experience. The service needs to be meaningful to both the student and the consumer. The service needs to give students the opportunity to use generalist social work practice knowledge and communication skills to perform tasks that enhance the life of the consumer. The service is community-based and community-driven. While both the university and community collaborate on the parameters of the service to be provided, it is the community that is the host for the service.

Third, having community members work alongside students and engage in the service can be beneficial to both parties. While the student engages in the civic responsibility of volunteerism, community members are broadening the student's worldview of poverty, powerlessness, and marginalization. For instance, students can serve as models for adolescents recovering from substance abuse, while community members can share their consumer perspectives and life wisdom.

Fourth, community members receive service directly or indirectly. Most students work directly with a limited number of community residents; however, students are often able to work with a small number of people for the indirect benefit of the community at large. For example, students who use guided questionnaires to interview community members for a community assessment may produce a report that can be used to support a grant application for a residential facility for crystal methamphetamine users.

Fifth, the organization actively facilitates the service-learning experience on-site by orienting the student to the community in general, the organization in particular, persons to be served, special populations, student responsibilities, other service providers, and relevant social, political, economic, health, and educational issues. The student needs to be aware of the community and its history, population, leadership, issues, and resources; the organization and its purpose, clientele, staff, policies, and funding; the clientele's needs, strengths, limitations, and uniqueness; the responsibilities and expectations of community and staff members; the service providers not only in the organization but also outside in the local and greater community; and the relevant issues that impact the community and consumers being served. For example, if a disproportionately large number of parents die in their fifties due to diabetes and cardiovascular problems caused by obesity, resulting in poverty for surviving spouses and teenage children, then perhaps the student needs to know about this health issue so as to work more efficaciously with these community residents.

Sixth, students should be supervised regularly, with academic, practice, and reflection guidelines agreed upon by both the faculty member and supervisor. The importance of encouraging reflection should be clear. Supervisors should have easy access to faculty members, and instructors should feel free to visit the service-learning site.

Finally, supervisors should have means by which to evaluate students and services performed on the micro level. The university may provide this evaluation tool and consider it when grading the student. An evaluation of the service-learning program should also be carried out.

University and Faculty Roles and Responsibilities

The third partner is the university, which most often, through its faculty or service-learning staff, takes the initiative to propose and prepare for the experience long before the term begins.

First, social work faculty members must be familiar with service learning and how it can be used successfully as a form of pedagogy in micro practice.

In addition, most instructors engage in preliminary service-learning experiences by initiating relationships with organizations to identify appropriate sites and create and maintain community partners. Capacity building and community building may also occur well before the student is placed at the service-learning site.

Second, the faculty member designs the syllabus whereby the micro course purpose, objectives, content, readings, assignments, and class activities are integrated into and/or support the service-learning experience. In the author's course, students need to be able to connect expected competencies with what is applied while serving with and learning from an oppressed group in the community.

Third, social work faculty should prepare students for working with an at-risk population that likely has problems unfamiliar to the students. Instructors should provide students with a beginning knowledge of basic theories, frameworks, paradigms, stages, approaches, skills, values, and ethics for working with a special population at a particular life stage and for addressing issues and working with relevant programs and policies. For example, in the author's course, students need to possess practice knowledge, skills, values, and ethics that will help them work effectively at the micro level with their special populations. Knowledge of the theoretical underpinnings for micro practice, such as systems theory and the strengths and empowerment approaches, in addition to interpersonal, interviewing, and communication skills, can readily be used when working with community members. Students need to understand the planned change process and basic social work values related to confidentiality and informed consent. An appropriate pedagogical tool in conjunction with the service activity might be an in-class or online discussion of ethical dilemmas and the use of an ethical dilemma framework to guide practice.

Throughout the term, classroom-learning activities, such as exercises, simulations, case studies, and role-plays, can complement the lectures and readings while fortifying the service-learning experience. Instructors may develop assignments that encourage students to apply course knowledge and skills while providing service.

Fourth, instructors must help students reflect on their experiences, growth, discoveries, and disappointments. Students who engage in service learning should be assigned to reflect in journals, papers, class discussions, or presentations through use of guided questions. Instructors should make an effort to respond to these assignments appropriately to foster further student growth and development.

If service learning is optional and not all the students in the class are so engaged, then it is critical that the instructor regularly provide time for in-class reports from the service-learning students that answer reflection questions, such as What is happening in the community? Why is it happening? Who did what? How does this link to the textbook and lectures? Is there an imbalance in this community? What can I do for social justice? How do I feel about serving? What stereotypes and myths are dissolving? and How am I growing personally and/or professionally?

Fifth, the instructors are responsible for grading students. The service-learning assignment generally forms only part of the course requirements, and it is the faculty member who ultimately evaluates and grades the students' service-learning assignments. While the community organization supervisor is oftentimes asked to complete an evaluation of students, and while the instructor takes that evaluation into consideration when determining the grade, the instructor ultimately gives students the service-learning grade or score as well as the course grade. The author frequently uses service-learning assignments as 10 to 25 percent of the course grade. Some instructors give points for completing the required number of service hours; others award additional points for the development of a PowerPoint presentation about the service-learning experience. Some presentations include application of course content and reflection highlights.

Finally, both formative and summative evaluation should be an integral part of the service-learning experience. Formative evaluation should be ongoing throughout the term and can include telephone or e-mail communication several times a term to assure that things are going as planned. Summative evaluation should be conducted at the end of the term by all three stakeholders in an effort to assess the impact of the service activity on the community or measure the learning experience of students. Evaluation should also help to improve the service-learning enterprise for the student, community, and university. Evaluation generates ideas for how better to prepare the next service-learning student, serve the community, or facilitate reflection in the classroom. Evaluation gives direction for improvement, growth, and change for the community, students, and university.

COLLABORATIVE RESPONSIBILITIES OF SERVICE-LEARNING PARTNERS

When the three service-learning partners perform their responsibilities and fulfill expectations, then the student learns and serves in ways not possible in a traditional classroom setting, the community identifies its own needs while working with students and receiving relevant service not available otherwise, and the university provides a successful form of social work education pedagogy that helps students gain a deeper understanding of social work course

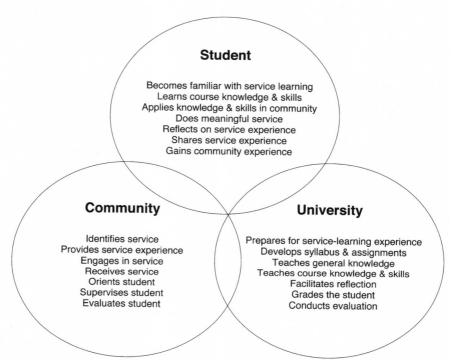

Figure 2.1.   Responsibilities of Service-Learning Partners

content. Figure 2.1 summarizes the collaborative responsibilities of service-learning partners.

COMPARISON OF A TRADITIONAL VERSUS SERVICE-LEARNING MICRO PRACTICE COURSE

Social work practice courses that offer service learning as an option or as a requirement differ from non-service-learning courses in several ways. While additional time and effort are needed to make the service-learning experience available, the benefits for all three partners are considered worthwhile by many. Students will make wonderful discoveries and gain deeper understanding related not just to their social work education but also to their lives. The instructor should be prepared for students to testify about their growth and development due to service-learning involvement. Community partners will appreciate the service received, and instructors will be

Table 2.1. Comparison of Traditional and Service-Learning Micro Practice Courses

Course Descriptors	Traditional Practice Course	Service-Learning Micro Practice Course
Lectures	Prepare for lectures	Prepare for lectures
Prepare for service learning	Not applicable	Collaborate with organization
Syllabus objectives	Usual learning objectives	Add service-learning objective
Syllabus assignments	Traditional assignments (i.e., research paper)	Add service-learning and reflection assignments
Service-learning orientation	Not applicable	Student, faculty, and community person involved
Assignments	Traditional assignments	Student completes service-learning experience and reflection assignment
Course knowledge	Customary lectures, textbook, apply knowledge in role-play with peers	Customary lectures, textbook, apply knowledge with community members
Course skill	Apply skills in role-play	Apply skills with community members
Community-based experience	Not applicable	Student provides meaningful service while applying course content; student records observations and integrates course content, records professional and personal growth; student shares experiences with class and community
Faculty oversight	Not applicable	Monitors service-learning experience
Reflection feedback	Not applicable	Students synthesize their understanding of the experience, describe self-growth, and note social injustices in a reflection assignment
Class presentation	Not applicable	Students present their service-learning experience
Evaluation	Faculty grades student	Faculty, community, and students evaluate; community recommends a grade; faculty grades student

able to model advocacy for those without a voice. Table 2.1 provides a comparison of traditional and service-learning approaches in a micro practice course.

CONCLUSION

As some final advice, when designing a service-learning syllabus, faculty may want to consider (Heffernan 2001):

- including service as an expressed objective
- clearly describing how the service-learning experience will be measured
- describing the nature of the service-learning experience
- specifying the roles and responsibilities of students at the site (e.g., transportation, time requirements, community contacts)
- defining the needs the service-learning experience meets
- specifying how students will be expected to demonstrate what they have learned at the site (e.g., journal, papers, presentations)
- developing course assignments that link the service experience and the course content
- including a description of the reflective process
- including a description of the expectations for the public dissemination of students' work, and
- using the service-learning experience as a preparatory bridge for entry into the social work internship.

With the social work profession's emphasis on values development, working with people, and advocacy for social and economic justice for the powerless, service learning can logically be an especially effective form of pedagogy in social work education. As more faculty members include service learning in their courses, there will be greater benefits for students, the community, and the university.

Early effort and organization are needed to include service learning in a course, and ongoing effort is required. Sometimes things do not work out as planned. The instructor does not control much of what happens, and crises can occur. Nonetheless, the benefits are inspiring. This author's students repeatedly say, "This was the best assignment I have ever had!" "I gained so much more from this experience!" "Why can't more classes have service learning?" Community members grow in self-confidence and learn from their "social work friends." Instructors enjoy the successful use of a pedagogy that draws out professional commitment to service and social justice.

While service learning may seem to fit practice courses best, it can be used effectively in perhaps any social work course. Service learning can well be used throughout the social work curriculum in required and elective courses at both the baccalaureate and graduate levels. This volume presents many such examples.

REFERENCES

Anderson, D. K., and Harris, B. M. (2005). Teaching social welfare policy: A comparison of two pedagogical approaches. *Journal of Social Work Education, 41*(3), 511–26.

Bennett, G., and Green, F. P. (2001). Promoting service learning via online instruction. *College Student Journal, 35*(4), 491–98.

Berry, H. A., and Chisholm, L. A. (1999). *Service-learning in higher education around the world: An initial look*. New York: The International Partnership for Service Learning.

Bringle, R., and Hatcher, J. (1995). A service learning curriculum for faculty. *Michigan Journal of Community Service Learning, 2*, 112–22.

Butin, D. W. (2003). Of what use is it? Multiple conceptualizations of service learning within education. *Instructors College Record, 105*(9), 1674–92.

Chapin, J. (1998). Is service learning a good idea? Data from the national longitudinal study of 1988. *Social Studies, 89*(5), 205–11.

Cohen, J., and Kinsey, D. (1994). Doing good and scholarship: A service-learning study. *Journalism Educator, 48*, 4–14.

Compton, B. R., Galaway, B., and Cournoyer, B. R. 2005. *Social work processes* (7th ed.). Belmont, CA: Brooks/Cole.

Dale, O., Smith, R., Norlin, J. M., and Chess, W. A. (2006). *Human behavior and the social environment: Social systems theory*. Boston: Allyn and Bacon.

Darling, R. B. (1998). The value of a pre-internship observation experience. *Teaching Sociology, 26*, 341–46.

Dorfman, L. T., Murty, S., Ingram, J. G., and Evans, R. J. (2002). Incorporating intergenerational service-learning into an introductory gerontology course. In M. J. Mellor and J. Ivry (Eds.), *Advancing gerontological social work education* (219–40). New York: Haworth Press.

Enos, S. L., and Troppe, M. L. (1996). Service-learning in the curriculum. In B. Jacoby and Associates, *Service-learning in higher education: Concepts and practices* (156–81). San Francisco, CA: Jossey-Bass.

Feinberg, J. R. (2002). Service learning in contemporary Japan and America. *Social Education, 66*(6), 368–72.

Forte, J. (1997). Calling students to serve the homeless: A project to promote altruism and community service. *Journal of Social Work Education, 33*, 151–66.

Gamble, D. N., and Well, M. O. (1995). Citizen participation. In *The encyclopedia of social work* (483–94). Washington, DC: NASW Press.

Gutierrez, L. M. (1994). Beyond coping: An empowerment perspective on stressful life events. *Journal of Sociology and Social Welfare, 21*(3), 201–19.

Heffernan, K. (2001). *Fundamentals of service-learning course construction.* Providence, RI: Campus Compact.

Hegeman, C. R., Horowitz, B., Tepper, L., Pillemer, K., and Schultz, L. (2002). Service learning in elder care: Ten years of growth and assessment. In M. J. Mellor and J. Ivry (Eds.), *Advancing gerontological social work education* (177–94). New York: Haworth Press.

Hollis, S. A. (2002). Capturing the experience: Transforming community service into service learning. *Teaching Sociology, 30*, 200–13.

Howard, J. P. F. (1998). Academic service learning: A counternormative pedagogy. In R. A. Rhoads et al. (Eds.), *Academic service-learning: A pedagogy of action and reflection* (21–30). San Francisco, CA: Jossey-Bass.

Jacoby, B., and Associates (1996). *Service-learning in higher education: Concepts and practices.* San Francisco, CA: Jossey-Bass.

Lee, J. A. B. (1994). *The empowerment approach to social work practice.* New York: Columbia University Press.

Miley, K. K., O'Melia, M., and DuBois, B. (2004). *Generalist social work practice: An empowering approach.* New York: Allyn and Bacon.

Peterson, L., and McCook, K. D. L. P. (2003). Using a homeless shelter as a library education learning laboratory: Incorporating service-learning in a graduate level Information Sources and Services in the Social Sciences course. *Summer, 42*(4), 307–10.

Poindexter, C. C., Saunders Lane, T., and Capobianco Boyer, N. (2002). Teaching and learning by example: Empowerment principles applied to development, delivery, and evaluation of community-based training for HIV service providers and supervisors. *AIDS Education and Prevention, 14*(5), 391–401.

Rocha, C. (2000). Evaluating experiential teaching methods in a policy practice course: The case for service learning to increase political participation. *Journal of Social Work Education, 36*(1), 53–64.

Rogers, A. T. (2006). *Human behavior in the social environment.* Boston: McGraw-Hill.

Saleebey, D. (2006). *The strengths perspective in social work practice.* New York: Pearson.

Saltmarsh, J., and Heffernan, K. (2000). *Introduction to service-learning toolkit: Readings and resources for faculty.* Providence, RI: Campus Compact.

Serow, R. C., Calleson, D. C., Parker, L., and Morgan, L. (1996). Institutional support for service-learning. *Journal of Research and Development in Education, 29*(4): 220–25.

Staples, L. (1999). Consumer empowerment in a mental health system: Stakeholder roles and responsibilities. In W. Shera and L. M. Wells (Eds.), *Empowerment in social work practice* (119–41). Toronto: Canadian Scholars Press.

Strage, A. (2004). Long-term academic benefits of service-learning: When and where do they manifest themselves? *College Student Journal, 38*(2), 257–61.

Swift, C., and Levin, G. (1987). Empowerment: An emerging mental health technology. *Journal of Primary Prevention, 8*(1/2), 71–94.

Wade, R. C., and Saxe, D. W. (1996). Community service learning in the social studies: Historical roots, empirical evidence, critical issues. *Theory and Research in Social Education, 24*, 331–59.

Weah, W., Simmons, V., and Hall, M. (2000). Service learning and multicultural/multiethnic perspectives. *Phi Delta Kappan, 81*, 673–78.

Weigert, K. M. (1998). Academic service learning: Its meaning and relevance. *New Directions for Teaching and Learning, 73*, 3–10.

Williams, N. R., King, M., and Koob, J. J. (2002). Social work students go to camp: The effects of service learning on perceived self-efficacy. *Journal of Teaching in Social Work, 22*(3/4), 55–70.

Williams, N. R., and Reeves, P. M. (2004). MSW students go to burn camp: Exploring social work values through service-learning. *Social Work Education, 23*(4), 383–98.

Woolcock, M. (1997). *Constructing a syllabus: A handbook for faculty, teaching assistants and teaching fellows* (2nd ed.). Providence, RI: Brown University.

Zastrow, C., and Kirst-Ashman, K. K. (2001). *Understanding human behavior and the social environment* (5th ed.). Belmont, CA: Brooks/Cole.

Zlotkowski, E. (Ed.). (1998). *Successful service learning programs*. Belmont, MA: Anker Publishing.

Chapter Three

Service Learning across the Social Work Curriculum

Virginia Majewski

In the preceding chapters, the authors define service learning for the purposes of this volume and elaborate on the fundamental components of service learning. In addition, they frame this pedagogical approach using the most basic principles of contemporary social work education—a systems approach to practice, empowerment through intervention, and the strengths perspective.

In some ways similar to the social work field experience, service learning places the "learner in the situation" by integrating "the two elements of learning, the knowledge derived from experience with the knowledge generated by theory and research" (Goldstein 2001). However, as Amy Phillips points out in chapter 1, service learning is distinguished from the social work practicum primarily by (1) the student's role as a community participant rather than a service provider, and (2) the reciprocal and reflective nature of the experience relative to, and inclusive of, community partners.

This chapter proposes to take the readers of this volume a step further by considering the implementation of service learning across the social work curriculum. To this end, the author explores the continuum of possibilities determined by the amount of time the instructor wishes to invest and the level of resources available for such implementation. Afterwards, the author provides a series of factors to consider when selecting a service-learning project or otherwise deciding to use service-learning pedagogy in the social work curriculum. The chapter wraps up with a brief look at the foundation program objectives of the current Council on Social Work Education's *Educational Policy and Accreditation Standards* (2001) as they link curriculum content areas. The reader is then invited to peruse subsequent chapters, which present models of service learning in these areas.

A CONTINUUM OF POSSIBILITIES FOR INTEGRATING SERVICE LEARNING

R. L. Sigmon's (1994) well-known and often-referenced continuum describes the types of experiential learning (volunteerism, service learning, and internship) and the emphasis and beneficiaries associated with each. This chapter presents a continuum that tackles the many approaches to service learning itself, all of which emphasize service and academic learning with the student, community, and university as beneficiaries. Figure 3.1 encapsulates the basic premise that any educator can find a place along the continuum of service-learning possibilities by taking into account the time and resources available or potentially available for such initiatives.

Service Learning as Adjunct to the Curriculum

At one end of the continuum are models paralleling requirements for volunteer or community service that carry no course credit. Volunteer hours may be a prerequisite for admission to the baccalaureate social work major or part of the admission portfolio to a master of social work program. Often students seek out their own volunteer activities and document participation. That they might be considered service learning, these activities could become more formalized with a reflection component. Although these models represent a departure from most definitions of service learning in that academic credit is not attached, they nonetheless offer opportunities for action and reflection within the context of academic learning in a broader sense.

For example, while on the faculty of a small regional university, this author worked with other social work faculty and students to design such an ap-

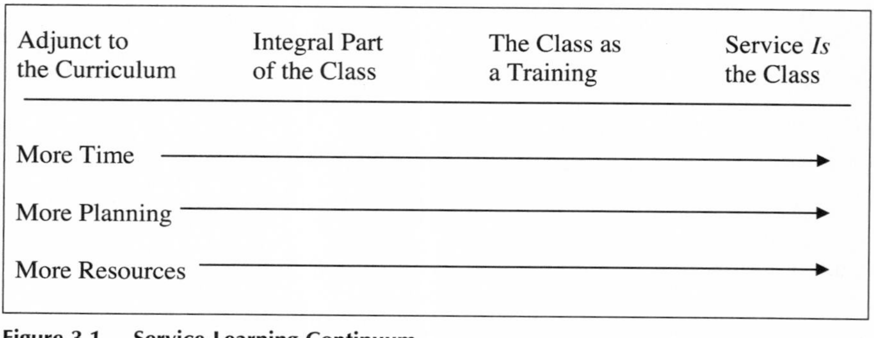

Adjunct to the Curriculum	Integral Part of the Class	The Class as a Training	Service *Is* the Class
More Time			⟶
More Planning			⟶
More Resources			⟶

Figure 3.1. Service-Learning Continuum

proach—a community-service information outlet. The design was based on a model utilized by university YMCAs in the 1960s and 1970s. Groups of students interested in the same service area, for example, hunger prevention or juvenile justice, engaged in structured service activities designed by YMCA staff and community partners. Central to the service activities in the YMCA model were monthly meetings and reflective sessions with facilitators, who were either faculty members or advanced graduate students.

This author's model included a yearly student retreat hosted by the student-run Social Work Organization. The students invited representatives from community agencies, such as the literacy council, senior citizen center, homeless shelter, and youth organization, to discuss opportunities for service in formal presentations. Then, in breakout sessions, representatives from each organization met with faculty and students with an interest in that service area. In this model, as in the YMCA model, students themselves took leadership in organizing and coordinating service activities, holding regular meetings to reflect on experiences, and encouraging faculty members to allow them to bring these experiences into the classroom as applications of social work knowledge, values, and skills.

While it is by most definitions just an extension of volunteerism, this model nonetheless affords social work faculty and students an entrée for experimenting with key service-learning components, such as building community partnerships and engaging in reflection activities. The model allows faculty members who are new to service learning to gain some experience with fewer time and resource demands.

Service Learning as an Integral Part of the Class

Along the continuum, there are a number of ways to integrate service learning into credit-bearing courses. Part II of this volume is replete with models illustrating how social work faculty have accomplished this integration in all social work curriculum areas. As part of course design, individuals, groups, or entire classes may engage in service learning. Typically, at least one course objective addresses the service-learning component. The instructor creates related assignments, such as journals or analytical papers, and sets aside time during class for reflection activities. For example, a course entitled "Poverty and Related Social Problems" involves activities at a local food bank or soup kitchen. As part of processing the experience, the instructor allows multiple opportunities during the semester for students to report back and reflect on what they have learned in the context of course themes. Reflection activities may also involve agency staff or recipients of services as students sort out the theoretical content of the course as applied in this setting. Continual feedback from the instructor sets the tone for critical reflection by students and fosters personal and professional development.

The Class as Training for a Community Service

Along the continuum are models that give immense weight to preparation or training for service. These models of service learning require a course syllabus with objectives, reading materials, course assignments, and methods for evaluation and feedback directly related to this training. Students receive academic credit for the class, but the class differs from other academic courses in that it includes objectives related to students' capacity to engage in a service upon completion. Completion may involve earning some sort of certification in addition to an academic grade.

In one institution, students in the social work program organized to provide peer counseling and a twenty-four-hour hotline for victims of sexual assault on campus. The faculty facilitated this activity by creating a course on sexual-assault intervention and counseling. Students taking the course (forty-five contact hours) received three elective credits and a certificate in sexual-assault counseling from the state. While in the course, students helped raise funds for the hotline and performed other organizational tasks. The course required students to serve as peer counselors for at least one semester after completion of the course. Trained students also continued to assist with fundraising and organizational development and engaged in advocacy at the state and national levels. The program grew under the auspices of a universitywide advisory committee composed of students, faculty, and staff members from the university community. Reflection activities occurred in monthly meetings as well as during class time.

At another institution, students enrolled in a one-credit course on critical-incident stress management before engaging in a service-learning course to assist hurricane survivors. During the service activity, students integrated knowledge and skills acquired in the course with the situations and people they encountered in the disaster area. Given the nature of the experience, reflection sessions occurred upon return from the site.

Community Service *Is* the Class

Because service learning links service with academic learning, this model is perhaps one of the best understood, and in many circles it is often described as an internship when implemented on an individual student basis. This mode of service learning is distinguished from an internship, however, by the experience's nature as a group or class activity with the community as a full partner and the beneficiary of a service. Perhaps the best descriptor for courses at this end of the continuum is "immersion," and they are generally conducted off-site, outside the traditional classroom setting. This model still requires a course syllabus, course objectives and assignments linked directly to activities, clear expectations for grading, and instructor feedback.

Service-learning courses on this end of the continuum may or may not have a classroom aspect. Nonetheless, the instructor finds the time and a venue to prepare students for the project and to debrief students afterward. Many such courses use online technology, such as Blackboard or WebCT, for preparation. Reflection sessions might be built into group meetings on-site or in chat rooms. While on-site, reflection occurs formally and informally throughout the experience. Projects usually involve an entire group, but students may have individualized service assignments and select individual research projects, as well as relevant readings to apply in their area of academic interest.

This author, along with a colleague, created a three-week immersion course on an American Indian reservation. For the first two years, the core service project involved working with elementary school teachers in a drug-free summer school program for children in grades kindergarten through six. In the third year, faculty members invited community members to identify other projects in addition to this project. Students helped clean up around a senior housing complex, reconstructed a ceremonial site, set up and maintained a refreshment stand for a teenage drop-in program, and visited a juvenile detention center and women's shelter. Because the course was multidisciplinary, each student had his or her own research project related to a major course of study (social work, biology, anthropology, psychology, or nursing). The integration and reflection activities revolved around understanding how people from another culture perceive social problems and solutions to those problems, how outsiders are perceived and how they can provide service in culturally appropriate ways without imposing their own values, and how the existing literature often portrays life on American Indian reservations as compared to the realities experienced by the students while working with community members. The long-term evaluation of this course is described in chapter 12. In chapter 9, Meryl Nadel illustrates another immersion project in greater detail.

Today, there are nonprofit organizations that partner with universities to provide a variety of immersion-type service-learning experiences. Amizade Global Service Learning (www.amizade.org) is one such organization that partners with universities and faculty members, assisting with the service-learning components by providing trained facilitators and allowing faculty members to focus on academic content in their respective disciplines. Increasingly, universities are adding service-learning offices to their administrative infrastructures to assist faculty members with projects along the entire continuum presented here.

FACTORS TO CONSIDER IN PLANNING A SERVICE-LEARNING COURSE

While faculty members must decide where along the continuum they are most comfortable, they must also take into account other factors when adopting service learning as a pedagogical approach. These factors include the following: the institutional environment for service learning, their own philosophical or political motivations, course objectives, the availability of a community partner, commitment to action and reflection, time constraints, and resources (Majewski and Hawranick 2003). This section will briefly discuss each of these considerations.

The Institutional Environment for Service Learning

Institutions of higher education vary in their commitment to service learning. Thus, it is important to understand the climate within which one is attempting to implement a pedagogical approach that involves significant investment of a faculty member's time, perhaps some financial resources, and an out-of-the-classroom community-service expectation of students. In planning terms, the faculty member must assess the opportunities and constraints associated with developing a service-learning component in a course. Some of the most pressing questions include the following:

- Is service learning part of the institutional mission?
- Does the institution have any prior experience with service learning?
- Is there an office of service learning, by this name or another, on campus?
- Is there a faculty development office that has information on instructors who typically engage in experiential learning activities?
- Will the time spent designing and implementing a service-learning course component be a benefit for promotion or tenure or positively (at least not adversely) affect a merit pay raise?
- What are the institutional guidelines (especially insurance coverage) for involvement with students in an activity outside the classroom?

I. Harkovy and L. Benson, in discussing the theoretical bases for academic service learning through the works of John Dewey, Francis Bacon, and Benjamin Franklin, state, "Strategic, academically based community scholarship and service involves the integration of research, teaching, and service, and aims to bring about structural community improvement (for example, effective public schools, neighborhood economic development, strong community organizations) rather than simply to alleviate individual human misery (for example, feeding the hungry, sheltering the homeless, tutoring the 'slow learner')" (1998, 17). University administrators may find in this emphasis a certain congruence between service learning and the mission of the institution (Lucas 2000). In addition, K. Ward suggests several strategies for faculty members who wish to influence the institution to favor service learning, including making sure that all campus administrators are aware of service-learning activities on campus, creating faculty committees for service learning, connecting service learning to other university activities, working with "curriculum committees to stress the academic side of service learning," addressing faculty reward structures, and providing data about the benefits of service learning (1998, 78–79).

Philosophical and Political Foundations for Service

The author believes that service learning requires some introspection on the part of the instructor. The faculty member should reflect on his or her own values, philosophy, and political basis for utilizing service-learning pedagogy. Two major paradigms seem to prevail in academic service learning: philanthropic and social justice paradigms. Readers might refer back to Phillips' description in chapter 1 of Joseph Kahne and Joel Westheimer's (1996) conceptual matrix of "change versus charity" in service learning. Across disciplines and professional programs, the philanthropic paradigm is perhaps the more prominent, promoting the "giving" side of service, with reflection resting primarily with the faculty member and students within the halls of the academy (Brody and Nair 2000; Forte 1997). Language describing actual service experiences within this paradigm includes "helping others in need," "feeling good about oneself," and "gaining a sense of civic responsibility." The community is the beneficiary of students' altruism, while students are the beneficiaries of the community's openness to their involvement in activities that they can link to their academic learning and to their professional and personal growth.

The social justice paradigm stresses "change" through community engagement, and community members and recipients of service often assume a role in reflective activities (Redman and Clark 2002; Wade 2001; Warren 2000; Maybach 1996). Social work fits well into this paradigm with its emphasis on systems functioning, identifying student, client, organization, and community strengths, and subsequently working toward the empowerment of students and service recipients alike. Language describing actual service experiences within this paradigm includes "advocating," "mobilizing," "challenging the status quo," "confronting injustice," and "mutually empowering."

Why is it important for the faculty member to explore and articulate his or her underlying philosophy and politics? There may be some greater associated levels of risk when the instructor embarks on service learning within the social justice paradigm (Marullo 1996). While it is not well documented in the service-learning literature, there seems to be some inherent threat when outsiders attempt to raise consciousness or change the status quo. S. Marullo suggests that there may be both "institutional backlash and community skepticism": "If the service-learning program is effective in creating students who think critically and who are empowered to act as agents of change, they are bound to upset those who benefit from the status quo" (1996, 133). The instructor should be well equipped to mentor students through adverse reactions to their community-engagement activities, as well as proactive in averting negative reactions within the educational institution. Educators must also be prepared to guide students through their critical inquiry about social inequities and perceived avenues of remediation (Lucas 2000; Hayes and Cuban 1997; Cone and Harris 1996).

Course Objectives

Course objectives and related expected outcomes ground the service-learning experience by providing the necessary framework for its academic and experiential aspects. Does the instructor want the student to learn and apply specific skills? Is it a primary underlying objective that the student develop self-efficacy? Will the experience help students clarify their values and uncover stereotypes and their own prejudices? Will it help them understand the dynamics of oppression and injustice?

In addition to the traditional course objectives, the instructor might add one or two that specifically relate to the service-learning experience for the class. In some social work programs, there may be a process for including additional objectives or offering an alternative version of a course when it incorporates service-learning pedagogy. The instructor, cognizant of the institutional and departmental environment for service learning, may want to allow sufficient time before the start of the course to seek any necessary sanctions.

Availability of Community Partners

While there are a number of excellent examples of service-learning components in social work programs that extend beyond the semester, the norm for any such experience is one semester. With this in mind, the instructor should do some homework related to the availability of a community partner. Over time, it is likely that the instructor will develop a relationship with one or more partners to facilitate entry into a meaningful experience. Developing partnerships involves approaching community or citizen organizations, as well as the institution's office of service learning. When there is sufficient time or if the course objectives dictate that students actively pursue a potential project as part of skill development, the instructor might develop an exercise to help students find an appropriate venue.

Being aware of service-learning activity across campus is essential in developing community partnerships. Some communities and organizations, especially those in close proximity to campus, may feel "overused" by numerous departments, either as a result of mandatory volunteer activities or service learning. Instructors should be sensitive to invasive practices that exhaust meaningful experiences or consume too much agency staff member time. One agency director reported to this author that students often had short time requirements, such as fifteen hours over a semester, which were more of a hindrance to the agency than a benefit. The agency staff and service recipients spent more time establishing new relationships than meeting goals in an effective manner.

Time Constraints

The instructor must, in each instance, take stock of the time investment, both in terms of the number of weeks needed to complete a project and the amount of class time students must devote to planning and reflection. Back planning is a good technique to help instructor and students budget their time so they can reasonably achieve course objectives. How much out-of-class time will the project require of the students and the instructor? Students likely have required course readings, papers, and exams. The instructor also needs preparation time for the usual academic parts of the course—lecturing, leading discussions, and grading. Projects that require too much out-of-class time are likely to result in stress and dissatisfaction with the learning experience or to impact other courses. Reflection is not only one of the most important components in service learning, but it distinguishes service learning from other experiential classroom activities. How much class time can the instructor devote to student discussion of the experience? If the reflection will largely be individualized in a journal or paper, will there be some forum for sharing and group problem solving that can be built into the class structure?

Commitment to Praxis

According to Paulo Freire, *praxis* means "reflection and action upon the world in order to transform it" (1970, 33). Praxis is the espoused basis of most service-learning activity, although the term is often misinterpreted by the instructors most dedicated to this pedagogical approach. Freire's expression of praxis supports the basic social work allegiance to social justice rather than charity.

Praxis requires time in the course schedule and, even in the evaluative elements, for reflective exercises. A commitment to praxis on the part of the instructor means challenging students to think critically about their role in the community, to examine their relationships with community members, consumers of the service provided, and even with the instructor, and to probe the intended and unintended consequences of actions taken in the community setting. Several resources exist in the education literature to help the instructor plan reflective exercises along these lines (e.g., Eyler, Giles, and Schmiede 1996).

The author's own particular style includes gaining agreement from the community partner to participate in group reflection. As an experiment, in one graduate-level course taught by this educator, three community members were invited to attend class, providing input and participating in reflection activities throughout the term. The instructor's commitment proved much higher than the students' motivation to receive such feedback, creating a sense of insecurity among the students when community members pushed them to evaluate critically their preconceived ideas of what was beneficial to the community.

Resources

Finally, the faculty member must determine the level of investment required to carry out the project. What is needed in terms of financial resources, transportation, facilities, and even the involvement of another faculty member or graduate assistant? Some institutions provide small grants for innovations in course development. A well-thought-out proposal that anticipates needs often goes a long way toward securing the support needed from within the institution.

SERVICE LEARNING ACROSS SOCIAL WORK CURRICULUM AREAS

One of the basic premises of this volume is that faculty can incorporate service learning into any course in the social work curriculum. To demonstrate this, the editors invited seasoned social work faculty to write about their service-learning projects. They selected model projects in order to address the foundation objectives of the Council on Social Work Education's *Educational Policy and Accreditation Standards* (EPAS) (2001). As a guide, table 3.1 presents the social work curriculum content areas with associated EPAS founda-

Table 3.1. Service Learning across the Social Work Curriculum Based on Curriculum Content Areas and Foundation Objectives in the EPAS

Program Objective 1. Apply critical thinking skills within the context of professional social work practice. This is basic to service-learning pedagogy, where students, faculty, and community partners engage in praxis, action plus reflection.

Curriculum Area	Foundation Objectives (Numbered According to Their Order in the EPAS)	Illustrated in Model Program
A. Values and Ethics	2. Understand the value base of the profession and its ethical standards and principles, and practice accordingly.	All contain some elements
B. Diversity	3. Practice without discrimination and with respect, knowledge, and skills related to clients' age, class, color, culture, disability, ethnicity, family structure, gender, marital status, national origin, race, religion, sex, and sexual orientation.	Yoakam & Bolaños (chapter 8); Nadel (chapter 9); Majewski & Turner (chapter 12); Ames & Diepstra (chapter 7); Sather, Carlson, & Weitz (chapter 6)
C. Populations-at-Risk and Social and Economic Justice	4. Understand the forms and mechanisms of oppression and discrimination and apply strategies of advocacy and social change that advance social and economic justice.	Nadel (chapter 9); Yoakam & Bolaños (chapter 8); Majewski & Turner (chapter 12); Watkins, Charlesworth, & House (chapter 5); Sather, Carlson, & Weitz (chapter 6)
D. Human Behavior and the Social Environment	7. Use theoretical frameworks supported by empirical evidence to understand individual development and behavior across the life span and the interactions among individuals and between individuals	Ames & Diepstra (chapter 7)

(continued)

Table 3.1. (*continued*)

Curriculum Area	Foundation Objectives (Numbered According to Their Order in the EPAS)	Illustrated in Model Program
	and families, groups, organizations, and communities.	
E. Social Welfare Policies and Services	5. Understand and interpret the history of the social work profession and its contemporary structures and issues.	Droppa (chapter 4); Sather, Carlson, & Weitz (chapter 6); Allen et al. (chapter 10)
	8. Analyze, formulate, and influence social policies.	
	12. Function within the structure of organizations and service delivery systems and seek necessary organizational change.	
F. Social Work Practice	6. Apply the knowledge and skills of a generalist social work practice perspective to practice with systems of all sizes.	Watkins, Charlesworth, & House (chapter 5); Sather, Carlson, & Weitz (chapter 6); Nadel (chapter 9); Malinowski (chapter 11)
	10. Use communication skills differentially across client populations, colleagues, and communities.	
	11. Use supervision and consultation appropriate to social work practice.	
G. Research	9. Evaluate research studies, apply research findings to practice, and evaluate their own practice interventions.	Sather, Carlson, & Weitz (chapter 6)

tion objectives. What follows in this chapter is a brief discussion of some objectives that permeate most service-learning projects, namely, those associated with critical thinking, values, and ethics. The remaining chapters illustrate model programs in the various curriculum areas, as well as evaluation studies, and offer a look at the larger picture.

Critical Thinking

As Sharlene Furuto describes in chapter 2, reflection is one of the key components of service learning. Reflection requires students to think critically about their experience; how the experience relates to the knowledge, values, and skills emphasized in the specific course; and how they themselves are transformed through the experience. According to R. Paul and L. Elder of the Foundation for Critical Thinking, "Critical thinking is, in short, self-directed, self-disciplined, self-motivated, and self-corrective thinking. . . . It entails effective communication and problem-solving abilities and a commitment to overcome our native egocentrism and sociocentrism" (2004, 1). Thus, by the very nature of the enterprise, service learning as pedagogy emphasizes critical thinking.

Reflective activities also require an investment by the instructor to help students address the basic elements of critical thinking as posited by Paul and Elder, including raising and formulating vital questions, gathering and assessing information, reaching well-reasoned conclusions, thinking open-mindedly about alternative approaches, and communicating effectively with others (2004, 1). Freire contrasts critical thinking with naïve thinking: "For the naïve thinker, the important thing is accommodation to his normalized 'today.' For the critic, the important thing is the continuing transformation of reality, on behalf of the continuing humanization of men" (1970, 81). Contemporary service-learning theorist C. Rosenberger emphasizes that students should engage in problem posing with the instructor, "unveiling and problematizing reality for the purpose of searching for more humane and just ways of living" (2000, 41). The instructor must also understand that "reflection involves a hard balancing act. A teacher must be willing to intervene, pose tough questions, and propose often uncomfortable points of view for a student's consideration. A teacher must also be ready to back off and give support in order to nurture the independence and autonomy that are the lifeblood of experiential learning processes" (Cooper 1998, 54).

Freire contends that praxis needs theory to illuminate it (1970, 119–20) and that its basic dimensions are cooperation and communication (168), unity (172–73), organization as a natural development of unity (180), and cultural synthesis, or the "investigation of the people's generative themes" (182). The instructor, who is the university partner and initiator of the service-learning pedagogy, plays the central role in assuring critical-thinking outcomes through the design of reflective exercises and modeling critical thinking for students and community partners through dialogue. "Only dialogue, which requires critical thinking, is also capable of generating critical thinking" (Freire 1970, 87).

The author has observed that many service-learning courses rely solely on reflective papers and journals, rather than dialogue. This author suggests an examination of how written work can lead to dialogue, beginning with timely feedback from the instructor. To further the objective that students will be able to apply critical-thinking skills, social work faculty may want to give more thought to their own application of such skills in the formal and informal settings of university and department meetings, field instructor trainings, and professional conferences. Such introspection may guide the service-learning instructor to model and stimulate critical dialogue more effectively among students and between students and community partners.

Values and Ethics

Preparing students to practice within the values and ethics of the social work profession is a cornerstone of social work education. Educators initiate processes that help students take stock of their own personal values, recognize at any given time dominant societal values and how they influence policy direction, and reconcile personal and societal values with those of the profession. M. E. King discusses social work values "reflected in the pedagogical elements underlying service learning": respecting diversity, self-determination, collaboration, social justice, a person-in-environment focus, and accountability in practice (2003, 40). As noted by Furuto in chapter 2, a strengths perspective and empowerment imperative constitute additional values embraced by contemporary social work practice that also figure prominently in service learning.

In the chapters that follow, readers will observe how an emphasis on values and ethics is paramount in most social work service-learning models. Educators recognize how service components and related reflection socialize students into the profession in a profound way well before the internship experience. For example, Robin Allen, William Rainford, Roy Rodenhiser, and Kara Brascia in chapter 10 demonstrate how service learning in a large general education class orients students to the values base of social work practice and enables them to make decisions about pursuing social work as a professional degree. Watkins, Charlesworth, and House describe in chapter 5 the values and ethics associated with youth development programs and the connection to social work practice that students experience as they engage in projects in an introductory course. In chapter 11, Rose Malinowski makes the application of social work values and ethics a central theme in her evaluation instruments.

This author suggests that values and ethics should become a central focus in all social work service-learning courses through explicit course objectives. The instructor might design reflection exercises on value conflicts with community partners and ethical dilemmas encountered in the project. Such conflicts and dilemmas often arise without warning, and the instructor should be prepared to recognize them and prepare for individual or group processing as necessary through what many faculty often refer to as "teachable moments."

Remaining Curriculum Content Areas

The final column in table 3.1 provides the reader with information on where in this volume to find illustrations of service-learning models for each curriculum area and related foundation objectives, although many model programs cut across several areas. Objectives and applications related to policy, research, and practice areas are too numerous to discuss here; however, since many service-learning projects also address diversity and populations-at-risk, the author feels compelled to make a few final points related to these curriculum areas.

Encouraging an appreciation for and valuing of people's diverse backgrounds and circumstances constitutes a major building block for preparing effective social work practitioners. Diverse populations are defined by race, ethnicity, gender, age, culture, sexual orientation, religion, physical or mental ability, and socioeconomic class. Natalie Ames and Stephene Diepstra, for example, demonstrate in chapter 7 how an oral history project with elders helped students broaden their knowledge and awareness of diversity, gerontology, populations-at-risk, and generational ties. John Yoakam and Patricia Bolaños discuss in chapter 8 several projects in which students helped with advocacy efforts on behalf of gay, lesbian, bisexual, and transgender people and communities. Many instructors design service-learning projects with community partners that expose students to diverse populations. Ideally, students should not just provide a service to a specific population but work side by side with members for service planning, delivery, and evaluation. In chapter 6, Paul Sather, Patricia Carlson, and Barbara Weitz illustrate their program's long-term commitment to two communities of color in their city. Reflection sessions in social work service-learning courses should include discussions about diversity, focusing on respect for difference and understanding the inherent strengths of people from different cultures, backgrounds, and circumstances.

There is often a tendency to treat diversity and populations-at-risk in the same course units or to lump them together as one and the same content area. Of course, it is often the case that many of the diverse groups that instructors discuss in classes also constitute populations-at-risk. The key to addressing diversity and populations-at-risk as one unit rests in helping students understand the social dynamics that place certain groups at risk. Service learning, in a hands-on way, opens the door for such understanding, while at the same time celebrating diversity in society.

The curriculum content area that combines the concepts of populations-at-risk and social and economic justice engenders discussions of advocacy and social change. For example, in her chapter "Populations-at-Risk/Immersion Experience," Nadel illustrates how an immersion project at a summer camp for HIV-affected families provides students with an opportunity to see this population's larger social and economic context. The reader will find these themes infused in many model programs presented.

This volume presents models for incorporating service-learning pedagogy in the areas of human behavior, social welfare policy, social work practice methods, and research. The editors trust that educators and practitioners will find these discussions useful and that they will document and share their own successes in service learning.

REFERENCES

Brody, R., and Nair, M. (2000). *The art of volunteering and service learning.* Wheaton, IL: Gregory.

Cone, D., and Harris, S. (1996). Service-learning practice: Developing a theoretical framework. *Michigan Journal of Community Service Learning,* (Fall), 31–43.

Cooper, D. D. (1998). Reading, writing, and reflection. In *New directions for teaching and learning.* No. 73. San Francisco, CA: Jossey-Bass.

Council on Social Work Education. (2001). *Educational policy and accreditation standards.* Alexandria, VA: Author.

Eyler, J., Giles, D. E., and Schmiede, A. (1996). *A practitioner's guide to reflection in service-learning: Student voices and reflection.* Nashville, TN: Vanderbilt University.

Forte, J. A. (1997). Calling students to serve the homeless: A project to promote altruism and community service. *Journal of Social Work Education, 33*(1), 151–66.

Freire, P. (1970). *Pedagogy of the oppressed.* New York: Herder and Herder.

Goldstein, H. (2001). *Experiential learning: A foundation for social work education and practice.* Alexandria, VA: Council on Social Work Education.

Harkovy, I., and Benson, L. (1998). Theoretical bases for academic service learning. In R. A. Rhoads and J. P. F. Howard (Eds.), *Academic service learning: A pedagogy of action and reflection* (11–20). San Francisco, CA: Jossey-Bass.

Hayes, E., and Cuban, S. (1997). Border pedagogy: A critical framework for service-learning. *Michigan Journal of Community Service Learning,* (Fall), 72–80.

King, M. E. (2003). Social work education and service learning. *Journal of Baccalaureate Social Work, 8*(2), 37–48.

Lucas, E. T. (2000). Linking social work and service-learning. *Journal of Baccalaureate Social Work, 5*(2), 167–78.

Majewski, V., and Hawranick, S. (2003). *Infusing service learning into the social work curriculum.* Curriculum workshop developed for the Council on Social Work Education Annual Program Meeting and presented in Atlanta, GA, February, 2003, Anaheim, CA, February, 2004, and New York, NY, February, 2005.

Marullo, S. (1996). The service-learning movement in higher education: An academic response to troubled times. *Sociological Imagination, 33*(2), 117–37.

Maybach, C. W. (1996). Investigating urban community needs: Service learning from a social justice perspective. *Education and Urban Society, 28*(2), 224–36.

Paul, R., and Elder, L. (2004). *The miniature guide to critical thinking: Concepts and tools.* Dillon Beach, CA: Foundation for Critical Thinking.

Redman, R. W., and Clark, L. (2002). Service-learning as a model for integrating social justice in the nursing curriculum. *Journal of Nursing Education, 41*(10), 446–49.

Rosenberger, C. (2000). Beyond empathy: Developing critical consciousness through service learning. In C. O'Grady (Ed.), *Integrating service learning and multicultural education in colleges and universities* (23–43). Mahwah, NJ: Lawrence Erlbaum Associates.

Sigmon, R. L. (1994). *Serving to learn, learning to serve: Linking service with learning.* Washington, DC: Council for Independent Colleges Report.

Wade, R. (2001). ". . . And justice for all": Community service-learning for social justice. *Issue paper: Community service/service-learning.* Retrieved June 25, 2003, from www.ecs.org/clearinghouse/29/13/2913.htm.

Ward, K. (1998). Addressing academic culture: Service learning, organizations, and faculty work. In R. A. Rhoads and J. P. F. Howard (Eds.), *Academic service learning: A pedagogy of action and reflection* (73–80). San Francisco, CA: Jossey-Bass.

Warren, K. (2000). Educating students for social justice in service learning. *Journal of Experiential Education, 21*(3), 134–39.

Part II

MODELS FOR SERVICE LEARNING ACROSS THE CURRICULUM

Chapter Four

Social Welfare Policy and Services: Service Learning through Social Policy Projects in Human Service Organizations

David C. Droppa

Although service learning has been used as a pedagogy to teach social work policy practice since the mid-1980s, there have been few descriptions of how it might be employed and few studies of its effectiveness. This chapter explores a model for teaching policy practice in partnership with human service organizations, including the model's origins in the Cedar Crest Democratic Academy, its implementation in a social policy course, its outcomes, the advantages and challenges of this pedagogy, and recommendations for teaching and research.

Prior to this study, the instructor had taught an undergraduate social work policy course for three years, with the requirement that each student write a policy paper describing a hypothetical policy project in an area of his or her interest. Although the project and paper seemed to help the student connect theory and concepts to a hypothetical policy, the exercise lacked real-life relevance. None of these student-designed projects was implemented following the course.

During the 2002–2003 academic year, the instructor was invited to participate in the Cedar Crest College (Allentown, Pennsylvania) Participating in Democracy Project. This project was a three-year, $1.2 million initiative designed to increase the importance students attach to attitudes about civic engagement and participation in democracy. In 2002–2003, Cedar Crest College field-tested the model at four United States colleges and universities, involving seventy-two faculty members and twelve hundred undergraduate students across many disciplines.

Those teaching the course were to select from three pedagogical strategies:

1. *Classroom engagement module*: Students participated directly in course governance and were encouraged to take responsibility for their learning.

2. *Community engagement module*: Service learning was employed with the goal of helping students develop a sense of responsibility for the well-being of their communities and affirming the value of public service as a responsibility of citizenship.
3. *Political engagement module*: Students were encouraged to participate actively as agents of social change at one of three levels: organizational, community, or legislative.

The findings of the field test by Cedar Crest in 2002–2003 are reported in *The Democratic Academy and Engaged Citizenship: An Assessment of Student Learning Outcomes* (Cedar Crest College 2003).

All students completed a pre- and posttest of attitudes and behaviors about democratic participation, and the same instruments were administered to a random sample of students not enrolled in a course using a democratic pedagogical strategy.

As part of the Cedar Crest project, the instructor decided in 2002 to implement both the classroom and political engagement modules in his undergraduate social work policy course at Seton Hill University, a small liberal arts university located in southwestern Pennsylvania. This course, usually taken in the junior year prior to the five-hundred-hour senior field practicum, had two unique features: it was run as a democratic classroom, with some decisions typically made by the instructor given over to the students, and all students were required to engage in a policy project with a human service organization partner. The instructor believes that the community engagement and political engagement models both employ strategies of service learning as students are involved in providing a service designed to meet the need of a community partner and learn about the culture of the organization and/or community. This service is based on and integrated with classroom learning. Democratic classroom principles were employed in the course as students reviewed the syllabus in the first class and had the option of selecting evaluative methods: exams versus papers, quizzes versus chapter questions, and how the final grade was scored. The service-learning aspects of the course are discussed in more detail below.

Based on the results of the first course, the instructor has continued to use the policy project model and to evaluate its impact on students and collaborating organizations. This chapter reviews the methods and outcomes of the project over four academic years.

LITERATURE REVIEW

The literature concerning community policy projects in social work education is sparse. J. L. Wolk et al. (1996) studied political practice in academic social work programs, finding that of 131 baccalaureate social work (BSW) programs responding to their survey, only 26 percent provided practica in government relations and 15 percent in policy advocacy and development, although 29 percent were planning to add political practica over the next three years. The numbers were higher in master of social work (MSW) programs (47 percent, 33 percent, and 43 percent, respectively). The authors concluded that there is a need for more political practica in social work education.

C. J. Rocha and A. K. Johnson (1997) describe the implementation of policy practice in the community with groups of MSW students at Case Western Reserve University and the University of Tennessee, Knoxville, in 1993 and 1995, respectively, based on a project developed by S. S. Butler and P. A. Coleman at the University of Maine in both an undergraduate and a graduate social work program in 1985. Rocha then compared outcomes of this experiential policy practice model with those of a control group in a policy course at the University of Tennessee, Knoxville, in 1995–1996 and found that "the experiential group was significantly more likely to perceive themselves as competent policy practitioners and to perform policy-related activities after graduation" (2000, 1). M. S. Sherraden, B. Slosar, and M. Sherraden (2002) described student involvement in a five-year collaborative policy project that included social work researchers from four universities, along with practitioners and advocates from various human service and banking organizations. H. A. Ishisaka et al. (2004) described a model in which MSW faculty and students from the University of Washington partnered with health and human service organizations in Seattle's International District to increase and improve class advocacy, social justice research, proposal writing, and community capacity building. Finally, D. K. Anderson and B. M. Harris (2005) compared two experiential approaches in teaching social welfare policy to BSW students. In the first approach, six third-year students partnered with the instructor and the staff of a health clinic serving immigrant families in a service-learning project using community-based research. In the second approach, ten fourth-year students took the social welfare policy course concurrently with their senior practicum, with the goal of integrating social policy in class and the field. Content analysis of student journal entries and a postgraduation survey of students regarding policy-related values and skills revealed that the approaches appeared to be similarly effective: in both pedagogical models, the students understood and were able to apply policy concepts and were involved in similar levels of policy activities following graduation.

Of the student social work policy projects described in the literature, all were group projects, and only two were carried out with undergraduate social work students. The study described in this paper appears to be the first reported in the literature matching BSW students, individually or in pairs, with human service organization partners.

GOALS

The instructor's goals in the policy service-learning project with community organizations or political entities were as follows:

1. The required policy project will become real, in the sense that the students will select an organization partner that had already identified a policy initiative in which the student can play a part, whether small or large.
2. Third-year social work students will relate in a more intensive fashion to a community organization or entity, bridging the gap between the twenty-five-hour service-learning experience required in four social work courses at Seton Hill University and the five-hundred-hour field practicum.
3. Students will report having gained more knowledge, skills, and confidence in their ability to engage in policy practice and policy advocacy after they participate in the policy service-learning project.

STRATEGIES

The students were required to work with an organization chosen from among six types: nonprofit, for profit, health care, educational, government, or legislative. Over the four years of this study, twenty different projects were completed by twenty-three students working in partnership with fifteen different organizations. Ten of the projects were developed by the instructor prior to the start of the course without student input, seven were developed by the instructor based on student suggestions, and three were developed by students with the instructor's approval. The instructor, who is also the social work field coordinator at the university, contacted either the head of the organization or the field supervisor by e-mail to ask whether the organization had a policy project in which a student could partner with someone from the organization. Sometimes there was a follow-up telephone conversation, but frequently the communication was entirely by e-mail. In the first year, about half of the organizations contacted agreed to participate, and each year the list of prospective organizations grew, with most new organizations added due to student interest. Over the last two project years, types of organization contacts initiated by students included a private day care center, an after-school youth program, and a Catholic grade school. Sometimes students asked for a type of organization in which they had career interest, either to explore their career choice further or to develop connections in the field. It is interesting that of the twenty-three students, seven (30 percent) worked directly with the head of the organization (the executive director of a nonprofit or the principal of a school), an experience they otherwise would not have had.

The organization's representative, usually an administrator or supervisor involved in the proposed policy, interviewed the student, having been informed in advance that he or she could decide that the student was not a good match for the project, though none did so. Most of the time, the organization in which the student was interested ended up being the one chosen, but, on rare occasions, the instructor arranged for an organization that could accommodate the student's strengths and weaknesses. For most of the projects, the instructor did not meet with the student and organization together, although the instructor usually met before the project began with organization representatives with whom he was not familiar.

The student could join the policy work at any stage, from building the agenda to evaluating or revising a policy that had already been enacted or revised. Of course, the less complex the policy, the more of the process the student experienced. The frequency of meetings between student and organization varied widely, ranging from two or three meetings for a project in which the student was doing primarily Internet-based research on a policy to a maximum of fifteen for a project that required more intensive collaboration. The average number of meetings was around eight. Most of the meetings were in person, although, on some projects, use of e-mail and the telephone decreased the number of meetings.

During the four academic years covered by this study, a total of twenty-three students completed policy projects. There was some diversity among the students: nineteen were white females, of whom three were single parents; the remaining students were a white male, an Asian female, a black female, and a black male. Sixteen were of traditional undergraduate age, and seven were of nontraditional age (between thirty and fifty years old). Students partnered in groups of two on five different projects. In the five projects with student partners, the work was shared equally in three projects, and in the other two, one student did more of the work. Table 4.1 shows a chart with the type of organization, the type of project, and the number of students in each type of organization.

B. S. Jansson's (2003) model of policy practice served as a guideline for developing the required paper. Course content pertaining to the stages of policy practice was keyed to the sections of the paper, which were due after each topic was assigned in the text and presented and discussed in class. The paper had nine sections, each worth up to ten points:

1. description of the problem or opportunity
2. description of the agenda
3. description of the proposal
4. enactment/approval or implementation

David C. Droppa

5. contextual factors
6. description of how feedback was and will be utilized
7. description of the skills used or needed
8. assessment of the policy
9. assessment of the student's contribution

Up to ten additional points were given for written expression, and up to five extra points were given for attachments. Students were permitted to revise each section, based on instructor comments, and the complete paper was submitted at the end of the course.

Table 4.1.   Partners and Projects: Four Academic Years (2002–2006)

Organization	Projects
Nonprofit	
• Domestic violence center and shelter	Diversity policy
• Multi-county United Way affiliate	211 project
• Child abuse prevention & education agency	Accreditation policies
	Recommendations for program re-alignment due to funding cutbacks
	Parent handbook for after-school program
• Spectrum of residential and non-residential, mental health, and youth & family services	Incentive policy for staff trainers
• Workshop and services for blind individuals	Defibrillation policy
• County community action agency	Initial accreditation policies
	Customer satisfaction system
• Planned Parenthood affiliate	Emergency contraception legislation
For-Profit	
• Day care center	Staff dress and conduct policy
Health Care	
• Community hospital	HIPAA-compliant release form
	Training policy and implementation
• Regional hospital/health system	Patient care accountability policy
Schools	
• Catholic elementary school	Bullying policy
Government	
• County child welfare agency	Merge adoption and foster care approval processes
	Streamline training policy
• County aging services agency	Board confidentiality policy
• County juvenile probation office	Develop placement outcomes tracking system
Legislative	
• State senator's office	Legislative referendum reform

The project was reviewed and discussed in class. The instructor frequently elicited examples from student projects to illustrate concepts and principles from the text; the students were periodically asked in class to share how their projects were progressing; and students sometimes asked questions about aspects of their policy work. The instructor was available to students to meet outside of class to help with any aspect of the process, and some students took advantage of this opportunity. The instructor, not the organization partner, assigned the grade for the policy paper.

STUDY DESIGN AND MEASURES

Assessment of the effectiveness of the policy project strategy included feedback at the end of the course using three approaches.

1. Students participated in a structured focus group.
2. They also completed a postcourse, printed survey adapted from the Cedar Crest Political Engagement Module survey.
3. Organizational partners filled out postproject surveys, supplemented by either face-to-face or telephone follow-up questions by the instructor.

FINDINGS

Student feedback at the end of the course was captured each year using a structured focus group, with the instructor facilitating the discussion. Results included the following:

- Students said that working on a policy with an organization in the community helped them understand the course content. They reported that working with organizations in the community helped them better understand local, state, and federal government and improved the process of becoming a policy advocate. One said, "I'm now on the same ground as political science majors."
- Students also reported that the course increased their desire to promote social change, including involvement in policy practice. They perceived that the policy project would enhance their marketability to prospective employees and graduate programs after degree completion.
- Students thought that the democratic classroom pedagogy increased their interest in and commitment to the course. They liked having input into

course design, including how they were evaluated, whether by chapter questions or quizzes, exams or papers.

- They reported that they learned a lot about social policy and writing a policy proposal. Comments from students about the previous version of the course had included requests for more examples of agency policies and policy proposals than were presented in the text. With the policy service-learning projects, students brought into class real-life examples from their organizations. Students said that discussing their policy project work in class as it evolved brought the content to life and made readings from the text clearer. They added that the policy projects gave them a sense of accomplishment.
- Students noted the importance of the instructor's being available for consultation and support. They also liked the option of working with another student on the policy proposal.
- Students reported anxiety about the expectations, in that the policy project initially felt like it was "too much." Students reported some anxiety about how to initiate a project with an organization and what they might be working on.
- Students recommended that more guidance and support be provided in the partnering process. During the first year of the study, students recommended that the instructor preselect organizations that really want to work with them, while retaining students' option to self-select an organization, with the instructor making the introductory contacts.
- Students also recommended that the instructor steer future students away from large projects that were in the initial design stages ("more amorphous"). They found it difficult to figure out how to get involved.
- The students recommended that in future years, an initial meeting be held with the organization, instructor, and student for all projects in order to strengthen agreement about goals and expectations. Several students reported having to wait for their assigned staff members to finish a meeting or task to meet with them as scheduled, as well as being asked to do what they considered busy work. They also advised that all project assignments be finalized before the first class.
- Some students recommended that the university give an extra course credit for the policy project, which they compared to a lab in a science course.
- They also suggested that the organization partnership approach be used in more courses. One said, "We care more about what we learn if we experience it." Likewise, the students reported that the democratic classroom approach should be used in upper-level courses in the university, but they cautioned that this pedagogy might not work with courses with twenty or more students due to the time required to build consensus.

Surveys of organization partners were done during the first year using a form provided by Cedar Crest College, which was revised by the instructor for use in the second and subsequent years. Of the twenty projects, the organizations rated six (30 percent) as having no or minimal impact on the organization and fourteen (70 percent) as having moderate or substantial impact. The areas of impact are presented in table 4.2. Of the twenty projects, 55 percent resulted in new materials, products, policies, or forms; 45 percent resulted in new procedures; 30 percent resulted in completing a project, often one that the organization was having difficulty finding time to complete; and 25 percent positively impacted services to constituents. Other projects were seen as having an impact on mission, vision, or values (a project in which students located and organized demographic data in a way that contributed to the development of an organizationwide diversity policy), and legislation (a voter referendum).

Examples of successful projects may be instructive. At a community hospital, a release form was developed independently by two students who were granted permission by a regional, university-related teaching hospital to adapt its form. The revised form, along with a policy for use and for training staff, completed legal review and was implemented hospitalwide. At a county child protective services agency, a staff training policy was revised to comply with changing state regulations. The student sought input from supervisors who were to be given additional responsibility for training when the policy was implemented. The organization reported that the policy was completed and implemented sooner because of student involvement. In the same organization, policies were revised to merge training of prospective foster parents and adoptive parents. The organization reported that the resulting training was more efficient than when the two groups were trained separately, and the resulting policy was disseminated to other county human service departments as a model.

One student worked with a local office of Planned Parenthood on a statewide legislative initiative to require all hospitals to make emergency

Table 4.2. Areas of Impact on the Organization

Area of Impact	Number of Projects	Percent of Total Projects
Services to constituents	5	25
Completing a project	6	30
Mission, vision, or values	2	10
Organizational procedures	9	45
Connections with the community	1	5
New products, policies, or forms	11	55
Legislation	1	5

Note: Total number of projects = 20. More than one selection was permitted.

contraception available to women who were the victims of incest or rape. The initiative did not pass, but the student was instrumental in lobbying and training others across the state to work on the initiative. Another student was asked by a youth and family nonprofit organization to assist in determining what incentives might be more effective to encourage supervisory staff to continue to act, or to increase their time spent, as staff trainers. She worked with the instructor to design and conduct a survey of regional nonprofits to learn what incentives they employed to encourage their staff to engage in training activities, and she shared the results of this survey with her partner organization. Two students at a for-profit day care center worked with management and staff to design a set of policies covering the dress and conduct of direct-care staff. A student worked with the principal and parents of a parochial elementary school to develop a bullying policy that included the reporting and management of allegations.

Organization partners provided their opinions about what helped the project to work. Student-related variables were chosen most frequently: for half of the twenty projects, the respondents selected "verbal information from the student," "the student's interest or enthusiasm about the project," and "the student's overall attitude." Of the respondents, 40 percent selected "the student's ability to interact with supervisor or other staff" and "the student's ability to complete tasks or assignments"; 25 percent cited "written/e-mailed information from the student" and "the student's reliability or dependability"; 20 percent selected "written information from the instructor." Of respondents selecting the "other" category, two organizations mentioned that the students asked good questions and brought a different perspective; others said that the student showed initiative, kept the supervisor moving, or began to work on the policy at a good time, or that student and staff motivated each other (one organization each). One organization reported that weekly meetings helped keep things moving. Another noted that there was a learning curve for the student, who was more helpful as the project proceeded. On the other hand, another organization commented that its student was able to start and produce results quickly. One organization liked that a student had learned about legal issues, regulations, organization policy, and their interconnectedness and that she understood the reasons for developing a policy.

Organization partners also noted obstacles. The primary obstacle selected was a lack of information from the instructor about what was expected before the start of the project (25 percent of the projects). The next most frequently chosen option included student-related variables, such as "student was not dependable; for example, missed meetings or did not follow through with assignments" (20 percent of projects), "student did not have enough time to devote to the project" (15 percent), and "student did not assume enough responsibility or take initiative" (15 percent). The selection of "not being dependable in attending scheduled meetings and following through with assignments" was particularly true for students who were single parents or working and attending school full-time. Comments in the "other" category included "the organization selected a project that was in its infancy and required a good bit of student initiative to move forward," "poor student writing skills," "lack of consistency of the student's time with the organization," "schedule conflicts between the student and organization," and "would have liked more time." One organization reported that the project had to be narrowed to fit the student's available time. Another reported that the two students assigned to the project appeared more interested in finding out what the project would accomplish if it were implemented, rather than working to accomplish project implementation tasks.

Recommendations for improvement, an open-ended question on the post-project organization survey, corresponded to the obstacles mentioned by the organization partners. Organizations responding mentioned a desire for more information prior to the start of the project for 35 percent of the projects. Two would have preferred this to occur in a face-to-face meeting with the instructor; three would have wanted the student to be included as well; another preferred more information in writing rather than face to face. Although written information about the project scope and expectations was provided to each organization prior to the start of the project, it was clear that this was not enough for most organizations. Two strategies will be considered for the next project year: the written information will be clarified as to expectations of student, organization, and instructor, and whenever possible, a face-to-face meeting including all three will be held to review the expectations.

Two of the organizations recommended a more formal process for students with less initiative; one of them, in which two students, by design, worked fairly independently of the organization on an outcomes project, recommended that students should submit a written report and meet with the organization at the end of the project. This recommendation was implemented, and the policy paper was modified for the fourth project year to require that the students report on the organization's satisfaction with the results of the project. Other recommendations were to select students with strong interest in either the organization or project, more effective communication with the students, longer planning lead time for the project, and improved student writing skills.

All students who finished the course completed a confidential postproject survey about the course and project. The data reported below are from the surveys completed by all students in the second through fourth project years, whether or not they completed their projects. The surveys used a five- or six-point Likert scale, varying by type of item. All but one student agreed or strongly agreed that the work they had done in this course had made them more marketable in their chosen profession after graduation; the remaining respondent selected "neither agree nor disagree." All but one said that the opportunity to learn outside the classroom and the instructor's ability to promote the integration of active learning and classroom readings and assignments were "very good" or "excellent"; the remaining respondent selected "good." All rated the instructor's enthusiasm as "very good" or "excellent." The survey also asked the students to report the average number of hours a week spent on the course, compared with the number of hours they considered valuable in advancing their education. After discarding one outlier, an average of 7.9 hours was reported to have been spent on this course per week (ranging from 2.5 to 18.5 hours), of which students believed an average of 6.4 hours (81 percent of hours spent) to have been valuable in advancing their education.

DISCUSSION

The goals of the policy project outlined earlier were substantially achieved.

- Regarding goal 1, all of the students successfully completing a service-learning project played a part, whether small or large, in working on a real policy in a human service organization.
- Regarding goal 2, students developed relationships with community organizations or entities, bridging the gap between previous service-learning experiences and the five-hundred-hour field practicum. They reported that they were able to come to know an organization in the semester prior to entering the field practicum and were, therefore, more knowledgeable about whether to pursue a field placement with that type of organization. Over the four years of this study, three of twenty-four students (13 percent) entered field placements in the organization where they had completed their policy project.
- Regarding goal 3, students reported having gained more knowledge, skills, and confidence in their ability to engage in policy practice and advocacy after the collaborative policy projects. As in the Cedar Crest College Participating in Democracy Project, students taking the policy course reported that they were more likely to become involved in certain aspects of the political process, including writing letters to the editor and policy practice. Although this outcome was not one of the three initial goals, students reported an unanticipated advantage of the policy projects: they could list the project on student portfolios and resumes. References to their service-learning policy projects might be considered more prestigious than internships or other student activities to the extent that they were real-life projects developed in partnership with local community organizations.

Instructors may be correctly concerned that using this model requires more of their time. For each of the first three years, the instructor's time investment increased because of the organization partners' and students' desire for more preproject information and preparation. The time investment remained about the same for the fourth year for two possible reasons. First, as the course is taught, systems are developed that work and can be revised or used "as is" in subsequent years, including assignment handouts, checklists, and e-mail communication with prospective organizations. In the two most recent academic years, a precourse meeting with students was held to explain the policy project and to start the matching process between students and organizations; this proved helpful in making earlier student contact with potential organization partners. Second, organization partners with experience using the model agreed to take students in subsequent years, and when students selected these organizations, less instructor time was needed to orient them to the project.

After having taught the policy course using organization partners for four successive academic years, the instructor has found that a number of organizations now anticipate having students work on policy projects, and some engage in planning about how best to utilize student energy and skills. Of the eight organizations serving as partners in the third project year, all responded on the postproject survey that they would be willing to participate in this type of project again; six of them committed to the fourth project year.

The instructor believes that because this is a particularly effective method of teaching policy practice, it is worth whatever additional time is required. Experiential learning is reported to be more effective than passive learning as it increases faculty-student interaction. Use of the policy project model requires more faculty-student contact in and out of class, respects diverse talents and ways of learning, uses problems as points of entry into the subject, and makes courses assignment centered rather than merely text and lecture centered, all of which are hallmarks of effective pedagogy (Walvoord, Barry, and Laughner 2001). The instructor also enjoyed soliciting examples from the students' policy work with the organization partners as examples in class discussion since they were more relevant to the students than examples from the text or other sources.

This model has two advantages over a community partner model that involves the class in one large project. First, students can select a project of interest, which, for some, appears to enhance commitment to the process and to effective learning. Second, students get to know an organization well enough to determine whether they want to seek a field placement in that organization or type of setting, while group projects may not afford the same level of perceived connection. These are areas for further study.

TEACHING RECOMMENDATIONS

Instructors wishing to test this model are advised to preselect more organizations than there are students in order to facilitate effective matching and student choice. Partnering with political entities, as well as nonprofit organizations engaged in community development, will provide additional policy sites for students. Legislative offices offer this option, and the state offices of membership organizations like the National Association of Social Workers may also be explored. Ideas for engaging students in policy projects at the state or local level are available at Influencing State Policy, the national committee of social work educators dedicated to teaching policy practice. The instructor found this resource particularly valuable (www.statepolicy.org).

This policy project model might be considered for other undergraduate social work courses, particularly those focusing on work with organizations and communities. However, application of the model to large classes would dramatically increase instructor time and require additional teaching support or modifications to course design.

CONCLUSION

Both social work programs and human service organizations are encouraged to try collaborating on student service-learning policy projects. The investment of time in initiating such projects and keeping them on track appears to pay dividends in active learning and the accomplishment of policy initiatives that, for lack of student involvement, might not be addressed. The author hopes that his experience with this service-learning policy project will be useful to those who try and that they will share the results of their innovations with others in both the academy and in human services.

REFERENCES

Anderson, D. K., and Harris, B. M. (2005). Teaching social welfare policy: A comparison of two pedagogical approaches. *Journal of Social Work Education, 41*(3), 511–26.

Cedar Crest College. (2003). *The democratic academy and engaged citizenship: An assessment of student learning outcomes.* Retrieved January 3, 2005, from Cedar Crest College website at www.cedarcrest.edu/redesign/democracy/pdf%20files/Comprehensive%20Assessment%20Report%20AY%202002-2003.pdf.

Ishisaka, H. A., Sohng, S. S. L., Farwell, N., and Uehara, E. S. (2004). Partnership for integrated community-based learning: A social work community-campus collaboration. *Journal of Social Work Education, 40*(2), 321–36.

Jansson, B. S. (2003). *Becoming an effective policy advocate: From policy practice to social justice* (4th ed.). Pacific Grove, CA: Brooks/Cole.

Mendes, P. (2003). Teaching social policy to social work students: A critical reflection. *Australian Social Work, 56*(3), 220–33.

Rocha, C. J. (2000). Evaluating experiential teaching methods in a policy practice course: The case for service learning to increase political participation. *Journal of Social Work Education, 36*(1), 53–63. Retrieved from the Academic Search Elite database (2793467), 1–11.

Rocha, C. J., and Johnson, A. K. (1997). Teaching family policy through a policy practice framework. *Journal of Social Work Education, 33*(3), 433–44. Retrieved from the Academic Search Elite database (402429), 1–12.

Sherraden, M. S., Slosar, B., and Sherraden, M. (2002). Innovation in social policy: Collaborative policy advocacy. *Social Work, 47*(3), 209–21.

Walvoord, B., Barry, K., and Laughner, T. (2001). *Teaching well using technology: A faculty member's guide to time-efficient choices that enhance learning.* Notre Dame, IN: Kaneb Center for Teaching and Learning, University of Notre Dame.

Wolk, J. L., Pray, J. E., Weismiller, T, and Dempsey, D. (1996). Political practica: Educating social work students for policymaking. *Journal of Social Work Education, 32*(1), 91–100.

Chapter Five

Social Work Practice: Nurturing Beginning Practice Skills while Mobilizing Partnerships between Youth Development Agencies and Social Work Education

Marie L. Watkins, Leanne Charlesworth, and Annemarie V. House

As social work education wrestles with its responsibility to educate students about the human service demands of the twenty-first century, a more explicit link between education and practice is required in the early and formative years of students' social work education. This chapter describes how the application of classroom learning, guided by service-learning experiences based in youth development agencies, enhances student understanding of the history, as well as the premises, principles, and practices, of the profession of social work.

The youth development model was established within the context of settlement house social work with youth. Today, this model remains an untapped resource for social work education. The authors suggest that embedding youth development premises, principles, and practices within a service-learning component of an "Introduction to Social Work" course helps students make the connection between social work's rich service history and the reality of current service provision within youth development agencies. A growing number of social work educators have voiced concern about the youth development model's lack of representation in social work education (Barton, Watkins, and Jajoura 1998; Morrison, Alcorn, and Nelum 1997; Watkins and Iverson 1997; Watkins, Morrison, and McCarthy 1999). On the other side of the social work education's "town-gown" equation, youth development professionals urge social work education to move beyond the treatment-oriented, problem-centered knowledge, skills, and values that are contradictory to the "assets-based" and "preparation for adulthood" model of youth development (Watkins 2000, 2006). Service-learning partnerships between youth development professionals and social work educators confront these issues by providing forums to share expertise, receive information with which to examine current practice, and shape human service delivery systems related to best practices with diverse youth populations (Greene 1996). Service-learning partnerships between social work educators and youth development agencies are also very timely because the service activities respond to the youth development agencies' shrinking resources while simultaneously providing learning that is strengths focused, culturally competent, community based, and, most importantly, youth centered (Watkins 2006).

Recent reports indicate that the need for youth development services is increasing while agency funding is diminishing (McLaughlin 2000; National Research Council and Institute of Medicine 2002). Contemporary settlement houses and other community-based agencies, such as Boys and Girls Clubs, Big Brothers/Big Sisters, YMCAs and YWCAs, and Girls, Inc., have increased their efforts to provide effective emotional, physical, and academic support and supervision to more children and adolescents as parents, schools, and communities are less available to fulfill their roles as nurturers in healthy youth development (Carnegie Council on Adolescent Development 1995; Delgado 2004; DeWitt Wallace Reader's Digest Fund 1996; Hechinger 1992; Merry 2000; Watkins 2000). F. Hechinger's words of more than a decade ago continue to ring true as the poverty rate for children in our country remains alarmingly high: "Youth service organizations are assuming a crucial new role for children and youth at high risk, and that role is to supplement incomplete or inadequate families and families who are simply too poor to provide for their children's needs" (1992, 191).

This chapter discusses the viability of a service-learning partnership between a youth-development-grounded, century-old settlement house and an "Introduction to Social Work" course taught at Nazareth College of Rochester, New York. This partnership illustrates the ways in which youth development agencies can provide undergraduate social work students with service-learning opportunities, facilitating knowledge and skill development in the areas of youth empowerment, advocacy, and community involvement (Boyd 2001; Jarman-Rohde et al. 1997; Libby, Rosen, and Sedonaen 2005). Our discussion also explores the concept of youth development and the operational mechanics of initiating and sustaining service-learning partnerships focused on achieving course objectives within an "Introduction to Social Work" course. Service and social work learning opportunities, as well as examples of the impact of youth development service-learning partnerships on student learning outcomes, are highlighted.

THE YOUTH DEVELOPMENT MODEL
AND SOCIAL WORK EDUCATION

A theoretical congruency exists within the literature on resiliency and the premises of youth development, the history of the social work profession, the youth services provided within a settlement house, and the objectives of an "Introduction to Social Work" course.

The youth development model offers a framework for social workers to believe in, think about, and practice the core tenets of strengths-based micro, mezzo, and macro social work practice with youth. The youth development model advocates a set of premises, principles, and practices to "prepare a child" (Pittman 1996). According to K. Pittman, "We must change how we look at youth and expect young people to be not just problem free, but fully prepared. To be fully prepared, young people need people, places, possibilities, preparation, practices, participation, permission, promotion, and perspective. And that equals power" (1996, 7).

The youth development model does not operate in a vacuum. The model takes into account the existence of adversities and developmental challenges that may impact children in different ways in many circumstances. At the same time, the youth development model suggests building on the competencies of youth and "emphasizes the manifest potentialities rather than the supposed incapacitates of young people—including those from the most disadvantaged backgrounds and those with the most troubled histories" (Damon 2004, 16). While taking into account the varied circumstances that may be present in the lives of youngsters, youth development focuses on the achievement of positive youth outcomes. Positive youth outcomes have been defined as psychosocial and competency-based outcomes (Academy for Educational Development/Center for Youth Development and Policy Research 1996). *Psychosocial outcomes* include a sense of safety and protection, a sense of self-worth or positive self-concept, mastery, autonomy, a sense of belonging, spirituality, and self-awareness. *Competency-based outcomes* include personal competency or efficacy, physical health, mental health, cultural and social competence, and employability. Moreover, healthy development outcomes have been articulated as the Forty Developmental Assets (Search Institute 1995), assets critical to preparing young people for adulthood. Thus, social work grounded in the youth development model offers relationship-building, programmatic, and policy-development opportunities to

- build on youth competencies
- prepare youth for adulthood
- promote holistic mastery-building and relationship-enhancing opportunities to increase the number of positive youth outcomes (Bloomberg et al. 2003; Catalano et al. 2004), which in turn minimize the "rotten" outcomes (Dryfoos 1990)

The rationale for youth development services is deeply reflective of the values of the social work profession and its methods; it therefore reinforces the focus of the "Introduction to Social Work" course. During this introduction to the social work profession, students learn the core, contemporary social work knowledge, values, and skills. In addition, students are expected to acquire a basic understanding of fundamental professional principles, including the meaning and relevance of concepts like cultural competency, empowerment, and social justice. Furthermore, students are introduced to systems thinking and the strengths perspective and are expected to acquire a beginning-level ability to apply this knowledge. Thus, the intended student learning outcomes of the "Introduction to Social Work" course are supported by the underlying premises, principles, and practices of youth development:

- Youth development is all inclusive; its philosophy embraces difference. Youth development approaches and strategies embrace all youth, including those who have not chosen healthy behaviors.
- Youth development operates within the total environment of the individual, emphasizing a holistic approach to change. Youth development approaches engage youth, families, community-based organizations, government, and others in the community as full partners, working together to make a difference.
- Youth development links individuals with resources. Youth development approaches recognize that all youth need opportunities in order to acquire and sustain healthy behavior and attitudes.
- Youth development capitalizes on the hope and belief that all people have the potential to change and grow. Youth development approaches support the long-term sustained efforts vital to the development of behavioral change toward healthy lifestyle choices (Partners for Children 2000, 9–10).

In summary, the youth development model supports many connections to social work, primarily its ecological and strengths perspective approaches, through a belief in the resiliency and potential of the youthful spirit: "Youth development happens everywhere. The process is enduring, comprehensive, and engages youth. All youth are developing; all youth have strengths; all youth have needs; all youth can contribute to their communities; all youth are valued" (Pittman as cited by Partners for Children 2000, 15).

FRAMEWORK FOR SERVICE-LEARNING INTEGRATION

The "Introduction to Social Work" course is a prerequisite for all other social work courses within the baccalaureate social work curriculum. It has historically provided students with the foundation needed to understand and fulfill virtually all of the Council on Social Work Education's *Educational Policy and Accreditation Standards* and baccalaureate program objectives through other coursework.

The placement of a service-learning opportunity within this "prefieldwork" social work course enables students to experience and integrate the basic principles of the social work profession. As a result, student exposure to social work's settlement house tradition grounded in the principles of youth development became the focus of the service-learning opportunity. The impetus for the academic service-learning experience was a series of collaborative, community-based events sponsored by the Nazareth College Office of Multicultural Affairs, Nazareth College's Center for Service-Learning, the college's Department of Social Work, and the community-based settlement house. These events celebrated the legacy of settlement house work in the Rochester area. As a result of these activities, the faculty who taught the "Introduction to Social Work" course, funded by Nazareth College's Center for Service-Learning, committed to a three-year service-learning partnership with an after-school youth education/employment program conducted by the settlement house.

Three action steps were used to build partnerships among the faculty members, agency staff, students, and the service recipients—the youth. These action steps included

- developing the partnership
- integrating the experience into course content
- adding a macro-level dimension to the course

Developing the Partnership

To develop the partnership, an initial focus was matching the agency's strengths and the academic institution's requirements, using the expertise of the faculty and the settlement house staff. This matching process produced an interdependent synergy to achieve mutually determined interests, capacities, and needs. The faculty engaged agency representatives in the design of the course's service-learning requirements in order to

- establish commonalities between the outcomes of social work education and the youth development mission statement of the agency
- achieve a collective agreement on the guiding conceptual framework (i.e., the congruency between youth development principles and the empowerment/strengths perspective)
- redefine individual institutional boundaries to incorporate the scope of partnership

- achieve mutual agreement on outcomes, goals, resources, and methods of operation congruent with the requirements of the "Introduction to Social Work" course, while honoring the mission of the agency and the integrity of the youth development model of service delivery
- help students translate social work concepts, such as psychosocial assessments, resistant clients, coping strategies, and other case-management strategies, into youth development opportunities for relationship building, youth-adult partnerships, and asset-based advocacy, with youth as resources, not recipients of service (Watkins and Braun 2005; Watkins 1998)

Integrating the Experience into Course Content

A second action step was the incorporation of youth development premises, principles, and practices within student learning outcomes and course learning objectives. The service-learning activities were embedded in the "Introduction to Social Work" course to demonstrate to students the connection between settlement house–based youth development and the history of social work practice. Therefore, the practices of youth development infused within service-learning activities, combined with the "Introduction to Social Work" course outcomes, provided the structure, coherence, and congruency for the relationship among the youth development agency, Nazareth College's Department of Social Work, and the college's Center for Service-Learning.

The knowledge, skills, and values of youth development were integrated within the "Introduction to Social Work" course objectives in the following manner:

- Generalist social work practice skills (interpersonal, groups, community organization, research) and curriculum content were based on the strengths-oriented, youth development, and developmental asset-based frameworks.
- The integration of the theory-based social work curriculum, combined with the realities of youth development agencies' daily operations and the youth members' well-being and social functioning, provided a coherent educational approach to teaching generalist practice skills.
- Critical thinking skills were important competencies as students applied theory to youth situations.
- Opportunities for increased appreciation and application of skills related to person-in-environment, cultural competency, and social and economic justice were infused into students' educational skill-building experiences.
- Relevant and appropriate individual and social group work services to youth were offered through respectful, collaborative, mutual relationship-

building between youngsters and social workers, rather than problem-focused treatment interventions.

- Advocacy knowledge and skills were taught to promote policy and legislative change within community-based, family-centered, youth-focused systems and institutions.
- The values and ethics of the youth development and generalist social work professions were transmitted (Watkins 1998).

Successfully integrating the experience into course content is a critical action step because students must understand that the service-learning experiences are intentionally designed to reflect the practice strategies derived from the daily realities and unique culture of the youth development agency while simultaneously integrating academic requirements. Frequently, students will ask, "How is playing basketball really a form of social work?" Another common lament is, "The kids won't sit and listen to me as I try to counsel them." The "unruly" behavior of youth who may or may not show up for a group activity may initially create confusion for "Introduction to Social Work" students who are intent on "assessing" and "helping" young people.

With intentionally designed service-learning activities to illuminate the strengths of youth, the connection between the social work concepts of "resiliency" and the "strengths perspective" and the youth development conceptual framework facilitate the students' achievement of the "aha" experience. The most common area of professional growth and personal development relates to the students' reaction to youth behavior. Students' interpretation of youth's "inappropriate and unruly behavior" becomes a teachable moment to examine the connection between the students' personal premises, principles, and practices and the role of a strengths-based social worker.

Adding a Macro Dimension

A third action step is to design service-learning activities that involve faculty, students, and agency staff with administrative macro-oriented projects that exist within the agency, in addition to "fun with a purpose," guidance-oriented activities provided for youth. Community-based, macro-oriented, service-learning activities facilitate students' initial understanding of the profession's historical and contemporary philosophy and knowledge, value, and skill base. Service learning enriches student ability in these areas through technical assistance, research, and community-outreach opportunities. Such research and outreach opportunities include assistance with program development and evaluation, grant writing, and community outreach. This array of macro service-learning experiences positively challenges students and provides faculty the possibility of research and service activities.

SERVICE-LEARNING YOUTH DEVELOPMENT ACTIVITIES

With background clarification and planning between agency staff, faculty, and students completed, the students committed to a ten-week, two-hour contract with the after-school education/employment program. The time commitment also included assignments for the course, planning and participating in a variety of activities, writing a reflective journal, and participating in reflective classroom discussions.

At the start of the partnership, an identified and significant need among the youth participants was the influence of a relationship with a "caring adult." The social work students served as caring adults, offering relationship-building skills, asset strengthening, mentoring, role modeling, goal development, and plain old fun. Activities engaged in by social work students and youth included the development and presentation of "dream boards." In this relationship-building activity, both teens and social work students visually depicted their hopes and aspirations for the future on poster board. Completed dream boards were presented to one another and displayed.

Social work students and youth also attended community and campus events together. These events included a citywide youth summit. In addition, students and youth collaboratively planned campus tours, pizza parties on campus, and the viewing of on-campus theater performances or similar extracurricular events. During one semester, social work students created a video entitled "A Day in the Life of a College Student" for the teens.

Students and teens also collaboratively planned many other diverse activities in response to teen interests, such as mock job interviews, academic or other "awards" ceremonies or celebrations for teens, a "night out" at a teen night club, and multicultural dinners. In addition, social work students consistently provided mentoring and homework tutoring when needed.

SERVICE-LEARNING YOUTH DEVELOPMENT OUTCOMES

A variety of youth competency-building and student learning outcomes are achieved through this type of partnership. Settlement house staff indicated that the service-learning component of the class not only exposed youth to positive adults (the social work students) but also stimulated interest in career and college exploration. The experience supported the sharing of important support and information regarding education and career choices, as well as hopefulness about the future among all participants.

Without a doubt, the students' participation in this service-learning activity brought course objectives "to life." Students, in their reflective discussion and writing, reported a variety of types of learning. Many students described their firsthand glimpse into a life outside of the familiar. Some students indicated that the experience represented their first exposure to the challenges of youth and families struggling with poverty and inadequate educational and social welfare programs. Many students began to understand the operation of a multifaceted neighborhood service center. Some students described their revisiting of the challenges of adolescence. For example, some students who initially identified with the youth attending the settlement house reported surprise at the generational differences they discovered.

Most significantly, many students began to assess their own values, fears of diverse populations and urban settings, and desire to pursue the field of social work. For some, the experience bolstered self-confidence and enabled self-discovery of varied talents and skills. Many students indicated that they were proud of themselves for overcoming their initial concerns and fears about youth who reside in urban neighborhoods or in a city. Student reflections suggested that many students would be more likely, in the future, to pursue similar educational or career experiences. Some students noted that the experience "opened their eyes" to their own relationship-building, organizational, or other skills, as well as stimulated their interest in potentially working with teens again in the future.

Student learning and revelations were most eloquently and honestly shared in reflective journals. The following samples are organized by course objective.

Demonstrate and Understand the History and Evolution of the Social Work Profession

As noted, students were exposed to a multipurpose, neighborhood-based, service-delivery setting. In addition to participating in the after-school program, the students learned the overall function of the settlement setting. Students had an opportunity to witness the manner in which modern settlement work has come a long way since the days of Jane Addams and Hull House.

Identify At-Risk Populations, as well as Their Strengths, Challenges, and Service/Advocacy Needs

Through service learning at the settlement house, social work students also began to gain a clear understanding of the concept of the "person-in-environment."

The students began to hypothesize about which youth were choosing healthy behaviors and which were not. They began to recognize how nonproductive choices could be directly related to a lack of support from family or community and to poverty. The social work students began to understand the importance of professional advocacy and community intervention to improve and develop long-term effective partnerships to enhance the potential of youth from underserved neighborhoods. The settlement house "opened its door" for social work students to develop practice skills in working with culturally diverse populations, which broaden their views of social work practice to include an awareness of the interconnectedness of other systems impacting the lives of youth. As one student reflected, the settlement house "provides many services to the Rochester community. The XYZ program in particular has helped to get children off the street and provide them with an afternoon activity as well as tutoring. I think that [the education/employment program] is a benefit to the community; however, more planning and organization [is] needed to occur to make it much more dynamic."

Identify Personal and Professional Values and the Relevance of Self-Awareness to Social Work

In each written student reflection, students were encouraged to "dig deeply" into their personal belief systems as they discuss their experiences at the settlement house. The first student reflection assignment was especially designed to encourage students to articulate their assumptions and concerns to establish a baseline of knowledge, skills, and attitudes. Emerging from the first reflection papers were themes about their personal values.

- "Due to stereotypes, I have to admit that I was a little intimidated. The kids are great. The energy and laughter helped move the group along."
- "Being from Rochester, I have heard many things about the children at [this settlement house]. I hope that by working with them I can prove the negative sayings to be false and confirm the positives."
- "Both sets of students (settlement house and Nazareth) are able to experience a truly human and honest contact. I feel that all the students can gain a better understanding of people and better understand their differences and similarities, which will impact on their lives forever."
- "Approaching the [settlement house], I was a bit reserved and nervous about meeting 'city kids.' My preconceived notions of kids living in the projects were that they were angry and lived a life of crime. Therefore, they were probably cold and hard and would probably see us as imposing on

their lives. . . . I found myself absorbing everything that was taking place and hoped that my prejudice was not showing."

Make an Informed Decision Regarding
Social Work as an Educational and Career Focus

As noted, the service-learning component of the "Introduction to Social Work" course provides the student with an opportunity to prepare for field practicum. There are often few possibilities early in the social work curriculum for students to connect with an agency to begin their micro/mezzo/macro practice skill development. Because of this "beginning" experience, the student can explore his or her own direction and focus, asking, Do I truly want to be a social worker? or Do I want to work with youth? The service-learning experience can solidify the student's desire to enter the field of social work and offer him or her the chance to make an enlightened decision about a career choice based on increased self-knowledge and understanding of the profession. In this case, student reflection entries indicated that the service-learning opportunity did, indeed, provide preprofessional experiences.

- "The experience helped me explore my use of self as a social worker."
- "I think it's a great experience and one that will help me in my decision of whether to go on to graduate school for social work or school psychology."
- "If I do decide to become a social worker, then this will help me to not judge people before I meet them so I can get to know them first."
- "I learned that you have to be ready for change and be flexible to new ideas. I did a lot of reflective and critical thinking. The service-learning project helped to relate the textbook to reality."

A BROADER PERSPECTIVE ON IMPACTS IN AN "INTRODUCTION TO SOCIAL WORK" COURSE

Multiple additional potential student learning outcomes may result from youth development service-learning experiences. In general, students have an opportunity to demonstrate proficiency with generalist practice knowledge, values, and skills in community-based, grassroots, youth development settings. That is, while students are learning about the history of the social work profession and the range of practice arenas, they also have the opportunity to see firsthand the challenges of the implementation of youth development principles (and their connection to the strengths perspective) across various fields of social work practice (e.g., child welfare, juvenile justice, school social work, community mental health practice with youth). For example, students learn quickly about the potential tension between social work practice from a youth development model as they are introduced to problem-based social work interventions in the "Introduction to Social Work" class. As one student succinctly stated, "I am amazed at the differences in the way that other professionals think about and treat kids—I never thought that youth development meant anything more than playing with kids, until we heard about the settlement house's staff's meeting with Joey's teacher and school counselor. I could hear the difference in their approach with him—now I get it [the youth development model]."

Other potential impacts of a youth development service-learning project include students' increased proficiency in applying youth development principles and social work practice intervention in the following areas:

- social work practice with individuals, as well as group skills relevant to the biopsychosocial developmental stages of youth
- understanding the intersection of race, socioeconomic status, gender, sexual/affection orientation, and social and economic justice principles in the provision of services to a diverse population of youth
- understanding community-based, family-centered, youth-focused systems interactions
- principles of client-centered, asset-based outcomes measurements and practice evaluation tools that reflect indicators of healthy development rather than decreases in social problems
- increased self-awareness and constructive and ethical use of self, as well as the application of structured supervision in social work practice with youth from diverse backgrounds
- the historical placement of settlement house group work as one foundation of social work practice (Watkins 1998)

In their reflection papers, students indicated that they were able to work with such general social work concepts and engage in more sophisticated discussions related to self-awareness, particularly their own attitudes and values. Furthermore, students indicated that the service-learning experience facilitated an opportunity to "step out of their comfort areas." In addition, students gained new information and experiences, facilitating enlightened decisions regarding career choices.

A less anticipated impact emerges when instructors journey along with the students as they become more self-aware and honest with themselves. The instructor may experience validation when students become more able to identify negative value judgments and share how beliefs and attitudes are beginning to change as a result of the service-learning experience. The instructor may find his or her own skills challenged in the course of "starting where the student is" developmentally and responding sensitively to student fears and concerns regarding urban settings and residents. The instructor's relationship-building skills may be challenged as students initially express high levels of fear, anxiety, and even anger regarding the service-learning requirement.

CONCLUSION

Youth development agencies continue to respond to the human service needs of millions of vulnerable families and youth who reside in many of our country's most underresourced neighborhoods. Unfortunately, the youth development model and traditional youth development agencies are typically overlooked and underrepresented in social work education. Service-learning opportunities provide a bridge of resources between these agencies and social work education.

It is our contention that social work education would benefit from the inclusion of community-based youth development agencies as partners in social work education. Many of the core services conducted by youth development agencies are congruent with the knowledge, skills, and value requirements of generalist social work practice and the principles of undergraduate social work education. Such partnerships would facilitate the achievement of academic outcomes for baccalaureate social work students, as well as enhance teaching, research, and service collaborations between youth development agencies and social work programs.

REFERENCES

Academy for Educational Development/Center for Youth Development and Policy Research. (1996). *Youth program/community outcomes.* Washington, DC: Author.

Barton, W., Watkins, M., and Jajoura, R. (1998). Youth and communities: Towards comprehensive strategies. In P. Ewalt, E. Freeman, and D. Poole (Eds.), *Community building: Renewal, well-being, and shared responsibility* (145–68). Washington, DC: NASW Press.

Benson, P. (1997). *All kids are our kids.* San Francisco, CA: Jossey-Bass.

Bloomberg, L., Ganey, A., Alba, V., Quintero, G., and Alcantara, A. A. (2003). An asset-based program for youth. *American Journal of Health Behavior, 27,* S45–S54

Boyd, B. L. (2001). Bringing leadership experiences to inner-city youth. *Journal of Extension, 39*(4). Retrieved October 10, 2006, from http://joe.org/joe/2001august/a6.html.

Carnegie Council on Adolescent Development. (1995). *Great transitions: Preparing adolescents for a new century*. New York: Carnegie Foundation.

Carnegie Council on Adolescent Development, Task Force on Youth Development and Community Programs. (1992). *A matter of time: Risk and opportunity in the nonschool hours*. New York: Carnegie Corporation of New York.

Catalano, R., Berglund, L., Ryan, J., Lonczak, H., and Hawkins, D. (2004). Positive youth development in the United States: Research findings on evaluations of positive youth development programs. *The Annals of the American Academy, 591*(1), 98–124.

Center for Youth Development and Policy Research. (1994). *Enriching local planning for youth development: A mobilization agenda*. Washington, DC: Center for Youth Development and Policy Research/Academy for Educational Development.

Damon, W. (2004). What is positive youth development? *The Annals of the American Academy, 591*(1), 13–24.

Delgado, M. (2004). *New frontiers for youth development in the 21st century: Revitalizing and broadening youth development*. New York: Columbia University Press.

DeWitt-Wallace Reader's Digest Fund. (1996). *Strengthening the youth work profession: An analysis of and lessons learned from grantmaking by the DeWitt-Wallace Reader's Digest Fund*. New York: Author.

Dryfoos, J. (1990). *Adolescents at risk: Prevalence and prevention*. New York: Oxford University Press.

Greene, R. (1996). *Intensive field units: Guidelines for development*. Unpublished manuscript, Indiana University School of Social Work, Indianapolis.

Hawkins, D., and Catalano, R. (1992). *Communities that care: Risk-focused prevention using the social development model*. Washington, DC: Developmental Research and Programs.

Hechinger, F. (1992). *Fateful choices: Healthy youth for the 21st century*. New York: Carnegie Corporation of New York.

Jarman-Rohde, L., McFall, J., Kolar, P., and Strom, G. (1997). The changing context of social work practice: Implication and recommendations for social work educators. *Journal of Social Work Education, 33*(1), 29–46.

Libby, M., Rosen, M., and Sedonaen, M. (2005). Building youth-adult partnerships for community change: Lessons from the Youth Leadership Institute. *Journal of Community Psychology, 33*(1), 111–20.

McLaughlin, M. W. (2000). *Community counts: How youth organizations matter for youth development*. Washington, DC: Public Education Network.

Merry, S. M. (2000). *Beyond home and school: The role of primary supports in youth development*. Chicago: University of Chicago, Chapin Hall Center for Children.

Morrison, J., Alcorn, S., and Nelum, M. (1997). Empowering community-based programs for youth development. *Journal of Social Work Education, 33*(2), 321–31.

National Research Council and Institute of Medicine. (2002). *Community programs to promote youth development*. Washington, DC: National Academy Press.

Partners for Children. (2000). *Promoting positive youth development in New York State: Moving from dialogue to action.* Albany: Office of Children and Family Services.

Pittman, K. (1993). *Stronger staff, stronger youth conference: Summary report.* Washington, DC: Center for Youth Development and Policy Research.

———. (1996). Community youth development: Three goals in search of connection. *New Designs for Youth Development, 3,* 4–8.

Pittman, K., and Fleming, W. (1991). *A new vision: Promoting youth development.* Washington, DC: Center for Youth Development and Policy Research.

Search Institute. (1995). *Forty developmental assets for healthy development of young people.* Minneapolis: Author.

Watkins, M. (1998). *Principles of collaboration to establish a youth development intensive field unit.* Unpublished manuscript presented at Council on Social Work Education Annual Program Meeting, Orlando, FL, March 8–10.

———. (2000). *Youth work is a REAL job.* Final report to Lilly Endowment. Indianapolis, Indiana.

———. (2006). *Mobilizing youth development in service-learning activities.* Unpublished manuscript presented at National Society of Experiential Education Annual Program Meeting, Nashville, TN, October 14.

Watkins, M., and Braun, L. (2005). *Service-learning: Making the connection between community and career development.* Indianapolis: JIST Publishers.

Watkins, M., and Iverson, E. (1997). Youth development research/teaching/service field units. In R. Greene and M. Watkins (Eds.), *Serving diverse constituencies: Applying the ecological perspective* (167–97). New York: Aldine de Gruter.

Watkins, M., Morrison, J., and McCarthy, R. (1999). *The principles of community-based youth development: Implications for social work education.* Presented at Council on Social Work Education Annual Program Meeting, San Francisco, CA, March 13.

Chapter Six

Research: Infusing Service Learning into Research, Social Policy, and Community-Based Practice

Paul Sather, Patricia Carlson, and Barbara Weitz

Baccalaureate programs in social work education are charged with the important, but daunting, task of preparing students to work effectively as generalist practitioners. This means that students completing an undergraduate degree in social work should be able to intervene strategically with individual clients, families, and groups, as well as be competent to assess social problems in the larger community and collaborate with others to respond to them. However, engaging and sustaining students' interest in the community practice dimension of social work has proven a difficult task for social work educators.

Although the latest *Educational Policy and Accreditation Standards* (2001) for undergraduate social work education emphasize a generalist model, a number of authors (Black, Jeffreys, and Hartley 1993; Midgley 1993; Mosca 1998; Rompf and Royce 1994) have noted that while students are often eager to acquire the skills necessary for the direct-practice dimension of generalist practice, they are less enthusiastic about the curriculum components dedicated to social welfare policy analysis, community-based practice, and research.

In particular, A. Johnson (1994) asserts that recent shifts toward community-based service delivery have not been matched by corresponding shifts in social work curricula. As a result, there is growing concern that students are ill trained for community-based practice. D. Bailey and K. Koney reported that the discussions of the Midwestern Deans and Directors Forum raised concerns about this issue: "The need to better integrate the educational sequences was argued so that learnings obtained from the community could trigger ideas for teaching and research and so that findings from these two areas could be fed back to the community, thus demonstrating a truly holistic approach to social work practice" (1996, 609).

The research of B. Kasper and C. Wiegand (1999) not only highlights the reluctance of social work students to embrace macro content in the curriculum but also notes the limitations of existing teaching methodologies used to acquaint students with the theory and skill base of macro social work practice. As D. Iacono-Harris and K. Nuccio state, "The task then, is to challenge students to stretch their notions of social work so that they begin to think, feel and practice the integrated model" (1987, 80).

In response to this teaching challenge, several social work educators have developed models to link particular courses in the macro sequence and include a more active learning approach in the teaching of these courses. For example, an advanced policy course developed by Johnson (1994) integrated significant content on task force approaches to responding to social problems. Students in this course functioned as a task force, examining the scope of an existing social problem in the community and, ultimately, sharing findings and recommendations in a final report to the public.

A model for linking research and policy content is proposed by J. L. Mosca (1998), who introduces students to a particular model of community-based treatment of the chronically mentally ill. Research results comparing the treatment outcomes of this approach to other approaches are then melded into an analysis of current local and national policy development regarding the chronically mentally ill.

K. Reardon (1994) incorporates community projects to teach the participatory action research model in his undergraduate research methods classes. Beyond learning research skills, he found that his students "learn to become more self-directed problem-solvers who adopt more proactive stances toward existing community issues. They also become more confident in their ability to provide needed leadership for family, community and workplace problem-solving" (Reardon 1994, 53).

A complex model designed by Walsh (1998) incorporates senior-level research and practice classes with a co-requisite field placement. Students are required to identify a "field agency problem issue," develop a research proposal to study the problem, conduct a research project, and report the outcomes in the course of their senior year.

The field placement is also utilized as the key practice arena in the design developed by Kasper and Wiegand (1999). In this model, students develop a required "macro project" as part of their field placement and synthesize this macro theory and practice project with a corresponding required senior practice course dedicated to macro content.

These approaches present interesting and valuable prototypes for engaging students more actively in the practice dimensions of macro social work and clarifying the linkage between practice, policy analysis, and research. However, the lack remains evident of a clearly articulated plan to engage undergraduate social work students in community-based practice activities that are tied to the community-based theory and practice content of the undergraduate program.

DEVELOPMENT OF A COMMUNITY-BASED CURRICULUM

We believe that service learning as an innovative educational approach introduced earlier and more consistently in the social work curriculum provides the student with more opportunities to integrate theory and practice and prepares the student for a more meaningful practicum experience. Our experience indicates that a service-learning approach to teaching macro social work principles and methods dramatically increases students' interest in this often misunderstood practice arena and provides community agencies with better assistance in responding to underserved clients. A curriculum that integrates community-based learning and insures a constant presence in the community will offer a more consistent approach to addressing community problems.

The definition of service learning that we use in our program, as adopted by the Service Learning Academy at the University of Nebraska at Omaha in 1998, states, "Service learning integrates community service with academic study. Typically, professors design service-learning projects in partnership with representatives of community organizations, planning activities that will meet genuine needs in the community and advance the students' understanding of course content. In the community setting, students work under the supervision of community agency staff; on campus, they reflect on that experience, considering its relationship to their reading and research as well as its impact on their personal values and professional goals" (2005).

The few published studies linking service learning with social work indicate successful collaborations. R. Pulice's (1998) Community Consultation Project linked students with community agencies. In survey results asking their opinions as to the contribution of this assignment relative to other learning experiences, nearly all (fifty-nine of sixty-two) of the students rated the project as making a highly significant contribution to their learning experience relative to other foci in the curriculum.

A study by T. H. Batchelder and S. Root (1994) indicated that participation in a service-learning program facilitated student development in several areas. Their research showed that the participants in service-learning courses made greater gains in several dimensions of thinking about social problems than students did in traditional classes. Service learning "influenced participant's use of prosocial decision-making and advanced forms of prosocial reasoning as well as their tendency to reflect on occupational identity issues" (Batchelder and Root 1994, 354).

In the overview of the social work curriculum presented in figure 6.1, this service-learning approach is implemented in two junior-level policy courses, a senior-level community-based practice course, and a senior-level research methods course. The incorporation of a service-learning approach in this course work was initiated in 2000 and continues to be a work in progress. Our experience mirrors the previously cited research noting the difficulties in capturing student interest in macro coursework and developing a meaningful method to integrate theory with practice.

The impact of the inclusion of the service-learning approach is best illustrated by comparing two graphics that highlight the differences in the amount of time students spend in a community practice activity as a result of adding a service-learning dimension to the macro course sequence and senior research methods course (see figure 6.1).

Clearly, the pre-service-learning curriculum model represents a "bookend" curriculum in terms of actual application of classroom content. Pre–social work students complete sixty-four hours of volunteer activity in preparation for admission to the BSW program. Once admitted, students have no opportunity to apply macro course content until beginning their practicum in the senior year. The problems inherent in this curriculum model are obvious. It is unlikely that many social work students would be able to retain macro content without more timely opportunities for application. A service-learning approach to teaching community practice offers a means for social work educators to aid students integrate conceptual frameworks with practice realities earlier and more consistently than the typical practicum placement. However, it should also be noted that service-learning-based coursework is not intended to replace the practicum component of social work education but can enrich this experience for the student by insuring that the student possesses a solid knowledge and skill base in community practice to utilize in a culminating practicum placement.

Equally important is the fact that students will continue to fail to gain an appreciation of the significance of macro social work practice unless they can consistently be involved with stakeholders and practitioners who are working to address social problems impacting their communities. L. Gutierrez et al. comment that "of particular importance are skills to develop cultural competence to learn from the community, which involves understanding one's own and the community's culture and social location, recognizing and building from community strengths, working as a partner, and dealing with conflict in and between groups" (1996, 503). Students need to develop this understanding of the context for their practice in the community.

W. Devore and E. Schlesinger (1991) address the need for culturally competent practice through a model that creates "layers of understanding." Students need a perspective that integrates values, knowledge, and skills with an understanding of the ethnic reality of clients' lives. Once again, however, the

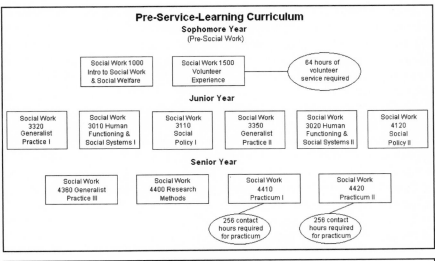

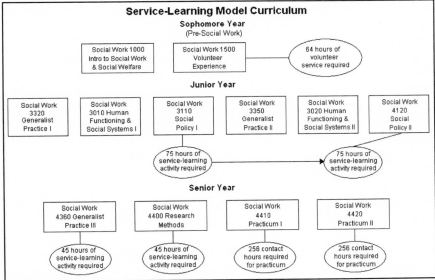

Figure 6.1. Overview of Social Work Curriculum

limitations of solely classroom-based learning are apparent. Students cannot absorb the complexities of culturally diverse communities without direct experience of them.

At the University of Nebraska at Omaha, the service-learning model curriculum is literally envisioned as taking the classroom into the community. In order to achieve this end, classroom sites have been developed in two communities of color. The selection of such communities is deliberately intended to build an understanding of cultural competency into the service-learning experience. It also offers the university the opportunity to be a consistent presence as a partner in addressing the community's ongoing problems. One site is located in a primarily Hispanic community, while the other is in a community composed of African Americans.

The model curriculum courses involved in the Hispanic community are the social policy two-course sequence in the junior year. The first course examines social policy development: historical aspects, value assumptions, social-political-economic context, and processes and skills required for analysis. The second course focuses on institutional racism and sexism as they relate to social injustice and seeks to increase students' understanding of strategies to address the institutional barriers facing people of color. The students engage in projects involving agencies such as the Nebraska Association of Farm Workers/Multicultural Human Development Corporation, the Chicano Awareness Center, and a family mentoring project. The students' projects include work in the following areas: at-risk Latino adolescents and their families, educational awareness about migrant families, gang prevention education, and advocacy with the Nebraska state legislature on the health issues of Latino families.

Students in their senior year experience service-learning components in their third social work practice course and their research methods course. These two courses use an off-campus classroom in the predominantly African American community on the north side of the city. The third practice course provides an introduction to the goal-oriented, planned change process with an emphasis on groups, organizations, and communities. The focus is on developing practice skills in planning, collaboration, empowerment, and advocacy to effect change. The research methods course introduces students to the scientific method used in social work research and builds beginning research skills and increased appreciation for the uses of research in generalist practice.

RESEARCH COURSE DESCRIPTION

The research course in our macro sequence is intended to build research skills using elements of the action research model (also called participatory or community-based research). By using a service-learning project drawing on the content of both research and practice courses, we believe we offer students an example of the successful integration of research and practice. K. Strand (2000) points out that undergraduate research is not only about introducing students to the basics of traditional research but is also intended to help them understand their role as researchers, especially when conducting a research project in a community setting. She sees this as a way of empowering students with confidence and experience by using these skills in a community context. She believes service learning and the action research model accomplish this goal. M. Wells's (2006) description of her use of service learning in a social work statistics course confirms Strand's position. Students in Wells's course gave high marks to the value of integrating course learning in the use of the Statistical Package for the Social Sciences with data analysis by working on a research project for a community organization.

A. Alvarez and L. Gutierrez (2001) emphasize the importance of fit when determining the suitability of using a participatory research approach. They point out that a key dimension is the involvement of community members in the process of identifying and defining the research work. Our work with community partners is based on their identification and shaping of the projects for our students. Alvarez and Gutierrez see participatory research as "quite compatible with the methods, goals and values of the community practice" (2001, 2).

The course instructors insure that the final descriptions of the projects as defined by the community partners contain tasks drawing on the content of both courses (see figure 6.2). Students are introduced to the process, language, and skills of the traditional research model through their textbook reading and classroom discussions. For example, as part of the course, students construct their own class survey; administer, code, enter, and analyze the data; and report to the class. Students in the research course need additional reading and discussions to deepen their understanding of the action research model as textbooks have not typically offered this material. The research instructor uses reserve readings, which offer content on the development of the action research model and how it may offer answers to criticisms raised about traditional research in communities of color.

Throughout the semester, the instructor is able to use the service-learning project work for examples when discussing course content. For example, students explore the use of the Internet for literature review as part of this class. One service-learning group looking for best practices in teaching the elderly about preventing falls brought thoughtful questions to class about the value of the content on commercial websites and about ways to access portions of census data.

The two instructors (those for the courses on practice and research) evaluate the service-learning projects separately for the use of specific course content. The service-learning project represents 25 percent of the course grade in each of the courses.

The service-learning projects developed for these two courses integrate the content of both courses while seeking to address needs identified by the community agency. Community partners not only identify problems for work but become teaching partners as well. Students are thus able to use a broad range of skills and resources to address core community problems. Figure 6.2 illustrates

Macro Practice Course Objectives	Service-Learning Projects	Research Course Objectives
To continue the development and utilization of social work knowledge, skills, and values in social work practice with a focus on groups, organizations, and the community	Individual Development Accounts (IDA) Project: • Develop a profile of current IDA participants • Research grant possibilities to expand IDA program • Develop report for board on how other states are funding IDA programs • Develop an educational program to promote IDA participation	To develop beginning skill in designing and carrying out an evaluation research project
To develop skills in culturally competent social work practice with gender, ethnic, and racial differences in groups, organizations, and communities		To develop moderate skill in evaluating research studies and applying findings to their own practice
To develop the ability to use available resource systems and to become knowledgeable about means to overcome their limitations	City Sprouts Project • Research community garden programs as a community development strategy • Evaluate the demonstration site: who is participating?	To develop an understanding of and commitment to ethical standards and application of social work values in the research process
		To develop familarity with the qualitative approach in social work research

Objectives	Service-Learning Projects
To develop moderate skill in planning, collaboration, empowerment, and advocacy to effect social change within groups, organizations, and communities To develop moderate skill in analyzing and differentiating settings in order to select appropriate and effective forms of intervention	• Explore how the garden is impacting the neighborhood • Consult with North Omaha Food Security Council; assist them in a needs assessment process • Develop strategies for promoting participation in the garden
To develop an understanding of the quantitative approach in social work research To develop an understanding of the impact of gender, ethnicity, race, sexual orientation, disability, religion, culture, age, national origin, and socioeconomic status on social work research	Workforce Investment Act (WIA) • Research WIA programs in other states and report on model programs • Interview job training participants in Women Mean Business Program • Develop a survey for program graduates

Figure 6.2. Course Objectives/Service-Learning Projects

how the objectives of each course related to the projects during one academic year.

CHALLENGES IN THE WORK

Developing a curriculum that places students in the community throughout their social work major presents a number of challenges for the school or department. For us, the challenges have involved our ability to evaluate the experience, the process of deciding which problems to address in the community and through which agencies, and the need for greater institutional support.

Formal evaluation tools for service learning as a teaching methodology have been developed by other higher education institutions (Myers-Lipton 1998; Olney and Grande 1995; Stacey, Rice, and Langer 1997) but are usually designed to assess more general outcomes of this approach, such as increases in students' civic-mindedness. While useful, these tools fail to measure desired outcomes specific to the social work curriculum. Moreover, there is an absence of outcome measures that address the impact of this approach on faculty or community partners.

In the macro practice class, students prepare weekly reflection papers on particular topics and links to their specific service-learning projects. These papers provide students insight into particular course content and the process of project implementation. Agency partners provide an evaluation through a post-course debriefing session with both instructors, which includes discussion of a written evaluation form completed by the agency partners. This information is used to adapt and improve the courses continuously. Shared reflective experiences involving both students and community partners have been attempted, but time limitations have made this approach difficult to pursue.

Qualitative reports in the form of student journal entries do indicate that students' grasp of community practice principles and techniques is enhanced through service learning, but without evaluation methodologies that can accurately and consistently identify the results of this approach for all parties involved, it will be difficult to gain needed external support for curriculum revision efforts.

It is also apparent that the nonprofit agencies serving as community partners for service-learning-based courses welcome the assistance students bring as they complete their class projects. But every agency is not necessarily a suitable partner for this approach to teaching and learning. The grassroots community agency can offer students many unique learning opportunities, but there is also a point at which an agency's need becomes too great. The service-learning approach works best when clearly identified goals are established for student projects that can be completed in a reasonable amount of time. Structure and processes need to be in place to ensure effective partnerships (Barringer and Harrison 2000). It is also vital that key agency personnel remain available to students for consultation throughout a semester time frame. When these conditions cannot be met, student satisfaction and learning are jeopardized. The development of an agency screening tool that establishes a set of criteria for agency selection as the partner in the service project would be a useful addition to the service-learning literature and a valuable assessment tool for social work educators.

Service learning as one approach to the teaching enterprise is gaining popularity across many campuses. As other departments implement service learning in particular courses, faculty and administrators often rely on social work faculty for help in developing contact with community agencies. These collaborations often hold great potential for agencies that could benefit from the assistance of, for example, marketing, communications, or accounting students. However, without an institutional means for developing and monitoring these endeavors, it is possible that students and agencies will gain little from their collaborations. This places social work educators in the difficult position of serving as the broker between agency and university without any means to facilitate a positive outcome for either party. The need for close academic involvement and support should be impressed upon other departments seeking such partnerships.

The issue of institutional support for service learning includes additional components. Service learning challenges students to move beyond the comfort zone of the classroom and to develop a tolerance for ambiguity as projects develop. "Indeed, both flexibility and adhered to processes for discussion and decision-making are especially important for partnerships to evolve and grow" (Mai, Kramer, and Luebbert 2005). Some students are delighted to apply what they are learning more directly and can manage the stressors of service learning without difficulty. Others never adapt to the changing conditions of community practice and are uncomfortable with a portion of their grade not being determined by a series of predictable exams and papers. Student evaluations of faculty teaching these courses may reflect these students' discomfort. Administrators of social work programs will need to bear in mind that adapting to service learning takes time for both students and faculty.

It will also be important to understand the unique demands of teaching service-learning courses when evaluating faculty teaching portfolios. Teaching service-learning courses involves a considerable time commitment. Developing relationships with agency partners, refining course syllabi, and defining student projects can take months prior to the start of the course. Maintaining regular communication with agency personnel and students during a course is equally time-consuming. Finally, if promotion and tenure decisions continue to be based primarily on faculty research and publication, faculty members may be forced to abandon this promising approach in order to meet these expectations.

CONCLUSION

Service-learning content infused across the undergraduate social work curriculum offers students the opportunity to practice skills learned in the classroom in community settings for the benefit of both students and community partners. The use of community agencies in communities of color allows students to gain experience and some level of comfort in working with diverse populations. At the same time, we believe this approach begins to address concerns about creating a more consistent and connected experience for students over the entire period of their undergraduate social work studies. Particularly for research, service learning offers students the opportunity to experience how research knowledge and skills are embedded in generalist practice. By placing classrooms in the communities we are working with, we believe we send a message that we are partners and not merely visitors. This curriculum allows the university to be a citizen of the community, sharing in the responsibility to address the strategic problems facing all of us as citizens.

REFERENCES

Alvarez, A., and Gutierrez, L. (2001). Choosing to do participatory research: An example and issues of fit to consider. *Journal of Community Practice, 9*(1), 1–20.

Bailey, D., and Koney, K. (1996). Interorganizational community-based collaboratives: A strategic response to shape the social work agenda. *Social Work, 41,* 602–11.

Barringer, B., and Harrison, J. (2000). Walking a tightrope: Creating value through interorganizational relationships. *Journal of Management, 26,* 367–403.

Batchelder, T. H., and Root, S. (1994). Effects of an undergraduate program to integrate academic learning and service: Cognitive, prosocial cognitive, and identity outcomes. *Journal of Adolescence, 17,* 341–55.

Black, P. M., Jeffreys, D., and Hartley, E. R. (1993). Personal history of psychosocial trauma in the early life of social work and business students. *Journal of Social Work Education, 29,* 171–80.

Council on Social Work Education. Curriculum Policy Statement. 2001

Devore, W., and Schlesinger, E. (1991). *Ethnic-sensitive social work practice.* New York: Macmillan.

Gutierrez, L., Alvarez, A. R., Nemon, H., and Lewis, E. A. (1996). Multicultural community organizing: A strategy for change. *Social Work, 41,* 501–508.

Iacono-Harris, D., and Nuccio, K. (1987). Developing the macro pool: Turning undergraduates on to macro practice. *Administration in Social Work, 11*, 79–87.

Johnson, A. (1994). Teaching students the task force approach: A policy-practice course. *Journal of Social Work Education, 30*, 336–47.

Kasper, B., and Wiegand, C. (1999). An undergraduate macro practice learning guarantee. *Journal of Teaching in Social Work, 18*, 99–112.

Mai, R., Kramer, T., and Luebbert, C. (2005). Learning through partnering: Lessons for organizational and community renewal. *Journal of Community Practice, 13*, 107–22.

Midgely, J. (1993). Promoting a development focus in the community organization curriculum: Relevance of the African experience. *Journal of Social Work Education, 29*, 269–78.

Mosca, J. L. (1998). Social policy considerations for community mental health services: A curriculum module integrating mental health research. *Journal of Baccalaureate Social Work, 4*, 87–97.

Myers-Lipton, S. (1998). Effect of a comprehensive service-learning program on college students' civic responsibility. *Teaching Sociology, 26*, 243–58.

Olney, C., and Grande, G. (1995). Validation of a scale to measure development of social responsibility. *Michigan Journal of Community Service Learning, 2*, 43–53.

Pulice, R. (1998). Responding to human service agency needs in a constrained resource environment: The role of the university and students. *Administration in Social Work, 22*, 65–73.

Reardon, K. (1994). Undergraduate research in distressed urban communities: An undervalued form of service-learning. *Michigan Journal of Community Service Learning, 1*, 44–54.

Rompf, E. L., and Royce, D. (1994). Choice of social work as a career: Possible influences. *Journal of Social Work Education, 30*, 163–71.

Stacey, K., Rice, D., and Langer, G. (1997). *Academic service-learning faculty development manual.* Ypsilanti, MI: Office of Academic Service-Learning, Eastern Michigan University.

Strand, K. (2000). Community-based research as pedagogy. *Michigan Journal of Community Service Learning, 7*, 85–96.

University of Nebraska at Omaha, Service Learning Academy. (2005). *Definition of service learning.* Retrieved October 4, 2005, from www.unomaha.edu/service learning/faq.php#whatis.

Wallace, J. (2000). The problem of time: Enabling students to make long-term commitments to community-based learning. *Michigan Journal of Community Service Learning, 7*, 133–41.

Walsh, J. (1998). A model for integrating research, practice, and field instruction in the undergraduate curriculum. *Journal of Teaching in Social Work, 17*, 49–63.

Wells, M. (2006). Making statistics "real" for social work students. *Journal of Social Work Education, 42*, 397–404.

Chapter Seven

Human Behavior and the Social Environment: An Oral History Service-Learning Project

Natalie Ames and Stephene A. Diepstra

This chapter describes the implementation and evaluation of an oral history service-learning project in undergraduate human behavior and the social environment (HBSE) courses at two institutions. It explores the ways in which an oral history project can enable students to apply theoretical content from HBSE courses, provides details on project implementation, and discusses evaluation of the project's impact on participating students. Additionally, the authors provide practical suggestions for others wishing to implement similar projects. The specific project the authors used matched students with older adults and offered them a real-life context for learning mandated HBSE course content, including the following: "theories and knowledge of biological, sociological, cultural, psychological, and spiritual development across the life span; the range of social systems in which people live (individual, family, group, organizational, and community); and the ways social systems promote or deter people in maintaining or achieving health and well-being" (CSWE 2001, 11).

ORAL HISTORIES AND SERVICE LEARNING

Oral histories can act as a vehicle for integrating service learning into HBSE courses. The oral history project described in this chapter added an experiential dimension to the educational process by engaging students in activities that required them to apply what they were learning in the classroom to meet the needs of a specific population (i.e., older adults) in the community. It was designed to link students' experiences with their partners to classroom instruction, and it provided structured opportunities for students to reflect, in discussions and written assignments, on their service-learning experience.

Benefiting both students and community participants is an important aspect of service learning and of the oral history project. Students gain in multiple ways. There is evidence that participation in oral histories promotes their empathy toward and understanding of their subjects (Penyak and Duray 1999). Students in L. M. Penyak and P. B. Duray's study "asserted that interviewing had taught them to respect people from different cultures" (1999, 70). C. R. Lee and K. L. Nasstrom highlighted oral history's value in teaching students about "aspects of their surrounding communities that they were previously unaware of, particularly when opportunities exist for cross-cultural understanding" (1998, 4).

Oral history assignments can act as a framework on which students can build intergenerational relationships. They enable students to practice their interviewing skills in a real-life environment and to carry out a structured examination of an individual's functioning within his or her social environment. Completing an oral history engages both the interviewer and the narrator (Grele 1998). "Oral history is at its core a collaborative relationship. . . . Students collaborate, broaden their focus to include the community and construct meaningful histories" (Lee and Nasstrom 1998, 3).

Oral history assignments can connect social work students with diverse populations. In fact, the literature indicates that oral history projects are particularly valuable when they pair students with individuals and groups historically silenced and/or marginalized in knowledge construction (Bial 1983; Delany and Delany 1993; Liebow 1993). The value of exploring these individual realities has been well documented (Germain and Gitterman 1980; Laird 1993; Martin 1995).

THE ORAL HISTORY PROJECT

The authors' oral history project required students to interact with older adult partners throughout a semester. It enabled them to explore systematically how their partners developed meaning in their lives within historical, social, economic, political, and cultural contexts often much different from those of the students. For the older adult partners, who were either in adult day care or subsidized residential communities, the students' repeated visits over the course of the semester provided social contact, a chance to reminisce and make meaning of their life experiences, and an opportunity to be acknowledged for contributing to the students' educational experiences.

The oral history project required seven interactions between students and older adult partners who were diverse in race, ethnicity, class, and economic status. These contacts provided students with opportunities to broaden their knowledge and awareness of diversity, gerontology, populations-at-risk, and generational ties. The project's component assignments were designed to facilitate learning about the impact of biological, sociological, cultural, psychological, historical, and spiritual factors on the individual's development across the lifespan and to help students integrate theory, knowledge, and practice.

THEORETICAL PERSPECTIVES

Theoretical approaches taught in HBSE courses emphasize the importance of the social environment in shaping human development and vice versa (Shriver 2004; Zastrow and Kirst-Ashman 2007). Theoretical content generally includes social systems, the ecological perspective, person-in-environment, and lifespan development. The project was designed to incorporate practical application of these theories and perspectives into the students' learning.

Social Systems Theory

O. Dale et al. describe social systems theory as "an application of the general systems paradigm to social phenomena" (2006, 26). A. D. Hall and R. E. Fagen (1956) define a system as incorporating a set of objects that exist in relationship with their attributes, as well as their environment, which ultimately leads to change. The abstract nature of systems theory often makes it difficult for students to grasp. Participation in an oral history project can help students understand how social systems theory applies over time to a specific individual's relationships with various micro-, mezzo-, and macro-level systems. For example, our students' partners included individuals who grew up during the Great Depression, fought in World War II, and/or took part in the civil rights movement. As partners shared their life narratives, the students became more aware of how historical events shaped their partners' lives as well as the impact their partners had on the world in which they lived. During reflective class discussions throughout the semester, students shared their experiences and learning related to systems theory, allowing them to see how social systems theory applied to other students' partners as well as their own.

The Ecological Perspective

Closely related to systems theory, the ecological perspective provides another theoretical construct through which students can view human behavior in the social environment. It is critical to students' understanding of the ecological perspective that they be able to conceptualize the dynamic transactions that take place between persons and the many systems in their environments (Ashford, LeCroy, and Lortie 2006; Longres 2000). Learning about how their partners have interacted, throughout their lives, with their environments can help students to comprehend that individuals "are not robots completely determined by their environment nor . . . independent actors operating solely on free will" (Longres 2000, 21).

The authors utilized a timeline assignment to provide a focal point for students to examine the impact of external historical events on their partners' lives. Placing milestones in their partners' lives side by side with historical events, movements, and eras helped students to comprehend the dynamic interactions between their partners and the physical and social environments in which they lived their lives. Additionally, by providing a historical context, this assignment highlighted "the interdependence among all parts of the environment" (Dale et al. 2006, 38).

Person and Environment

Debate exists within social work education about the nature of human behavior and the social environment (Shriver 2004). Central to this debate are questions about the power of individuals to shape their environment and the power of the environment to shape individuals. Although these fundamental questions cannot be answered definitively, engaging in an oral history project can encourage students to explore them. Students examine the relevance of biological, psychological, social, and spiritual theories of development alongside cultural, political, economic, and sociological theories of the environment. Ideally, they come to appreciate the importance of a holistic understanding of the social environment *and* human behavior.

Lifespan Development Theory

Exploration of lifespan development theory also contributes to an emphasis on the importance of holistic understandings of human behavior. Debate within this theoretical construct centers on the primacy and relevance of biology and/or environment in shaping individual development (i.e., nature versus nurture). Although neither the HBSE course nor the project can provide students with a final answer, both force them at least to grapple with the question. For example, a student may be partnered with an individual who has struggled with alcoholism. As the student learns there is a family history of alcoholism, a spontaneous classroom discussion may occur about whether alcoholism results from a biological predisposition, or social modeling within the family of origin, or a combination of these factors.

PROJECT DESCRIPTION

Before the semester began, the authors worked with organizations in their communities to identify sites where they might find older adults from diverse backgrounds to recruit as oral history partners. Those sites included two adult day care centers and two apartment complexes housing low-income, older adults. Other potential resources for locating older adults (or other populations an instructor might wish to expose students to) could include nursing homes, senior centers, local nonprofit organizations, support groups, and meeting places that serve specific population groups.

Assignments

The oral history project's component assignments were designed to incorporate key HBSE theoretical content. These assignments, described in detail later in the chapter, included a reflective journal, a genogram, an ecomap, a timeline, and a creative final product for the students to give to their partners at the end of the semester. Prior to beginning the project, the instructors prepared students by discussing some basic practical issues, including the following:

- *Appearance*: The authors discussed how the social values their partners grew up with might influence their views of such things as facial piercings, large or numerous visible tattoos (especially on women), and bare midriffs. Students were encouraged to consider these factors before each visit with their partner.
- *Safety*: Although some students met with their partners at adult day care facilities, others met in their partners' homes. Conducting their visits in pairs provided an added safety and security component for the students, particularly those making home visits. Students in HBSE courses typically have not yet done any fieldwork; thus, students understandably had some anxiety about "home visits." Discussing these safety concerns prior to their first visits with their partners seemed to allay most of these fears.
- *Respect*: Given generational customs related to the use of surnames, students were explicitly instructed on the importance of using formal titles

(i.e., Mr., Mrs., Ms.) as a demonstration of respect for the older person. Some students did develop first-name relationships with their partners, but this only occurred if the partners invited students to address them as such. Because students were not accustomed to making home visits, we also felt it important to point out that although they might be uncomfortable with the amount of clutter in a partner's home, drawing attention to this would not be respectful or appropriate.

- *Boundaries*: As the students developed relationships with their partners, the authors introduced the concept of boundaries and discussed how difficult it can be for students and beginning social workers to separate their professional and personal lives. Class discussions and journaling assignments allowed students the opportunity to process their thoughts and emotional responses to their partners and to explore the issue of maintaining appropriate professional boundaries with individuals for whom they had warm, positive feelings.

- *Termination*: The nature of this semester-long project mandated discussion of termination at the outset. These discussions explored the inherent difficulty, for social workers and service recipients, associated with ending relationships after investing time and effort in building them. They allowed students to voice, in a safe environment, the desire many had to continue relationships with their partners beyond the end of the semester. The "final product" assignment gave students a chance to construct unique and tangible remembrances of their relationships to present to their partners when they formally said goodbye at the end-of-semester celebration.

- *Readings*: Before discussing the service-learning components of the oral history project, students completed four brief readings on reminiscence and communicating with older adults [Kunz n.d.(a–d)] that illustrated the learning and service components of the oral history project. The readings helped students to understand that, in addition to giving them knowledge about course content, the project would enable them to practice the listening and questioning skills central to interviewing. The readings also highlighted the role of reminiscence and life review in helping older adults recognize and acknowledge the strengths and resources they used to cope with difficult times, as well as the fundamental importance of having listeners for their stories.

The reading "Older Adult Development" [Kunz n.d.(b)] summarized the developmental stages to be covered in the course. Discussion of this reading included what students could learn from their partners, particularly about the strengths, knowledge, and understandings adults gain over their lives; the significance of viewing one's life realistically by accepting past events and experiences and feeling satisfaction in one's accomplishments; and the ways in which people experience and cope with loss.

The Journal Assignment

Reflection is a critical component of service learning (Long et al. 2001; Nystrom 2002; Roschelle, Turpin, and Elias 2000). The journal assignment served as a tool to help students integrate classroom material with what they were learning from their experiences with their oral history partners. It also provided a mechanism for focusing class discussions throughout the semester. In the first entry, students described their first visit with their partner: who was present, what happened, who said what, and what they felt and thought before and after the visit.

The second journal entry included the same elements as the first. In addition, students wrote about (1) any changes in the perspective described in the first entry that resulted from contacts with the oral history partner, (2) what accounted for any changes or for the fact that no changes had occurred, and (3) what they believed they could learn from the project that would promote personal or professional growth. For each subsequent visit, students described in their journals (1) who was there, what happened, and who said what; (2) feelings and thoughts before, during, and after the visit; and (3) the relationship between their observations and thoughts and the material covered in class and in the textbook.

Students' final entry reflected on the personal strengths and weaknesses that helped or hindered them in completing the project. They gave examples of aspects of the project they found enjoyable and those that were difficult, and they summarized what they had learned that could promote their personal and professional growth.

Reflective Discussions

Research indicates that service learning is most effective when instructors encourage class discussion, explicitly connect the service experiences to the course's subject matter, and prepare students for the experience before they begin the service participation (Astin et al. 2000). Class discussions at the beginning of the semester focused on answering students' questions and addressing their concerns about completing the oral history project. Topics included confidentiality, interviewing techniques, communicating with older adults, older adult development, reminiscence, and life review. Discussion of the service aspect of the assignment included summarizing the research findings on the beneficial effects of life review and consideration of the importance of social contact as adults age and experience the loss of the people in their lives with whom they can review significant life events. Instructors also provided students with topical guidelines to aid them in initiating conversations with their oral history partners.

The classroom discussions that took place throughout the semester allowed students to support one another when they encountered similar frustrations and learning experiences and enabled them to challenge each other's responses in ways the instructors could not. Discussions offered a basis for expanding students' understanding of development across the lifespan as they considered the ways in which typical functioning differed among their partners and compared their partners' development to the life stages covered in the course. These discussions broadly allowed the students to consider how environmental considerations, such as historical events, family constellations, and societal changes, shaped their own lives, as well as those of their partners, and how individuals, in turn, shape facets of their environments. As they reflected on the differences among their partners' responses to similar historical events and personal situations, students were able to examine interactions between person and environment.

The Ecomap, Genogram, and Timeline Assignments

At mid-semester, students produced ecomaps, genograms, and timelines detailing the lives of their partners. These assignments were intended to help students identify the social, cultural, and historical factors that had shaped their partners' lives. They also provided a structure for students to examine the personal and environmental challenges their partners had faced, the strengths they had exhibited throughout their lives, and the historical contexts within which they had lived. The genograms and ecomaps gave students two separate formats for examining their partners' interactions with their physical and social environments and the biological, psychological, and social forces that shaped their development and behavior across the life course.

The purpose of the ecomap assignment was for students to explore the connections among the systems that influence a person's life, including areas of conflict and areas of support (Ashford, LeCroy, and Lortie 2006). The assignment required students to place their partners within a social context that included organizations and factors that had significantly affected their lives (Sheafor and Horejsi 2006).

To prepare for constructing the genogram, students visited websites with examples representing a variety of family constellations, such as www.multi-culturalfamily.org/genograms and http://faculty-web.at.northwestern.edu/commstud/galvin/Genograms/Welcome.htm#welcome. The genogram required students to incorporate at least three generations of the partner's family (i.e., parents, siblings, children), briefly describe significant physical and mental health issues for each individual, and indicate the social relationships between their partners and other individuals.

To help students see their partners' lives in historical context, the timeline assignment required students to correlate milestones in the partner's life with important historical events. Students were directed to websites with relevant examples of timelines (e.g., http://havingoursay.com/TimeLine.htm) and information on historical events (e.g., http://timelines.ws). This assignment also gave students the opportunity to reflect intentionally on the importance of history in the life of an individual, as well as, more broadly, on the functioning of society.

The "Final Product" Assignment

Instructions for the last assignment of the semester, the "final product," were much less specific than for the earlier assignments. Students were directed to be creative in using the information they had gathered to develop a written and/or visual piece celebrating their partners' lives and the events and circumstances that had shaped them. Although students submitted this product to the instructors for evaluation, it was designed to be given to their partners at the end of the semester as a memento of the oral history experience. Examples of these creations included a beautifully framed family tree with photographs collected from the partner's daughter hanging from its elaborately drawn branches; a shadow box with carefully chosen items symbolizing significant relationships and events in a partner's life; a colorful, hand-bound book, hand-printed in calligraphy, of humorous sayings a partner had delighted the students with during visits; and a student-directed video paying tribute to a partner's accomplishments and strengths.

The final products were presented at parties each class held at the participating facilities at the end of the semester. Project participants, their family members and friends, facility staff, and other clients of the facilities were invited to attend. Amid smiles and tears, students introduced their partners to the group, highlighted what they had learned from the experience, and presented their partners with their creations as a symbol of appreciation for their participation in the project.

PROJECT EVALUATION

To collect data on the effects of the project, the authors designed an evaluation component. Study participants were sixty-three students enrolled in the authors' HBSE courses in Council on Social Work Education–accredited baccalaureate social work programs at two institutions, a large public university in the Southeast (two sections) and a small religiously affiliated college in the Midwest (one section). The students who participated in this project resembled the national profile of students enrolled in undergraduate social work programs (Lennon 1999). They ranged in age from nineteen to forty-one, with a mean age of twenty-two years; 93 percent were female, and 85 percent were Caucasian.

Project evaluation included both quantitative and qualitative measures. Pre- and posttests assessed students' perceived level of ability to work with older adults, interest in working with older adults, interest in learning more about older adults, and attitudes toward older adults. There was no statistically significant change in the last three measures at the end of the semester. However, the pre- and posttest results of students' perceived level of ability to work with older adults did show a statistically significant change ($p <$ 0.01). At the end of the semester, students felt more confident in their perceived level of ability to work with older adults.

Evaluation of students' perceptions of the project's usefulness yielded more definitive results. Table 7.1 summarizes these findings.

As part of the posttest, students were asked to respond in writing to four open-ended questions. A number of strong themes and several weaker ones emerged from this qualitative data, as summarized here.

Table 7.1. Student Evaluations

Questions: How Useful Was this Project in Helping You	Very Useful	Somewhat Useful	Slightly Useful	Not at All Useful	N
Identify the impact of age, race, ethnicity, religion, culture, and social class on development across the lifespan?	N=25 43%	18 31%	13 22%	2 3%	58
Identify the social contexts that affect human development and behavior?	26 44%	22 37%	9 15%	2 3%	59
Apply the strengths perspective?	17 29%	29 49%	11 19%	2 3%	59
Develop communication skills for gathering information from someone with whom you have little in common?	44 75%	11 19%	4 7%	—	59

Note: Summed percentages may not equal 100 due to rounding.

In response to the question, "What did you learn about yourself from participating in the oral history project?" two themes were noted:

1. Students learned about their desire/ability to engage with older adults.
2. Students gained insight into their own life circumstances, personal characteristics, and values.

The second question asked, "What did you learn about development across the lifespan from participating in this project?" Again, two themes emerged:

1. Students learned how interrelationships and interactions between person and environment affect individuals' development.
2. Students learned about positive and negative aspects of aging.

The next question also dealt with course content, asking, "What did you learn about aging and older adults from participating in this project?" The following two themes were discerned:

1. Older adults have strength, resilience, and wisdom.
2. Aging involves loss of family members and friends, as well as loss of physical and mental abilities.

When students were queried about suggestions for improving the project, fewer responses were forthcoming. Nevertheless, several weaker themes may be noted:

- change procedures for selecting and screening older adult partners
- find partners closer to campus
- good experience; no suggestions

OUTCOMES

Service-learning projects can provide social work students with a real-life context in which to apply and integrate knowledge, values, and skills learned in the classroom. An oral history service-learning project offers the potential for students to

- practice and enhance their communications skills
- increase their knowledge of and experience with diversity, including recognizing and confronting their own stereotypes

- learn about the impact of the social environment on human development
- develop an empathetic understanding of the lives and experiences of people whose realities are very different from their own

One unexpected and interesting evaluation finding was that 63 percent (*n* = 38) of the students who participated explicitly described an increase in their perceived sense of competence and confidence in their ability to interact and communicate with older adults. This suggests the possibility that, in addition to its service-learning benefits, an oral history project has the potential to increase students' sense of self-efficacy.

Oral history assignments can be a vehicle for connecting social work students to diverse populations with which they might not otherwise interact. Students' journals chronicled their initial reluctance toward, and fears about, interacting with older adults, as well as the positive changes in those feelings that occurred over the course of the semester. By the end of the semester, many reported having learned that they could initiate, sustain, and enjoy a relationship with individuals different from themselves. They reported increased understanding of what it means to grow old. A number of students reported having identified and confronted their own stereotypes about aging and older adults.

Oral histories give social work students practical opportunities to develop and apply their knowledge and skills with diverse groups. At the same time, they give socially marginalized individuals a chance to tell their life stories in ways that affirm who they are. The authors believe that the project described in this chapter could be adapted, with similar benefits, to include populations other than older adults, such as gays and lesbians, people with physical or mental disabilities, and immigrants. Using an oral history service-learning project offers instructors a creative format for teaching HBSE content and provides students with a real-life context for learning.

REFERENCES

Ashford, J. B., LeCroy, C., and Lortie, K. I. (2006). *Human behavior in the social environment: A multidimensional perspective* (3rd ed.). Belmont, CA: Wadsworth/ Thompson Learning.

Astin, A. W., Vogelgesang, L. J., Ikeda, E. K., and Yee, J. A. (2000). *How service learning affects students*. Los Angeles: Higher Education Research Institute, University of California.

Bial, M. (1983). Oral histories: A nursing home project. *Practice Digest, 6*, 7–8.

Council on Social Work Education (CSWE). (2001). *Educational policy and accreditation standards*. Alexandria, VA: Author.

Dale, O., Smith, R., Norlin, J. M., and Chess, W. A. (2006). *Human behavior and the social environment* (5th ed.). Boston: Allyn and Bacon.

Delany, S., and Delany, E. (1993). *Having our say: The Delany sisters' first 100 years.* New York: Kodansha.

Galvin, K. (2000). *Basic genogram components, genogram clues: Understanding relationships and patterns, more genogram examples, creating your own genogram.* Retrieved July 24, 2006, from http://faculty-web.at.northwestern.edu/commstud/ galvin/Genograms/Welcome.htm#welcome.

Germain, C. B., and Gitterman, A. (1980). *The life model of social work practice.* New York: Columbia University Press.

Grele, R. J. (1998). Values and methods in the classroom transformation of oral history. *The Oral History Review, 25*(1–2), 57–69.

Hall, A. D., and Fagen, R. E. (1956). Definition of a system. In *General systems yearbook,* vol. 1 (18–28). Ann Arbor, MI: Society for the Advancement of General Systems Theory.

Kunz, J. (n.d.-a). *Communicating with older adults.* Retrieved July 13, 2006, from www.members.aol.com/johnkunz/hand4.htm.

———. (n.d.-b). *Older adult development.* Retrieved July 13, 2006, from www.members .aol.com/johnkunz/hand2.htm.

———. (n.d.-c). *Reminiscence and life review.* Retrieved July 13, 2006, from www .members.aol.com/johnkunz/hand1.htm.

———. (n.d.-d). *Reminiscence approaches utilized in counseling older adults.* Retrieved July 13, 2006, from www.members.aol.com/johnkunz/art1.htm.

Laird, J. (1993). Women and stories: Restoring women's self-constructions. In M. McGoldrick, C. Anderson, and F. Walsh (Eds.), *Women and families* (427–50). New York: W. W. Norton.

Lee, C. R., and Nasstrom, K. L. (1998). Practice and pedagogy: Oral history in the classroom. *The Oral History Review, 25*(1–2), 1–7.

Lennon, T. (1999). *Statistics on social work education in the United States: 1998.* Alexandria, VA: Council on Social Work Education.

Liebow, E. (1993). *Tell them who I am: The lives of homeless women.* New York: Free Press.

Long, A. B., Larson, P., Hussey, L., and Travis, S. S. (2001). Organizing, managing, and evaluating service learning projects. *Educational Gerontology, 27*, 3–21.

Longres, J. F. (2000). *Human behavior in the social environment* (3rd ed.). Itasca, IL: F. E. Peacock.

Martin, R. R. (1995). *Oral history in social work: Research, assessment, and intervention.* Thousand Oaks, CA: Sage.

Multicultural Family Institute. *Standard symbols for genograms.* Retrieved July 25, 2006, from www.multiculturalfamily.org/genograms.

Nystrom, E. A. (2002). Remembrance of things past: Service learning opportunities in U.S. history. *Oral History Review, 29*(2), 61–68.

Penyak, L. M., and Duray, P. B. (1999). Oral history and problematic questions promote issues-centered education. *Social Studies, 90*(2), 68–71.

Roschelle, A. R., Turpin, J., and Elias, R. (2000). Who learns from service learning? *American Behavioral Scientist, 43*(5), 839–47.

Sheafor, B. W., and Horejsi, C. (2006). *Techniques and guidelines for social work practice* (7th ed.). Boston: Allyn and Bacon.

Shriver, J. M. (2004). *Human behavior and the social environment* (4th ed.). Boston: Allyn and Bacon.

Zastrow, C., and Kirst-Ashman, K. K. (2007). *Understanding human behavior and the social environment* (7th ed.). Belmont, CA: Wadsworth.

ACKNOWLEDGMENT

The authors wish to thank Nehal Outlaw, MSW, for her assistance with this project.

REPRINT INFORMATION

Portions of this chapter are reprinted from "Using Intergenerational Oral History Service-Learning Projects to Teach Human Behavior Concepts: A Qualitative Analysis," *Educational Gerontology, 32*(9) (2006), 721–35, with permission of Taylor and Frances, Publishers.

Chapter Eight

Human Diversity: Service Learning and Gender Studies within a Gay, Lesbian, Bisexual, and Transgender Context

John R. Yoakam and Patricia Bolaños

The impetus for service learning has its roots in student participation in social causes during the 1960s and 1970s. The student activism of the times brought attention to existing social problems and forced the education process to shift from a formal, static, teacher-centered endeavor to a more relevant experience (Stanton 1990; Flikkema 1998).

Many current professors and parents of today's college students were products of that period. As a result of having been involved in community struggles and social causes, these educators and parents have stimulated an interest in, and created programs that connect, campus and community.[1] Service-learning programs have sought not only to make the educational experience more relevant to students but also to provide a vehicle for sustainable change on the campuses themselves, as well as in the surrounding communities. Sustainable change within the context of the service-learning program means that the projects undertaken within the classroom will extend beyond the life of the course. For example, the desired outcome of "safe space" training for residential advisors in the dorms on campus, conducted as a service-learning project within the "Sexual Orientation and Gender Identity" course, was to create a welcoming atmosphere for gay, lesbian, bisexual, and transgender (GLBT) students that would continue in succeeding semesters and academic years.

Similarly, programs like Campus Compact were created to provide concrete resources, through conferences and publications of best practices, to newly established service-learning endeavors. Campus Compact, along with Edward Zlotkowski and the American Association for Higher Education, has provided models for service learning in various disciplines. However, one area among others yet to be addressed is gender studies, and more specifically, sexual orientation and gender identity.[2]

121

In a culture where equality among persons is valued, divergence of any sort is often overlooked. For example, the middle and upper classes may come into daily contact with the working poor, who work as cashiers at convenience stores or serve them at fast food restaurants. For the privileged, this group of individuals is, in essence, invisible: only their function is valued. The financial struggles or limited opportunities that these service workers face on a daily basis, therefore, do not attract the attention and understanding of the more affluent.

In similar fashion, another area of divergence from the dominant culture that is left unseen is sexual orientation and gender identity. The majority has little awareness of the limitation of civil rights or the hostility faced on a daily basis by people who are gay, lesbian, bisexual, or transgender.

THE SETTING

Set in rural Minnesota, the College of St. Benedict and St. John's University (CSB/SJU), with an undergraduate enrollment of approximately thirty-eight hundred, are private, residential, liberal arts colleges rooted in the Catholic university tradition and guided by the Benedictine principles of their founders. One of the principle Benedictine values observed in these colleges is respect for all persons. In 1993, CSB/SJU adopted a nondiscrimination policy in employment, conforming to the amended Minnesota Human Rights statutes, that includes protections in employment for persons based on sexual orientation and gender identity. People Representing the Sexual Minority (PRiSM) was recognized as an official student organization in the early 1990s. The Gender and Women's Studies Program for the colleges has also been part of campus life since 1982, when the first grants were written to incorporate gender studies into the curriculum. The gender and women's studies (GWST) minor was adopted in 1994 and the Joint Faculty Assembly approved a GWST major in 2006. Gay, lesbian, bisexual, and transgender studies fall under the aegis of the GWST program, although GLBT content within courses originates primarily from the departments, such as social work or English.

The colleges have a unique opportunity to explore gender issues given the fact that the two campuses are residentially segregated by gender (men at St. John's, women at St. Benedict's), although the academic, social, and extracurricular programs are fully integrated by gender. Courses can offer a "gender flag" if sufficient material within the course is devoted to exploring gender issues and women have authored at least half of the required texts. Table 8.1 depicts the four courses offered, the service-learning sites utilized, the numbers of students involved, and some results of these service-learning opportunities.

Table 8.1. Courses Offering Service-Learning Opportunities in a GLBT Context at the College of St. Benedict/St. John's University 2000–2003

Course Name	GLBT Service-Learning Sites	Number of Students at GLBT Sites	Results
First Year Symposium: Meaning of Difference	GLBT Programs Office, St. Cloud State University	4	Climate difference noted between universities having supportive programs and those without such programs
Sexual Orientation and Gender Identity	PRiSM at CSB/SJU; GLBT Programs Office, St. Cloud State University; Eclipse (GLBT Youth group), St. Cloud, MN	6	Students assumed more leadership roles with GLBT issues/concerns
Introduction to and Women's Studies	GLBT Programs Office, St. Cloud State University	2	Encounters with "real" GLBT persons supplemented texts
Community Psychology	GLBT Programs Office, St. Cloud State University	3	Students noted the numbers of allies attending GLBT-sponsored events

In order to create more visibility and awareness of GLBT individuals and their struggles, four different courses taught from the fall semester of 2000 through the spring semester of 2003 at the College of St. Benedict and St. John's University in Minnesota offered students the opportunity to complete a service-learning assignment in a GLBT context. This chapter examines the different approaches, populations, projects, and outcomes of the service-learning experiences in these courses. Based upon student evaluations, the authors also suggest how these service-learning opportunities might be improved.

FIRST YEAR SYMPOSIUM: THE MEANING OF DIFFERENCE

The general education requirements of the two institutions for incoming students include the First Year Symposium (FYS), a two-semester course aimed at helping students develop and improve their competencies in critical thinking, writing, oral presentation, and discussion, skills they will use and refine during their academic careers. Each symposium explores a specific topic, although the skills developed are common to all sections of FYS. One FYS section offered in the fall and spring of 2000–2001 explored the social construction of difference in American culture. The goals of this course were for students to obtain (1) a better understanding of how race, gender, sexual orientation, and social class are defined; (2) a grasp of problems facing each of the groups studied through a service-learning experience; (3) sensitivity to the challenges facing American society, given the demographic changes in its population; and (4) critical skills in examining and analyzing the role of race, gender, class, and sexual orientation in contemporary society.

Eighteen students enrolled in the "Meaning of Difference" FYS, nine males and nine females. During the first semester, the class worked to understand the terminology used to address diverse population groups. At the end of the first semester, representatives from three agencies spoke to the class, outlining the their program's functions and the communities they served in order for students to select the place where they would fulfill their service-learning requirement of thirty-five hours. Students were not only to assist the work of the agency but also to obtain data about the populations served for their research papers. These papers were to summarize and integrate the information they obtained from library and other resources on the St. Benedict's and St. John's campuses, as well as from their service-learning experiences. One of the three agencies where students could fulfill their service-learning requirements was the Gay, Lesbian, Bisexual, and Transgender Programs Office of St. Cloud State University (SCSU) (located four to eight miles from the St. Benedict's and St. John's campuses). Four students of the eighteen enrolled in the class chose to work with this program. They worked at the reception desk of the program's office and also did some filing with students from St. Cloud State. They assisted with the program's activities (coming-out groups for students exploring their same-sex attractions, educational programs, social functions, and advocacy).

At the end of the course, students wrote a ten- to twelve-page research paper in which they integrated and summarized research from a topic of their choice related to their service-learning experience. In addition, students were asked to conclude their papers with a reflective portion in which they pondered how the service-learning component had affected their academic experience and what service learning brought to the entire course experience.

SEXUAL ORIENTATION AND GENDER IDENTITY

In the fall of 2001, the Social Work Department at CSB/SJU offered a new course, "Sexual Orientation and Gender Identity." The course included a survey of theories about sexual orientation and gender identity, information on subcultures within the gay, lesbian, bisexual, and transgender communities, and a historical overview of GLBT cultures. Students also met with representatives from social service agencies working with GLBT individuals and their families to emphasize the importance of social work practice with this population.

The six students who enrolled in the course completed twenty hours of service learning in a program or project that focused on, and was staffed by, gay, lesbian, bisexual, and transgender persons. These projects included the following: the PRiSM group for GLBT students at St. John's and St. Benedict's; Eclipse, a support group for GLBT high school students in the St. Cloud, Minnesota, area; and the GLBT Programs Office at St. Cloud State University. Two students worked with the GLBT Programs Office; one student chose to use her work as an advisor to the Eclipse group (and its related adult task force on GLBT youth in St. Cloud, Minnesota); and the other three students worked with PRiSM on several projects, including staffing an information table and a rainbow ribbon campaign during National Coming-Out Week. It should be noted that these students were also members of PRiSM and served the group in a leadership capacity.

One weekend during the semester, the students and the instructor attended "Creating Change," a national conference sponsored by the National Lesbian and Gay Task Force held in Milwaukee, Wisconsin. There, they presented a workshop, "Making GLBT Issues Visible on a Rural, Catholic Midwestern Campus."

Students were required to write a ten- to twelve-page research and reflection paper. In this assignment students were to include a review of professional literature, as well as descriptions of programs similar to the ones where they had completed their service-learning assignments. For example, if the student discussed risk factors, such as suicide, for GLBT youth, then he or she was to describe programs that addressed these issues, such as the Eclipse group or programs supporting GLBT students in the Minneapolis and St. Paul school systems.

INTRODUCTION TO GENDER AND WOMEN'S STUDIES

"Introduction to Gender and Women's Studies" is a survey course, serving as the theoretical foundation for further courses a student may take in gender studies. Like the "Meaning of Difference" section of the First Year Symposium, special attention is given to the ways in which men and women differ. The course also uses the lens of race, class, ethnicity, and sexual orientation to examine how women and men shape their experiences.

The "Introduction to Gender and Women's Studies" course included a thirty-five hour service-learning requirement to be completed between the beginning of February and the end of April in a social service agency selected by the Service Learning Program of the colleges. As with other courses, the purpose of this requirement was to "fuse community service with academic reflection and analysis." Students were then to write a three- to five-page reflection paper, articulating the concepts they learned from the course that were related to the service-learning experience. The GLBT Programs Office at St. Cloud State University was the one GLBT-related site, which two students selected. (There were twenty-eight students in the class, and six other service-learning site options.)

COMMUNITY PSYCHOLOGY

In the fall of 2002, three students from the "Community Psychology" course taught at the College of St. Benedict/St. John's University fulfilled their twenty-hour service-learning requirement in a GLBT context. The students met with an intern at the GLBT Programs Office at St. Cloud State University to discuss work that they could do to benefit the St. Benedict's campus. They hoped to discover a context that would foster a good learning environment for GLBT students. The students worked with the GLBT Programs Office, which sponsored a drag (usually refers to cross-dressing men) show at SCSU. The students interviewed the performers and assisted with details at the event (selling tickets to raise money). They noted that half of the audience included GLBT supporters, not necessarily GLBT people themselves, such as friends of the performers and friends of the GLBT group in general. The St. Benedict students also worked with the assistant student-activities coordinator to develop and implement a safe-space training with the help of a Catholic sorority at SCSU. They made "GLBT Ally" and "GLBT Pride" buttons. They sat in on a few counseling sessions at the GLBT Programs Office. They assisted the PRiSM group on the CSB/SJU campus with a panel discussion/quiz show called, "Can You Guess the Straight Person?" Fifteen to twenty students attended this event.

In addition, they attended meetings of GLBT allies at SCSU and attended a conference on homophobia held at Augsburg College in Minneapolis. The goal of the students was to create a bridge between the GLBT Programs Office and the College of St. Benedict campus.

STUDENTS' EVALUATIONS OF
THEIR SERVICE-LEARNING EXPERIENCES

At the end of the semester, students from all of the above courses were asked to complete an evaluation from the Service Learning Department of the colleges about their service-learning experience. The evaluation consisted of the following items:

- What did your orientation include (if anything)? Was this adequate? Why or why not?
- Please demonstrate how a concept or theory from this course was evident in your service-learning project.
- What did you learn as a result of your service-learning project that you don't think you would have learned otherwise?
- Overall, describe the impact that this project had on you.
- How do you believe reflection affected your service-learning project?
- Is there anything that you would like to add about your service-learning experience that you think the Service Learning Department should know?

The results of these evaluations yielded some consistent and some divergent impressions from the students involved in service learning in a GLBT context. The following results summarize student evaluations from the four courses and responses to the evaluation questions described above.

Orientation: Most of the students found the orientation to their service-learning assignments to be adequate. The GLBT Programs Office staff at St. Cloud State was mentioned as being welcoming and helpful in describing the work of the center and the tasks the students were assigned to do.

Integration of theories and concepts from the course with service learning: Students saw the "hands on aspect" of service learning as beneficial to the overall knowledge gained from the course. In particular, they drew parallels between sexual-orientation and gender-identity discrimination and other forms of oppression based on race, gender, class, and ethnicity. They also gained information that helped them to examine and refute stereotypes about GLBT people and to educate others about GLBT civil rights. They saw the importance of providing safe space and fostering social support networks.

Added value of service learning: Students stressed the value of developing personal relationships with "real people" at their service-learning sites. They saw these relationships as an important supplement to the texts they read and to their experiences in the classroom. Several students noted the difference in the climate for GLBT students between St. Cloud State (where there was a visible, university-funded and-sponsored resource for GBLT students) and CSB/SJU, where no such program existed. They were able to see the effects of having an established, funded program. One student noted that the existence of the GLBT Programs Office at St. Cloud State fostered "citizen participation," while the absence of a similar resource at CSB/SJU led to less participation in the programs sponsored by PRiSM. (Author's note: The lack of a GLBT Programs Office also renders the GLBT community more invisible on the CSB/SJU campuses than at SCSU.)

Personal impact of the project: Students reported that their service-learning experiences had helped them to become more open and motivated them to become more involved and to assume greater leadership roles. However, one student reported becoming more suspicious of institutions, considering his or her cause to be lost cause, and contemplated giving up. Another student felt that the services the students offered, though not really needed, were nonetheless "appreciated."

Effect of reflection: The reflection aspect of the service-learning experiences came through student journals as well as discussions in class, with student workers from the Office of Service Learning facilitating. One reflection session was conducted in class during the semester. This session was conducted for approximately thirty to forty minutes, or about half a class period. Professors observed, but did not conduct, these sessions. Students were asked the following questions:

- What are some concepts or theories from class that you have seen in your project?
- How does your project help to improve your understanding of the coursework?
- What issues have you encountered through your service-learning experiences?
- What assumptions/preconceived notions/stereotypes did you have about the people you would be working with at the beginning of the semester? Has your service changed these assumptions/notions/stereotypes? Describe one event that stands out.
- How can the Service Learning Department, your professor, or the agency help you to have an even more successful experience?

Overall, students found the reflection component of service learning to be beneficial. Some reported that individual reflection (through journals) was of greater value than the group reflection in class. Others appreciated the opportunity to share "what was really going on" (from their work assignments) with their classmates and to compare experiences (from different service-learning sites). One First Year Symposium student commented, "It made me realize what I was learning. It was good to talk with other students about their similar experiences. It helped everything sink in."

Additional comments: Students found the experience to be "fun." Those at SCSU found the GLBT Programs Office a "great organization to work with." One student commented that the level of motivation for the GLBT service-learning project (in a "Community Psychology" course) varied among the participants and might have been improved had the group elected to work on GLBT issues (rather than being assigned to them).

OBSERVATIONS AND RECOMMENDATIONS

In the evaluations, students reported having benefited from completing a service-learning component as part of the four different courses in which they were enrolled. Their orientation to the service-learning projects, however, could have been more clearly defined in terms of agency expectations of the students and the tasks to be accomplished. The added value of service learning was often the relationship that students developed with others (sometimes across sexual-orientation lines). They also appreciated having a hands-on experience that integrated their textbook learning with the "real world." For the most part, the reflection component helped them to bridge the classroom experience and the service-learning environment.

Based on the student evaluations and the instructors' observations of the students' performance in their service-learning assignments, the authors make the following recommendations for improvement:

1. Acquaint students with the agency and the community they will be paired with prior to their beginning their assignments.
2. Clearly state and discuss the functions that the students will perform in the agencies to which they are assigned.
3. Formulate measurable criteria for the agency supervisor to assess the students' performance.
4. Provide for more than one reflection element throughout the service-learning experience. Students will think more clearly about what they are

accomplishing and still have time to make amendments to their assignments.

5. Provide the necessary opportunities for students to bring to the classroom experiences from the field and to relate them to the course content.

6. Provide the necessary transportation for students to travel to their assignments.

CONCLUSION

Sexual orientation, unlike race, age, and gender, is usually an invisible difference. Requiring students to work within a context where sexual orientation is visible and open enables them to explore that difference. The society surrounding the students participating in the above projects assumed heterosexuality as the norm. Two of the students from the "Sexual Orientation and Gender Identity" class identified themselves as heterosexual. By working in a GLBT context and by attending the "Creating Change" conference, they were able to experience, for a brief period, what it was like to be a sexual minority.

Academic education can acquaint students with historical, cultural, political, and sociological realities of what it is like to experience oppression and "otherness" as gay, lesbian, bisexual, or transgender. However, it was through personal relationships, students reported, that they were better able to understand differences and similarities between themselves and "the other."

In general, the goal of service learning here was to create sustainable outcomes from student involvement in programs, projects, and agencies. Mentoring and advocacy were sustainable outcomes that were achieved. Students who identified as gay, lesbian, or bisexual were able to empower themselves and others through organizing GLBT-related events on campus. Heterosexual students saw themselves as allies, helping to create safer, more open and understanding campus environments. GLBT students enrolled in the "Sexual Orientation and Gender Identity" course became mentors to other students who were exploring their sexual orientation. Heterosexual students who enrolled in the GLBT service-learning projects within these courses became identified as allies and influenced the opinions of their peers to end oppression and discrimination based on sexual orientation or gender identity. In addition, students developed ongoing personal relationships with the GLBT people they worked with on their service-learning projects.

When academic exigencies are bound with a service-learning experience, students are required to build relationships between acquired knowledge in a formal academic setting and the experience they gain from practice. In addition, benefits are derived from understanding diverse communities: a commitment to serve the community, a sense of personal empowerment, and ownership of the problems that are the source of misunderstanding and prejudice. Personal empowerment came through demonstrated leadership in developing GLBT-oriented programs on the CSB/SJU campus, participation in national and regional GLBT conferences, and observation of the effect of having a visible GLBT Programs Office at nearby St. Cloud State University. All of these benefits flow from the service-learning experience, especially when this experience occurs in a community where students may think that they have little in common with its members.

NOTES

1. Timothy K. Stanton, Dwight E. Giles, Jr., and Nadinne I. Cruz's chapter, "Mainstream or Margins," in *Service-Learning: A Movement's Pioneers Reflect on Its Origins, Practice, and Future* (San Francisco, CA: Jossey-Bass, 1999), provides an interesting insight into the process of institutionalizing service learning. It traces efforts in this direction made within the walls of academia by pioneers such as Jane Pernaul, Sharon Rubin, Garry Hesser, Dick Cone, Dick Couto, and Tim Stanton himself, as well as those efforts made from the trenches.

2. The AAHE series included the following disciplines: accounting, biology, communication studies, composition, engineering, environmental studies, history, management, medical education, nursing, peace studies, philosophy, political science, psychology, religious studies, sociology, Spanish, teacher education, and women's studies.

REFERENCES

Eby, J. (1995). *Service learning: Linking academics and the community.* Harrisburg, PA: Campus Compact.

Eyler, J., and Giles, D. (1999). *Where's the learning in service learning?* San Francisco, CA: Jossey-Bass.

Flikkema, E. (1998). Education for responsible citizenship at Drury College. In J. L. DeVitius, R. W. Johns, and D. J. Simpson (Eds.), *The spirit of community in liberal education* (21–22). New York: Peter Lang.

Stanton, T. (1990). Service-learning: Groping toward a definition. In J. C. Kendall et al. (Eds.), *Combining service and learning: A resource book for community and public service*, vol. 1 (65–67). Raleigh, NC: National Society for Internships and Experiential Education.

John R. Yoakam and Patricia Bolaños

Stanton, T., Giles, D., and Cruz, N. (1999). *Service learning: A movement's pioneers reflect on its origins, practice, and future.* San Francisco, CA: Jossey-Bass.

REPRINT INFORMATION

An earlier version of this chapter was published in the *NSEE* (National Society for Experiential Education) *Quarterly*, fall 2003/winter 2004.

Chapter Nine

Populations-at-Risk/Immersion Experience: Service Learning at Summer Camp

Meryl Nadel

THE CONTEXT FOR THE COURSE

Camp Viva materializes each summer for about a week. A world within a world, this intentional community invites service-learning students to experience an incomparable learning and service environment. As they live and work with HIV-infected and -affected families during the resident (sleep-away) camp session, students grow in their understanding of both micro and macro practice implications of life with HIV. In addition, the opportunity to hone group work skills is omnipresent in the twenty-four-hour-a-day group-living setting. Perhaps most importantly, students' relationships with their campers move beyond "clienthood" to "personhood" as they gain an appreciation for campers' resilience as well as the challenges they confront. This chapter illustrates a modality of service learning termed a *service intensive* because students are immersed in the experience.

HISTORICAL BACKGROUND

The summer camp—that opportunity for a change of pace and environment—has a long history in the United States, one intertwined with the history of social work. The earliest camps were established during the 1800s. While these first camps were private, settlement houses and other social agencies (often using rented or donated country houses) soon brought both children and adults to the country to provide respite from the city slums. The New York Children's Aid Society was associated with the Fresh Air Movement as early as 1872. Similar impulses inspired the Boys Club, Boy Scouts, and Girl

Scouts so that a number of camps were functioning by the early twentieth century. Other camps were sponsored by religiously affiliated groups like the Salvation Army, YMCA, Christian Herald Fund, Educational Alliance, Central Jewish Institute, and Jewish Working Girls Vacation Society. Still others were sponsored by ideologically committed groups, including socialists and Zionists (Ackerman 1999; Addams 1990; Eells 1986; Meadows 1995; Schwartz 1994a).

Given the involvement of settlement house and child-welfare workers, it is reasonable to assert that social workers were involved in resident camping from its early days. However, these camps focused largely on physical health and respite, rather than the "organized" programs and objectives that would develop later (Collins 2003).

As social workers became involved in developing group work theory and practice from the 1920s onward, their involvement in summer camps intensified. Camps provided an ideal setting in which to study small group interaction, group composition, and group programming. Social work luminaries, such as William Schwartz, Fritz Redl, W. I. Newstetter, and Gisela Konopka, among others, utilized the camp setting to advance group work theory and practice (Collins 2003; Mishna, Michalski, and Cummings 2001; Schwartz 1994b).

The social work presence in resident summer camps is also reflected in research studies conducted with campers or staff (Feldman, Wodarski, and Flax 1975; Marx 1988; Schniderman 1974; Williams, King, and Koob 2002; Williams and Reeves 2004). These and other studies examine such outcomes as changes in self-esteem, self-efficacy, values acquisition, and social competence.

Although F. Mishna, J. Michalski, and R. Cummings (2001) suggest that the social work profession's involvement in camps has decreased in recent decades, it is possibly evidence of social work involvement as documented by publications that has decreased rather than actual activity. Certainly, many community centers have continued to sponsor camps that are administered by social workers. Currently, social workers also function as consultants to camp staff in some residential camps (Joy Ganapol, personal communication, 2001; Judy Matthews, personal communication, 2000), as well as camp directors. Most notably, the growth of camps for "special" populations has provided a natural milieu for social work intervention.

Many camps, generally nonprofit, currently meet the needs of children and adolescents with physical, emotional, behavioral, and developmental challenges. Paul Newman's Hole-in-the-Wall-Gang Camp, serving children with cancer and other medical illnesses, is probably the best known of these programs. Mishna, Michalski, and Cummings (2001) have described a therapeutic camp for children and adolescents with learning disabilities and psychosocial issues, while N. R. Williams, M. King, and J. J. Koob (2002) and Williams and P. M. Reeves (2004) recently studied social work student involvement at a camp for burn victims. Additional developments include camps for families and seniors.

In the years since the recognition of pediatric HIV, resident camps serving the HIV-infected and -affected population have emerged in many parts of the United States. The Children Affected by AIDS Foundation (CAAF) estimates that about seventy-five such camps exist in the United States. CAAF has established a camp network, holds a yearly retreat for camp staff, and provides supportive services and some funding. Several different models are followed by these camps: some are for HIV+ children only, some are for HIV-infected as well as -affected children, some are for HIV+ children along with their family members, and some are for families that are HIV-affected and may or may not have a living member who is infected. Camp Viva is a family camp that fits into the last category. This means that campers may be children who are HIV+, parents who are HIV+, single adults who are HIV+, or family members who are HIV−. All the HIV-related camps share the goals of providing fun, respite, a break from the day-to-day stress of living with chronic—sometimes acute—illness, camper growth, and informal or formal education. Treatment of the disease is specifically not the goal of the camps (CAAF Camp Network 2006).

WHAT IS CAMP VIVA?

In 1993, a Ryan White CARE Act Planning Grant study revealed the need for respite services for Westchester County, New York, residents infected with and affected by HIV. These individuals and families were often isolated and lived in the inner-city areas of the county. Multiple agencies, under the direction of Family Services of Westchester, Inc. (FSW), collaborated to develop the camp and its year-round follow-up programs. The camp has met yearly since 1995 for about a week at the end of August, renting a summer campsite whose season has ended. Camp Viva's mission is to provide much-needed respite, support, and lasting rejuvenation to these children, families, and individuals.

From initial staff orientation sessions, through camp week, and in the course of year-round activities, an unwavering message is communicated: Camp Viva is a warm, supportive, loving family. Values and activities consistent with professional social work practice pervade the camp, and, indeed, numerous social workers, as well as other FSW staff, have been involved in the program since its inception. For example, confidentiality guidelines are carefully reviewed with all volunteers, levels of supervision are clear and explicit, and training in conflict resolution is included in the orientation process. The strengths perspective is also apparent: at each meal, for instance, campers and staff are encouraged to address the entire camp with a "shout out," a word of thanks or praise for another person or a positive accomplishment.

Viva offers children and adolescents the opportunity to experience a typical summer camp: the freedom and joy of a week in the country filled with activities, new relationships, and a hiatus from urban stressors. Adult campers experience the same benefits, as well as educational and supportive group and individual services. Medical supervision and counseling are provided to all who need it.

Children live in groups by age with their counselors, while adults live separately. All participate in numerous activities, such as swimming and boating, sports, arts and crafts, music, and fishing. Special activities include talent shows, carnival, disco night, a square dance, and other events. Good food is plentiful. As Viva's Web page states, "Kids are free to be kids and play with others without having to worry about what others might be saying about them or their families" (Camp Viva 2003). HIV and AIDS are only discussed with a child if the child initiates the conversation. Adolescents are engaged in education and prevention sessions. Once each day, Family Time brings together each family with an assigned volunteer staff member. The staff member guides the family in a structured activity, such as solving a puzzle or constructing a family tree, as he or she models constructive communication skills. Volunteer staff may be assigned to work with children, adolescents, or adults.

As noted above, these families tend to have difficult lives. Although the county in which they reside is considered wealthy, they live in its inner cities and face typically urban problems. Coming to camp means a radical change of environment. The week is intense: children, some with behavior problems, face adapting to group living; adults may find themselves confronting issues that they have avoided at home. A low staff-to-camper ratio means that social support is always available.

STAFF AND STUDENTS

Many campers and staff return summer after summer. They eagerly anticipate the session, some counting down the days. Reunions are scheduled between camp sessions. In addition, the camp provides a periodic newsletter, visits from volunteers, and a phone tree for important messages (sometimes the loss of a member of the camp family). In this way, support is maintained throughout the year. Staff members vary on many dimensions. Some are professionals, including teachers, nurses, social workers, lawyers, and businesspeople. About 10 paid staff and 40 to 60 volunteers serve about 75 to 120 campers each summer (depending on funding). Half of all new volunteers are students (from Iona College and the College of New Rochelle), and about 20 percent of the students return to camp without credit the following year. In all, the student/former student contingent has grown to about 30 percent of the volunteers. Students are recruited through on-campus publicity, class visits by the Campus Ministries coordinator, and word of mouth. All volunteers participate in orientation and debriefing sessions. Ongoing professional support and a lounge are available for staff respite during camp week.

The course titled "The Camp Viva Experience" is termed a service intensive because it consists primarily of an immersion service-learning experience in which students travel to the site at which they are studying and serving. Other such courses at the college have included an immigration law course on the Mexico-U.S. border and a Native American history course on a reservation. These courses integrate most of their academic class hours into the weeklong period of their "trip." During the service intensive, students expect and receive a highly concentrated, intense period of both learning and service. These offerings are consistent with the college's service mission.

Student involvement began when this author collaborated with the camp's volunteer coordinator to develop a service-learning course for Iona College students at Camp Viva. After being offered for several years as a special topics course, the class was presented to the Curriculum Committee and approved as a Social Work Department elective.

The course instructor wears a number of hats. An MSW social worker who is a graduate of our baccalaureate social work program, he also serves as volunteer coordinator for the camp. Thus, he is able to provide professional learning and supervision to students within a context he knows well as a staff member.

"The Camp Viva Experience" is a Social Work Department elective with no prerequisites, open to all students who successfully complete the application and screening process described below. The decision to open the course to all students acknowledges that the camp's community volunteers may well come without any relevant academic background, only the desire to serve.

RELATIONSHIP TO PROGRAM OBJECTIVES

Since "The Camp Viva Experience" is an elective course, it supplements the program objectives defined by the Social Work Department. Nonetheless, this course clearly addresses several of the Council on Social Work Education's curricular mandates. Most obviously, involvement with Camp Viva brings students into contact with an important population-at-risk: people infected with, or affected by, HIV/AIDS. As the face of the HIV epidemic has changed over the years, so has the camp's population. Currently, few of the children are HIV+, while most of the adults are HIV+. Some children attend with uninfected parents or caregivers (often grandparents) because the infected member(s) is (are) deceased. Some adults attend by themselves. At this point, many have lived with the stressors of HIV for years. Other risk factors are present in this population: most families are from impoverished, inner-city neighborhoods, most are people of color, some are isolated, and many have experienced substance abuse and other biopsychosocial challenges. Children are often being raised by single parents or grandparents. The ongoing interaction between students and campers that occurs during camp week enables students to garner an understanding of risk factors and populations-at-risk that goes far beyond what they can gain in the classroom. Campers are often relieved to share their struggles and obstacles with supportive service-learning students.

Students' commitment to social and economic justice increases as a result of their Camp Viva experiences. As they learn about their campers' lives, they are awakened to justice issues some of them have never faced. They may learn about injustice related to health care disparities and the discrimination that accompanies a diagnosis of HIV. Students who come from socioeconomic backgrounds similar to the young campers may see themselves as role models for these children.

As discussed previously, Camp Viva is suffused with social work values and ethics. From the start of the orientation sessions, the students and other volunteers learn the importance of individual dignity and worth, confidentiality, acceptance, respect, and compassion. The strengths perspective pervades the camp environment. The many experienced camp staff set a consistently high standard for community norms and values, and new staff (including service-learning students) quickly meet these expectations. The camp also provides a model for a diverse and peaceful community. The camp population varies in terms of age, ethnicity, religion, national origin, race, gender, sexual orientation, and family structure. It is rare to see any friction based on difference, and staff confront any that occurs within a group of children. Finally, this course provides significant group work practice experience for the students.

THE CAMP VIVA STUDENT EXPERIENCE

The Screening Process

"The Camp Viva Experience" offers three undergraduate credits when successfully completed. A thorough, three-stage application process includes careful screening of students by both Iona College and Camp Viva staff prior to acceptance. A general information meeting for all interested students is followed by submission of a written application and an interview with the volunteer coordinator/course instructor. The screening process allows the volunteer coordinator to assess the maturity and commitment of students. Iona College generally sends approximately eight students per year for credit, about half of whom are social work majors. Other student majors have included business, speech, education, psychology, or have been undeclared. In addition, students may return or attend for the first time without credit.

The student group is highly diverse, reflecting the makeup of the college. Traditional-aged students vary in ethnicity, socioeconomic status, and background. A number of returning adult students with extensive life experience have also participated. Students have included a Latino substance abuse counselor, a suburban homemaker, and students hailing from Africa, Asia, the Caribbean, and England, as well as New York City and its metropolitan area. Our students contribute to the multicultural environment at the camp.

Orientation

Once accepted, students are required to attend nine hours of orientation (six of which include all volunteers), complete a packet of additional readings related to the psychosocial aspects of HIV/AIDS, and read the extensive camp training manual. Orientation is conducted by the camp's professional staff, which includes social workers, a psychologist, educators, and others. The following content is included:

- information about HIV, universal precautions, and other safety issues
- an overview of the camp manual, schedule, and rules
- team-building exercises
- camper behavioral intervention and other strategies
- role-plays of potentially problematic situations
- learning about the support/feedback mechanisms incorporated into the camp structure
- course requirements
- an opportunity to ask any remaining questions of experienced staff

In addition, the introduction of the camp cheer and alma mater conveys to new volunteers something of the spirit and love they are about to encounter during camp week.

Camp Week

Students and the other volunteers arrive at camp the day before the campers do in order to help with camp preparation, acclimate themselves to the environment, meet fellow staff (a square dance is scheduled in the evening), and prepare for the campers' arrival. In addition to bunk assignments, each volunteer is assigned a particular camper family with which to work. Students report anticipation and apprehension: "I didn't know what an experience I was actually getting myself into, but it's not one that I will forget."

One student captured her feelings at the campers' arrival: "When the campers started to step off the bus, I got this feeling that I have never had before. I felt so good. My nervous and anxious feelings were replaced with feelings of joy and happiness. The campers' expressions were priceless. There were a few uneasy faces, but mostly faces filled with exhilaration."

The balance of professional structure and genuine warmth and acceptance is quickly evident. While respite and relaxation are important goals, a structured camp schedule insures that campers and staff are productively active. Likewise, while camper-staff interactions are highly informal, boundaries are clear and appropriate. All staff is held to strict expectations in terms of a daily feedback and supervision structure. Individual support and counseling are available to both campers and staff in recognition of the demands of the setting.

In their day-to-day functioning at camp, service-learning students are indistinguishable from the other volunteers. Most work alongside fellow counselors with a small group of children or adolescents of the same age. With them virtually twenty-four hours per day, students get the campers going in the morning, accompany them to activities, round them up for meals, invent skits, comfort them, cajole them, set limits with them, problem-solve, put them to bed at night, bond with them, and sometimes hear their deepest secrets. The students who work with adults encourage them to participate in various activities (sometimes for the first time in their lives) and to follow the camp schedule, and they act as willing listeners. The students cheer, sing, dance, laugh, and cry with the campers. All students become deeply immersed in the intense experience of camp week and emerge exhausted and enriched. For example, one student wrote about his (entirely voluntary) participation in a talent show as follows: "I did a skit explaining how Camp Viva was like a giant family where I had to deal with the children and how I met so many warm people."

Throughout the hectic, activity-filled week, the reality of the campers' everyday lives is never denied. A minister, the camp's "spiritual guy," sets the tone as the entire camp gathers twice daily for Circle. Recently, the themes he chose were "a time of joy," "a time of healing," "a time of peace," and "a time of love." The medical staff helps campers reevaluate and sometimes restart complicated medical regimens. In educational workshops, adult campers confront illness and loss, while celebrating strengths. Students learn through their daily interactions: "I was amazed at the adults that they were so energetic and full of warmth. I never would have thought that any one of them had AIDS."

The Academic Component

Expectations for the course are clearly laid out in the syllabus. When the course was presented to the college's Arts and Science Curriculum Committee for approval, care was taken to include the requisite number of "classroom hours." The course objectives are specified as follows:

At the completion of this course, students will have gained

- an introduction to and a greater understanding of the HIV/AIDS community
- the ability to think critically and to rethink stereotypical ways of understanding the HIV/AIDS population
- an appreciation for the benefits of building bonds and being of service to others
- a sensitivity toward people facing significant life challenges
- new skills for working with individuals, families, and groups
- the unique experience of living in the intentional community of a summer camp

Course assignments, in addition to the precamp activities already described, include keeping a daily reflective journal, participating in group and individual supervision, and submitting a five- to seven-page reflection/research paper (with references). Some suggested themes for the paper include "What Campers Taught Me" and "Crossing the Role Barrier in an Experiential Setting." Students also act as facilitators for Family Time each day, attend several of the adult education classes held during the week, participate in volunteer debriefing following the campers' departure, and satisfy additional expectations required of all staff. Students are also required to attend at least one camp reunion. Reunions, staged several times during the year, provide continuity and an opportunity for campers and staff to gather for a festive occasion.

OUTCOMES

Student Learning and Other Benefits

Definitions of service learning have been discussed in earlier chapters. As J. Schine notes, they appear to share the elements of "meaningful service, active participation, reflection, and learning" (1997, 189). The Camp Viva course easily satisfies these criteria and goes further. J. C. Kendall (1990) emphasizes the component of reciprocity: giving as well as receiving. Many times over, students of all ages have told us that they have gotten more than they have given. Although it is a week of hard work, students "also learn about themselves, their personality, how they relate and work with others, how they handle pressure and stress, as well as their ability to give to others" (Paul Schiller, personal communication, 2003).

The service-learning students also benefit from the opportunity to experience the bravery and spirit of people living with HIV. As one student wrote, "The most valuable lesson I learned from Camp Viva is that we need to live life to the fullest. . . . Parents at camp were infected . . . but they did not let it stop them from living." Another student was moved to reflect on her own relationships when one of the longtime adolescent campers expressed her heartfelt "wish" at a campfire that everyone would return to camp the following summer.

Kendall also discusses the aspect of students' "learning about the larger social issues behind the human needs to which they are responding" (1990, 20). Through reading about, discussing, and experiencing the challenges in their campers' lives, students are able to place these problems within the larger social contexts of poverty, racism, the lack of a reasonable health care system in the United States, and the need to pursue social justice. One course participant saw himself as a role model: a successful college student who has overcome challenges similar to those faced by his campers.

In their reflection papers, students often write about the significance of the relationships they develop during this brief period. They are deeply touched when campers say they hope they will return as counselors the following year. As one student wrote, "The 'Viva experience' was something that I will never forget. It sits with me every day and has helped me grow as a person, mentally and spiritually."

"The Camp Viva Experience" enhances the social work major while also appealing to nonmajors. A former student who has now returned for five summers commented on the difference between Camp Viva and field placement.

> At camp, even though you receive a grade, there is a lot less pressure. You don't get "evaluated" at camp. Even though it is only a week, I feel that you form greater bonds with the campers there than a year with your clients at your field placement. Campers at Viva absolutely love camp, and they look forward to it all year. Unlike most clients, Viva campers choose to be there and they really form bonds with each other as well as with the counselors. They will tell you personal things without your even asking. At camp, they can be themselves and that really helps in getting to know each other on a more personal level. . . . Since they feel comfortable, you see what they are really like. (Jill Jackman, personal communication, 2003)

On the camp experience as an introduction to the social work major (she first attended following her sophomore year), this former student commented:

> I definitely got a sense of social work as a major after going to camp. A lot of the counselors and staff are social workers. Just watching them handle certain situations served as a great model of what social workers do. Also, there are many times as a counselor that you must handle conflicts and that is also great experience. Family Time is also a good way to see family dynamics. Confidentiality, a big part of social work, also comes into play at camp since some campers will disclose personal information to you. . . . It is great communication experience, AND IT'S FUN! (Jackman, personal communication, 2003)

The former coordinator of service intensives at Iona contrasted "The Camp Viva Experience" course with other "trip" programs. She stated that, for students, this course affords a more in-depth connection to those served that is gained by living with campers, experiencing Family Time, and interacting on the individual, group, family, and camp levels. Furthermore, the supervision provided is more layered and intense, and the ongoing contact, through reunions, insures a deeper connection. Finally, the opportunity to return to camp the following year and the accessibility of the course to returning adult students also sets it apart from most other service-intensive courses (Katie Byrnes, personal communication, 2003).

Additional Contributions

This social work service-learning course has yielded benefits on many sides. Students have gained from the opportunity to experience shared positive relationships with campers and their family systems and at the same time increased their self-awareness, knowledge, and skills related to people infected and/or affected by HIV/AIDS. This intense connection in service to others translates into personal, at times transformative, growth and true experiential learning. For example, for some students the experience has confirmed or generated an interest in working professionally with people affected by HIV/AIDS.

As noted, while some students attend for one year, others return as experienced counselors/group leaders in subsequent years. In both cases, Camp Viva benefits from the genuine contribution of the students to the implementation of the camp program, as well as from the influx of energy and enthusiasm they bring to camp. Although students are seen as volunteer staff by all but their instructor/supervisor, student involvement "has ensured the availability [of staff] to serve the maximum number of campers with the optimal number of staff. Student participation has become a cornerstone of camp" (Schiller, personal communication, 2003). Iona College has benefited from the ability to offer its students a rare experience of community that is entirely consistent with the mission of the college and of social work. A year-round connection between Camp Viva and the Campus Ministries Center is currently being nurtured.

Although it is classified as an elective, "The Camp Viva Experience" contributes to the learning called for by the Council on Social Work Education's *Educational Policy and Accreditation Standards*. Students learn firsthand about populations at risk from HIV, poverty, and other factors. They emerge with an understanding of the importance of social and economic justice. They experience a diverse and resilient community. They are immersed in a setting guided by social work values, knowledge, and skills. While they may or may not consciously identify this aspect of camp, it is clear that all are positively impacted by consistent messages of respect, caring, and integrity. Finally, they gain a more multifaceted and holistic understanding of client systems (on a variety of levels) than is possible in many fieldwork settings.

Unique Added Value

It is difficult to convey on paper both the intensity and release of the resident summer camp setting. While staff (in the best camps) function as conscientious professionals with extensive responsibility for their charges, both as individuals and cabin groups, the safe, rural setting encourages openness and relaxation. Camp Viva's service-learning students benefit from this unique "utopian" opportunity.

As noted above, camps for diverse special-needs populations exist throughout the United States. Social workers are involved with a number of them on a variety of levels. The development of service-learning courses similar to "The Camp Viva Experience" could provide rich opportunities for such camps, for university students, and for the profession. As mentioned, two recent articles (Williams, King, and Koob 2002; Williams and Reeves 2004) discuss the use of service learning with MSW students at a camp for burn-injured children.

One student's reflection paper captures her experience from initial motivation through the close of camp. She concludes as follows: "I can't even begin to express how privileged I feel for taking part in this wonderful camp. I feel blessed in so many ways. Yes, I may have received credit for it, but to me it was so much more than that. It's a feeling that is hard to put into words, and believe me I tried. I know that making promises is against Camp Viva rules, but I already marked next year's camp on my calendar."

REFERENCES

Ackerman, W. I. (1999). Becoming Ramah. In S. A. Dorph (Ed.), *Ramah reflections at 50: Visions for a new century* (3–24). New York: National Ramah Commission.

Addams, J. (1990). *Twenty years at Hull-House*. Chicago: University of Illinois Press.

CAAF Camp Network. (2006). "Initiatives—Camp Network." Retrieved March 24, 2006, from www.caaf4kids.org.

Camp Viva website. (2003). "Camp Viva." Retrieved March 24, 2006, from www.fsw.org/camp_viva.htm.

Collins, L. (2003). The lost art of group work in camping. *Social Work with Groups*, 26, 21–41.

Eells, E. (1986). *History of organized camping: The first 100 years.* Martinsville, IN: American Camping Association.

Feldman, R. A., Wodarski, J. S., and Flax, N. (1975). Antisocial children in a summer camp environment. *Community Mental Health Journal, 11*(1), 10–18.

Kendall, J. C. (1990). Combining service and learning: An introduction. In J. C. Kendall et al. (Eds.), *Combining service and learning: A resource book for community and public service*, vol. 1 (1–33). Raleigh, NC: National Society for Internships and Experiential Education.

Marx, J. D. (1988). An outdoor adventure counseling program for adolescents. *Social Work, 33*, 517–20.

Meadows, R. R. (1995). *History of Virginia's 4-H camping program: A case study on events leading to the development of the 4-H educational centers*. Unpublished dissertation. Retrieved March 27, 2006, from Google Scholar database.

Mishna, F., Michalski, J., and Cummings, R. (2001). Camps as social work interventions: Returning to our roots. *Social Work with Groups, 24*, 153–71.

Schine, J. (1997). Looking ahead: Issues and challenges. In J. Schine (Ed.), *Service learning: Ninety-sixth yearbook of the National Society for the Study of Education, part I* (186–99). Chicago: National Society for the Study of Education.

Schniderman, C. (1974). Impact of therapeutic camping. *Social Work, 19*, 354–57.

Schwartz, W. (1994a). Camping. In T. Berman-Rossi (Ed.), *Social work: The collected writings of William Schwartz* (419–26). Itasca, IL: F. E. Peacock (original work published 1960).

———. (1994b). Characteristics of the group experience in resident camping. In T. Berman-Rossi (Ed.), *Social work: The collected writings of William Schwartz* (427–33). Itasca, IL: F. E. Peacock (original work published 1960).

Williams, N. R., King, M., and Koob, J. J. (2002). Social work students go to camp: The effects of service learning on perceived self-efficacy. *Journal of Teaching in Social Work, 22*, 55–70.

Williams, N. R., and Reeves, P. M. (2004). MSW students go to burn camp: Exploring social work values through service-learning. *Social Work Education, 23*, 383–98.

ACKNOWLEDGMENT

The author thanks Camp Viva's service-learning students, campers, and staff, especially Paul Schiller, for all their help and for welcoming her into the Camp Viva family.

Chapter Ten

General Education: Herding Cats and Making History in a Large General Education Social Welfare Course

Robin Allen, William Rainford, Roy Rodenhiser,
and Kara Brascia

GENERAL EDUCATION

At Boise State University, a strong collaborative relationship exists between the School of Social Work (which we will refer to as the School) and the campuswide Service-Learning Program (Boise State SLP). We maximize this relationship by incorporating a service-learning component into our "Introduction to Social Welfare" course. This chapter describes the nuts and bolts of how we integrate service learning into this course and how this course fits into the overall mission of the university. In addition, we provide a brief evaluation of how the service-learning experience impacts student learning, community agencies, and the overall quality of the course.

Boise State University has offered "Introduction to Social Welfare" both as a required course for social work premajors and as part of the university's general education requirements for over twenty-five years. As a required course for premajors, this freshman-level course provides a building block for achieving our compliance with the Council on Social Work Education's (CSWE) educational policies (CSWE 2003).

In addition, as an approved general education course, "Introduction to Social Welfare" provides us with opportunities to recruit students to the major, achieve credit-hour production to comply with university mandates, and build community relationships to support the institutional mission. By aligning "Introduction to Social Welfare" with the university's educational philosophy and objectives, we clearly show our program's fit with, and importance within, the university. This connection and visibility adds to the viability of the program, an important consideration, as a number of baccalaureate social work programs around the country have been closed in the last few years (Rodenhiser 2005; Williams 2005).

147

The School of Social Work plays an important role in the promotion of civic engagement on campus through its collaboration with the Boise State SLP. This campuswide program is an increasingly visible contributor to the institutional mission and to the reputation of the university as a metropolitan university of distinction as it seeks to "educate students to become informed and engaged citizens who will play a role in the betterment of society" (Coalition of Urban and Metropolitan Universities 2006). Service learning appeals to today's students because it provides them with applied learning experiences and job networking and gives their coursework personal relevance (Brody and Nair 2005; Eyler and Giles 1999; Litke 2002).

Service-learning pedagogy has proven successful in the social work curriculum due in large part to the support of the Boise State SLP. The Boise State SLP contributes to the success of service learning on campus by (1) offering comprehensive training, support, and maintenance programs for faculty, students, and community agencies, and (2) coordinating service-learning partnerships from a centralized staffing and database system. The university's commitment is evident in the staffing of the Boise State SLP, which includes one full-time professional, one half-time administrative assistant, and six part-time student assistants. A number of the students employed by the program are social work majors who also provide support to our social work service-learning courses.

NUTS AND BOLTS OF COURSE DESIGN

Typically, "Introduction to Social Welfare" enrolls about seventy-five students in each section. The service-learning requirement constitutes fifteen hours and is required of all students, be they social work majors or not. The service-learning staff and social work faculty carefully select agencies and projects to match the educational goals and objectives of the course. The instructors integrate the service-learning experiences of students with curriculum content through reflection activities that include both class discussions and written assignments. We should note that the School does not require faculty members teaching "Introduction to Social Welfare" to use service-learning pedagogy. Some choose not to do so.

Coordinating the community experiences of large classes requires thoughtful planning of course content, coordination of staffing, and ongoing communication between faculty, service-learning staff, students, and community partners. The desired result is that the student will be able to apply acquired classroom knowledge to the community experience, then return to the classroom able to communicate what he or she has learned. Thus, we consider several components in the planning process: (1) design of the course syllabus and lecture units, which includes consideration of the model of service learning the instructor will use (we describe three models in this chapter); (2) management of service-learning partnerships; and (3) facilitation of reflective learning.

Curriculum, Syllabus, and Lecture Units

The course description for "Introduction to Social Welfare" establishes critical thinking, reflective learning, and integration of theory as central to a service-learning pedagogical approach. The course rationale portrays the social work values of social justice and diversity as core concepts for the practice of democracy and the development of professional social work practice. Figure 10.1 illustrates the course description, rationale, and objectives.

"Introduction to Social Welfare" employs the dynamic pedagogical approach associated with service learning in which readings, class discussions, critical-analysis exercises, and a hands-on experience help the student successfully master course content as reflected in the course objectives.

We believe that successful service-learning outcomes require responsibility and maturity on the part of the student, perhaps even more so in the large classroom setting. For example, if the student fails to attend lecture, she or he lacks the exposure to the instructor's discussion of the theory intended for application in the community. A student may acquire an adequate grasp of theory by merely reading the course material; however, she or he may fail to maximize the experience when not involved in the interactive components of the classroom. Furthermore, we believe that a student's failure to complete the service-learning project will rob the student of the practical application of theory. The learning experience is thus left incomplete and the course objectives, unfulfilled. For this reason, we make mandatory, and closely monitor, attendance and completion of service-learning hours. For students who have a compelling reason not to participate in the service-learning component of the course, we use an alternative assignment/requirement, such as a term paper.

Less mature students may find such a course challenging. This is a freshmen-level course, and many of the students enrolled are transitioning to meeting the higher expectations of university-level education. However, we have not noticed an increased number of students failing this course compared to the number that failed prior to the implementation of the service-learning requirements. In fact, the engaged structure has helped some students to pass this course. We have taught this course in a variety of formats and feel strongly that a structured service-learning experience results

Course Description: Introduction to Social Welfare surveys contemporary social welfare programs, their historical development, underlying philosophy, and the need for social services in a modern society.

Course Rationale: Social Welfare is a required course for social work majors and offered as an elective for students not seeking a social work degree. The goal of this course is to provide the student with a broad overview of the field of social welfare including its history, mission, and philosophy. The course focuses on the historical and contemporary development of social welfare institutions and its impact on disadvantaged and oppressed populations. The development and implementation of social service delivery systems in promoting social and economic justice are examined. Special emphasis is placed on contemporary social problems that include information on the nature, extent, theories, and causes of such problems as well as social services designed to prevent, alleviate, or contribute to their solution.

Social Work Course Objectives—Students will be able to:
- demonstrate sensitivity to diversity through individualization, respect, and appreciation for differences;
- understand the history of social work and the policies, structures, and programs of social welfare as a social institution;
- demonstrate understanding of the dynamics of those social and institutional factors that inhibit healthy growth and promote oppression and discrimination;
- demonstrate the use of critical thinking;
- demonstrate the motivation for continued growth and expanding knowledge.

University Core Competency Objectives—Students will be able to demonstrate competencies in each of the following domains:
1. Critical Thinking/Problem Solving Skills
    Example: Students will clearly identify and analyze social welfare problems and identify possible solutions to these problems by utilizing methods of policy analysis.
2. Communication Skills
    Example: Students will read, interpret, analyze, and evaluate written discourse through assigned materials both independently and in groups.
3. Cultural Perspective
    Example: Students will explain their own cultural perspective and make meaningful comparisons between it and other cultural perspectives by comparing/contrasting different life experiences of dominant populations and classes to minority populations and classes. In particular, issues of racism, classism, ableism, ageism, and sexism and their impact on the social welfare system will be discussed.
4. Breadth of Knowledge and Intellectual Perspective
    Example: Students will articulate relevant basic assumptions, concepts, theoretical constructs, and factual information. Students will be exposed to an in-depth analysis of social welfare policies and programs in the United States. Included in this analysis are public assistance programs, the Social Security program, health and mental health care systems, civil rights, and the child welfare systems.

Figure 10.1.   Introduction to Social Welfare: Course Description, Rationale, and Objectives

in improved student learning, outcomes for which we provide evidence later in the chapter.

To receive academic credit, students must complete an orientation at the assigned agency, a service-learning contract, fifteen hours of service, five in-class reflection exercises, and a service-learning evaluation. These requirements, which must be monitored and graded, might seem too daunting to the instructor considering a service-learning component. However, the Boise State SLP provides support through a trained service-learning assistant (typically, an upperdivision undergraduate student) and a website to reduce the burden of certifying completion of assignments. The service-learning assistant works with the instructors to secure projects for students in community agencies, provides an orientation to the projects and the registration process on the first day of class, assists students who are having problems with enrolling for projects in the online database provided by the Boise State SLP,[1] and can assist the instructor with developing and grading reflections. The online database provides information on community agencies and the available projects, allows students to register for projects, and allows community partners to complete evaluations of each student's performance. Instructors can track where students are completing their hours and access agency evaluations. In addition, the instructors use Blackboard, a Web-based instructional tool, to facilitate the integration of students' reflection on and discussion of their experiences in agencies with classroom readings, lectures, and discussions.

Service-Learning Models Used in Large Classes at Boise State

In our large classes, we apply three models of service learning that we have named as follows: the single-site shotgun, multisite shotgun, and targeted models. We describe each of these models and discuss them in terms of the roles and responsibilities of the social work faculty and the Boise State SLP, as well as the strengths and weaknesses of each. Table 10.1 presents a summary of the discussion. The use of a particular model depends on the faculty member's preference in the particular semester. For example, if one faces an unusually busy semester, then the single-site shotgun model would be the appropriate choice. On the other hand, if a faculty member is working actively on a community organizing or research project, then the targeted model would be an excellent choice to achieve a high level of integration of teaching, scholarship, and service activities. The three models presented here emerged through a developmental process as we continually evaluated the course and sought to improve the learning experiences of our students.

The service-learning component of the course provides the student with the opportunity to experience firsthand how community-based programs apply social welfare policies to help service recipients function more effectively in

Table 10.1. Comparing and Contrasting Three Models of Service Learning

	Single-Site Shotgun Model	Multisite Shotgun Model	Targeted Model
Social Work Faculty Responsibilities	• Reflection/integration of course content • Coordination and collaboration with Service-Learning Program staff and community agencies	• Reflection/integration of course content • Coordination and collaboration with Service-Learning Program staff and community agencies	• Reflection/integration of course content • Coordination and collaboration with Service-Learning Program staff and community agencies
Service-Learning Program Responsibilities	• Set up agency projects • Provide service-learning assistant • Troubleshoot agency and student problems	• Set up agency projects • Provide service-learning assistant • Troubleshoot agency and student problems	• Set up agency projects • Provide service-learning assistant • Troubleshoot agency and student problems
Strengths of Model	• Simple—easy to implement • Can develop in-depth understanding of a topic, e.g., poverty or hunger	• Multiple sites enrich classroom discussion • Students can match interests with particular agency	• High level of integration of S-L experiences with course curriculum • Student development of activities at the Service-Learning site
Challenges of Model	• Need agency that can handle a large number of students • Service-learning tasks for students can be routine • Students may experience a lack of engagement • Requires the help of a service-learning assistant to coordinate logistics	• Integrating multiple issues into reflections and classroom discussion • Requires the help of a service-learning assistant to coordinate logistics	• Integrating multiple issues into reflections and classroom discussions • Time and energy intensive for faculty and S-L assistant • Finding agencies with resources to participate in intensive projects • Requires the help of a service-learning assistant to coordinate logistics

society. Careful, thoughtful selection of service-learning partners is necessary to ensure appropriate matching of theoretical content of the course with community-based practices. Our course instructors enjoy close collaborative relationships with community partners. We assert that successful service learning requires such relationships. To illustrate, we include examples of how these partnerships work in the discussion of each of model.

Single-site shotgun model. In this model, the instructor selects one service-learning site, generally an agency with an expressed need for a large group of students. In one section of the course, fifty students provided service to the Idaho Food Bank, where they completed a variety of tasks that were simple to organize and manage. The community partner supervised the large group in such activities as filling bags with food, stocking shelves with donations, and assisting in community fund-raising activities. The project provided students the opportunity to relate their work to material learned in the classroom around issues of poverty and social welfare. For example, one of the continuing themes of the course is understanding the role of values in shaping social welfare policy. Students completed a written reflection integrating this topic with their experiences at the Idaho Food Bank. Students reflected on their experience by responding to questions online via Blackboard. The use of a grading rubric helps to facilitate efficient grading of such a large number of student reflections. Table 10.2 provides an example of a reflection and the rubric used to grade it. In the single-site shotgun model, interaction among students, community partner, and the instructor is minimal.

We believe the single-site shotgun model is easy to implement and manage, requiring relatively little time or effort on the instructor's part. Another example of this model is a service-learning project that focused on solutions for homelessness. In the community surrounding the university, homelessness has become an identified and unresolved social problem, with many people living in city parks, along the riverbank, and in the nearby foothills. In response to the need for shelter and associated services, a faith-based community organization developed two shelter sites, one for men and the other for women. However, given constrained fiscal and human resources, the agency struggled to meet the demands of the homeless community. The instructor for one section of "Introduction to Social Welfare" had worked closely with the community organization to establish the shelters. After teaching students about homelessness, both historically and contemporarily, the instructor had agency staff visit the classroom along with a formerly homeless person to discuss the current context of homelessness in the community. Students were then required to complete fifteen hours of service learning in the agency, working side by side with agency staff in providing shelter services and support to homeless persons. The need of

Table 10.2. Example of Reflection Assignment and Grading Rubric

Throughout U.S. history, social welfare policies related to people who are poor have reflected the values of the period. How would you categorize the values that are influencing the current policies and programs for people who are poor today? How do these policies/programs impact (directly or indirectly) the lives of the people who are served by the agency where you are doing your service-learning hours?

Grade Earned	Above Standards 4	Meets Standards 3	Approaching Standards 2	Below Standards 1
Grading Standards	The reflection integrates experiences in the community organization with specific and relevant examples that demonstrate clear and accurate understanding of class material.	Most of the examples are specific and relevant and demonstrate a predominantly clear and accurate understanding of class material.	At least one example of an experience in the community organization is given and provides an unclear and/or inaccurate understanding of class material.	No examples given and/or no attempt to explain course material.

the agency for increasing capacity-to-serve was met, while students simultaneously benefited from experiential learning. Numerous students decided to major in social work (an unintended but positive outcome of service learning in the "Introduction to Social Welfare" course) as a direct result of their experiences in the shelter.

Multisite shotgun model. In this model, instructors select several sites that will provide projects to facilitate the application of course theory. This approach provides students with several sites and various projects from which to choose for their service-learning experience. A benefit of this model is that fewer students are assigned to each service-learning partner, thereby making the experience somewhat more personal. The instructor using this approach facilitates discussion between students serving at each site. In the classroom, students are able to compare and contrast the different agencies, their missions, and their approaches in dealing with social welfare issues in the community. However, coordination of the service-learning experience becomes more involved. With the need to manage interaction between the students and community partners, the instructor might rely heavily on the service-learning assistant to coordinate and facilitate communication and the completion of assignments and to troubleshoot problems that arise.

Using this model, one instructor incorporated a service-learning component to provide students with the opportunity to educate key stakeholders on policies related to social work in the community. The instructor, a legislative advocate in the community, identified several advocacy agencies that focus on state-level political advocacy and with whom he had an ongoing relationship. The community partners from each agency hosted five students and chose a community education project that fit with the agency's mission. For example, a women's rights agency used its students to conduct a campus educational day around domestic violence policies. Guided by agency staff, students in the project researched state and federal policies concerning domestic violence, created informational flyers and posters, and staffed an educational booth in a central location on campus for a day. Another agency concerned with human rights asked its assigned students to focus on abolishing the death penalty in the state. They were required to become experts on all aspects of the death-penalty debate. They then organized a death-penalty forum, with both pro- and anti-death-penalty advocates participating. The students were responsible for every aspect of the forum, from logistics to panel participants to media relations. The event was deemed a success, with over sixty attendees engaged in the discussion. In a stroke of brilliant organizing, the students had attendees complete a postcard to the governor demanding abolition of the death penalty. More than fifty cards were hand-delivered to the governor's desk at the statehouse.

As a final project in the classroom, each student group presented its project, from conceptualization to completion. The presentations provided students with a means to billboard their accomplishments in the community. One of the main themes of the "Introduction to Social Welfare" course, that policy is practice, seemed to be cemented in the students' learning experiences as evidenced by their enthusiastic, entertaining, and instructive presentations.

Targeted model. In this model, the instructor selects five different service-learning sites to provide students with a range of special, task-intense projects from which to choose. Each site receives approximately ten students. The community partners attend class the first day to introduce the agency, describe the service-learning project being offered, and field questions or address students' concerns. Afterwards, the instructor asks students to research the agency that interests them most via the Internet. What distinguishes this model from the previous one is that, during the course of the semester, the instructor visits each site, taking lecture and discussion to the site with assistance from the community partner (what we call "classroom in the community"). Feedback from community partners and students regarding this model has been very positive. Partners express satisfaction with student engagement at the service-learning site. Students themselves are enthusiastically engaged both in the classroom and at the site. Finally, the instructor enjoys greater connection to both student and community partner. Thus, the triad created by the targeted model heightens the positive effects of service learning, namely, integrated and engaged learning.

In an application of the targeted model, a faculty member identified one lecture topic from the course syllabus and used it as an underlying theme to teach about the use of social welfare programs and policies in redressing social ills. After identifying the theme of community poverty, specific community-based agencies that focus on eradicating poverty were targeted. Community partners came to the classroom and discussed with students the nature of their community-based programs and their service population. The course instructor, along with the community partners, led students through a two-week "poverty academy," using lectures, movies, readings, and reflective activities to afford students a solid understanding of the perceived causes, effects, and cures for poverty in the community. Students then signed up for the project and agency of choice.

One of the targeted agencies focused on hunger in the community. The students conducted research into the extent of hunger and food insecurity, relying on city officials, community agencies, and those experiencing hunger themselves as sources of information. The group of students then designed an educational booth that they operated in the statehouse during the legislative session. The intent of the booth was to ask legislators to carefully consider hunger in the community as a real and pervasive problem requiring governmental policies as redress. The students astutely provided legislators with donuts and coffee as a means of catching their attention. The booth was surrounded by legislators and their staff the entire morning.

COMPARING AND CONTRASTING THE MODELS

The time and effort required to manage community partnerships differs significantly among the three models described above. The single-site shotgun model with one community partner might present the least demanding scenario in terms of presemester planning and overall coordination. However, if the agency is new to service learning, the risks of misunderstandings and mismanagement are high. Time-tested community partners with significant experience managing college students in agency activities will likely be most effective with large service-learning classes. With Web-based student registration of projects, coordination and monitoring is needed only until students understand what is expected and get settled into their projects. Since all of the students are assigned to the same agency, problems, if they arise, tend to affect many students and therefore can be discussed and resolved all at once, rather than requiring individualized attention. For example, one semester the wrong directions for getting to an agency were given to students!

The Boise State SLP is key to the implementation of the single-site shotgun model, helping to locate agencies that can accept such a large number of students and troubleshooting the logistical challenges of placing and managing so many students. The service-learning assistant is the first contact when problems arise for either the students or the community partner. The assistant tends to shoulder most of the workload generated by the service-learning component of the course.

Because the multisite shotgun model involves multiple community partners, providing students with a wide range of topics, locations, and service times, the demands on the instructor increase. Most students appreciate options because they are likely to connect with an agency that matches their personal interests or learning needs. However, although students appreciate a choice, coordinating service learning through an array of agencies proves very time intensive to set up initially, as this model requires someone to recruit multiple agencies, orient them to working with students using the service-learning modality, and coordinate their classroom visits and subsequent agency orientations. Having established agencies decreases the planning time for each, but monitoring and troubleshooting seventy-five student/university/agency relationships still requires the ongoing time and attention of the faculty member and trained student assistants. The Boise State SLP assistant continues to facilitate the troubleshooting in the multisite shotgun model, but the instructor takes more responsibility for the integration of multiple sites into the students' learning experiences.

With the targeted model, the responsibility for partnership building, monitoring, and maintenance moves from the Boise State SLP staff to the instructor, in part because of the self-investment of the faculty member in the community issue. Boise State SLP staff may still have some role in orienting new agencies, helping them post projects online, and explaining service-learning forms and procedures. However, the faculty member is more directly involved in problem solving student/agency issues as selected projects tend to be extensions of his or her research or service interests. In addition, the faculty member typically arranges his or her own site visits to agencies for community classroom activities. Boise State SLP staff members are nonetheless available for consultation and troubleshooting if needed and will administer student evaluations of the service-learning experience, as well as take responsibility for making sure the agencies submit online evaluations of students' performance at the agencies.

FACILITATION OF REFLECTIVE LEARNING

The most rewarding element of service learning in a large class is the use of reflection activities and assignments to bridge experiential and classroom learning. Whether one chooses to have students write reflectively about their experiences, discuss them in groups, or respond to questions orally in class, the instructor is challenged to facilitate translation and communication of the student's experiences in a way that the student achieves introspective awareness of what she or he has learned. The literature makes clear that the learning process requires guided feedback from the instructor (Eyler and Giles 1999; Nitschke-Shaw and Ziesler 1998). Each of the models presents unique opportunities and challenges for reflection.

Reflection in the Single-Site Shotgun Model

With as many as seventy-five students engaged in a large community agency, individual students may feel overwhelmed and underappreciated. The tasks they are given at the site may seem mundane or repetitive—serving food in a shelter kitchen or hanging clothes at a thrift store. It is vital that the instructor help students connect course content (such as the effects of poverty) to the task at hand. Through the course structure and before the experience begins, the instructor requires students to read the textbook and scholarly articles or to view media that enables them to "look into the eyes" of those affected by the problems being addressed by the community agency. Having done that, the instructor then asks students to reflect on the lived experiences of service recipients before the student makes contact with the agency. The intent is that students will become more empathetic to the people they will encounter when they engage in agency activities.

Another reflection activity that helps students understand their place in the agency is having the community partner require students to reflect on the orientation at the agency. Students may reflect on their expectations, concerns, and issues related to the agency and individuals served. This exercise allows the community partner to have a greater role in reflection and to connect to students individually, responding to their possible anxieties or preconceptions about the nature of service and the population served. Written reflections are returned to the course instructor, who uses them for dialogue and discussion in the classroom during the initial weeks of the activity.

Reflection in the Multisite Shotgun Model

In this model, students are much more engaged in the service-learning site than in the first model. Here, students work in small groups to accomplish tasks that are project oriented. As an example of a reflection activity, if the students are completing projects with a statewide policy advocacy agency and they are tasked with designing a booth for the state fair to educate voters about tax policy, they might individually think about the course lectures and readings related to tax policy and create posters that incorporate course themes with agency perspectives. Under the guidance of the community partner, the group members come together and present their posters to each other, discussing how each poster contributes to the message they are trying to convey to the public. It is in the discussion, not the designing, of the poster that reflection leads to learning. To take it one step further, the group returns to the classroom, and each person presents his or her poster to the entire class, thereby connecting the project to the course learning objectives and enhancing the learning of all.

Reflection in the Targeted Model

As in all service-learning reflection, students communicate with each other and the instructor regarding how theory led to greater understanding of the agency's mission, the individuals served, and the impact of their service on the community. In the targeted model, a service-learning fair can be held where students, working with their community partners, design a presentation related to their group project. As they prepare their materials, group members discuss their experiences within the agency. The community partner facilitates the discussion, informed by her or his practice knowledge and materials provided by the course instructor that summarize what the students have learned in the classroom. The service-learning fair is a required attendance event for all students, who benefit from viewing their fellow students' projects and understanding what was accomplished. The students may evaluate the projects on both creativity and educational value. The class then reconvenes to discuss the projects as they relate to course themes.

In one application of the targeted model of service learning, the instructor approached reflection using three different methods. In the first method, the instructor posed reflection questions in class at five different points during the semester. Students responded to the questions in "two-minute papers." Following this, students formed groups of four to discuss their responses. Finally, each group reported back on the most salient observations discussed. In this way, seventy-five students were able to reflect and respond regarding integrated service learning. Two examples of such questions follow:

1. After introducing service learning in class in the first week of the semester, the following reflection was assigned as a two-minute in-class paper: Think about the service hours you will be doing at the Idaho Food Bank. What do you think you will be doing? What kinds of people will you be working with? Why do they need help? What does that help do for them? Write your answers in two minutes. Be thoughtful, but write quickly. Be ready to discuss your response with the class.
2. After students completed their service-learning hours at the Idaho Food Bank, the following reflection was assigned as a two-minute in-class paper: Why do hunger and food insecurity exist in Idaho? What are the effects of hunger (think about the individual, local-community, and state contexts)? How do we end hunger in Idaho? Be thoughtful, but write quickly. Be ready to discuss your response with the class.

The second method involved the "classroom in the community" described earlier. By meeting with ten to twelve students at a time, the instructor could lead a group reflection exercise in which students taught the instructor about the service-learning site, the tasks they had been performing, and how classroom learning applied to their work at the site. This small group interaction greatly facilitated integrated learning.

The third method involved the instructor's using Blackboard's Discussion Board to post questions to which students could respond in "bulletin board" fashion (a discussion thread with each posting visible to the discussants). While not a requirement of the course, quite a number of students took this opportunity to discuss their experiences, observations, and feelings with the instructor and each other.

OUTCOMES

Accreditation Standard 8 (Program Assessment and Continuous Improvement) requires that each social work program have an assessment plan and procedures for evaluating the outcome of each program objective (Council on Social Work Education, Commission on Accreditation 2003). "Introduction to Social Welfare" lays the foundation for subsequent social work courses and contributes to the achievement of overall program outcomes. Because of the inclusion of service-learning pedagogy, assessment of outcomes for this single introductory course provides valuable data for understanding overall program outcomes as enhanced by alternative methods of curriculum delivery. Such an assessment includes the focus on student learning within a service-learning context and, importantly, how communities benefit from the service-learning approach (Buchan et al. 2004).

One method of evaluating the service-learning component of "Introduction to Social Welfare" is the use of a service-learning survey developed by the Boise State SLP. The most recent data for sections of the course come from the fall of 2004. On this survey, students ($N = 97$) answered questions about their service-learning experience. Of the student respondents, 70 percent either strongly agreed or agreed that as a result of taking "Introduction to Social Welfare," they were more interested in helping solve community problems. When asked whether the course helped them see how course concepts can be applied to everyday life, 68 percent responded that they strongly agreed or agreed; 66 percent responded similarly that the experience fostered personal insights and growth.

In addition to completing the above service-learning survey, "Introduction to Social Welfare" students evaluated the course at the end of the semester. Specifically, students rated the overall quality of the course. On this question, instructors employing service learning in their courses consistently received scores of 3.5 or higher on a 4-point scale, leading us to conclude that students consider service-learning courses of high quality. Students also responded that they would recommend the courses to other students.

From our experience teaching this course, we find that students are more engaged and enthusiastic about the material compared to those who take the course without the service-learning requirements. This course, with its service-learning component (regardless of the model used), represents a major departure from most large, freshmen-level, general education courses at Boise State University. Our students and faculty are responding positively. Likewise, our community partners are enthusiastic about working with our "Introduction to Social Welfare" classes. The following statement illustrates typical feedback we receive from our community partners:

> Service-learning students bring new energy, ideas, and perspective to any organization. They impacted my organization by bringing new insights to the old way of doing things. New insights, new energy—any opportunity to revisit what we do helps us help clients more efficiently, effectively and with zeal that is not found in many non-student volunteers. Beyond just getting their hands dirty, service-learning students have the courage to make conversation with the homeless people that regular volunteers avoid.
>
> Having that eye contact and civil conversation with a young person is so good for our organization and makes a long lasting impact to the people we serve. (Hope Ryan, Director, St. Vincent de Paul Thrift Stores of Boise, personal communication 2006)

SERVICE-LEARNING BENEFITS
TO THE SCHOOL OF SOCIAL WORK

Offering a large, core (general education) course to seventy-five students affords a unique opportunity for students, especially prospective social work students, to learn about the applied nature of the social work profession. The service-learning pedagogy of the class provides students with unique applied experiences early in their academic careers that offer a rich context for them to understand the knowledge, skills, and values necessary for professional social work practice. The service-learning experience in a large class also helps all of the students understand the relationship of social work knowledge, skills, and values to the role of social work and other helping professions in the community. Students in this class gain a sense of connection with the community and an appreciation for civic engagement. For those who choose social work as a major, this understanding prepares them for more contextual service-learning activities in our curriculum and is a natural connection with the field practicum experiences that are the capstone of their academic educations.

NOTE

1. The database is available for adoption. For information, go to http://servicelearning .boisestate.edu.

REFERENCES

Brody, R., and Nair, M. (2005). *Community service: The art of volunteering and service learning* (3rd ed.). Wheaton, IL: Gregory.

Buchan, V., et al. (2004). Evaluating an assessment tool for undergraduate social work education: Analysis of the baccalaureate educational assessment package. *Journal of Social Work Education, 40*(2), 239–53.

Coalition of Urban and Metropolitan Universities. (2006). Coalition of Urban and Metropolitan Universities home page. Retrieved March 15, 2006, from http:// cumu.uc.iupui.edu/home.asp.

Council on Social Work Education (CWSE), Commission on Accreditation. (2003). *Handbook of accreditation standards and procedures* (5th ed.). Alexandria, VA: Author.

Eyler, J., and Giles, D. E. (1999). *Where's the learning in service-learning?* San Francisco, CA: Jossey-Bass.

Litke, R. A. (2002). Do all students "get it"? Comparing students' reflections to course performance. *Michigan Journal of Community Service Learning, 8*(2), 27–34.

Nitschke-Shaw, D., and Ziesler, Y. (1998). *Faculty guide to service-learning*. Unpublished manuscript, Bedford, NH.

Rodenhiser, R. (2005). Rochester Institute of Technology social work program. *BPD Update, 27*(1), 5–7.

Williams, C. J. (2005). BSW program closings from 1992 to 2004. *BPD Update, 27*(1), 3–4.

Part III

ASSESSING OUTCOMES OF SERVICE-LEARNING EXPERIENCES

Chapter Eleven

Process and Outcomes Evaluation in a Service-Learning-Intensive Curriculum

Rose Malinowski

The baccalaureate social work (BSW) faculty at Trinity Christian College uses service learning and the application of knowledge outside the classroom to empower students. A resulting question is, How does one then support and measure success in learning through social work student service-learning experiences? This chapter provides a description of the program's approach and a discussion of assessment tools implemented to measure learning outcomes.

COLLEGE SETTING

Trinity Christian College is a four-year liberal arts institution located in suburban Chicago with easy access to the heart of the city. Over 60 percent of its one thousand students live on the college campus. Trinity Christian College bases its mission on the heritage of the Reformation. The Reformed Christian tradition posits that God created the universe, including human beings, as good creation. Human beings fell into sin and sinful humankind has abused God's perfect creation; thus, human beings have failed to be good stewards of God's creation. Therefore, a significant responsibility of humankind's commission is to follow God's original purpose in transforming creation and ameliorating the effects of the abuse. This means that, within this tradition, the college is concerned with preserving and restoring the environment and rebuilding and restoring optimal functioning in all social institutions, from families to global interactions in the sharing of resources. In the Reformed tradition, human beings are appointed stewards; they are responsible for making the most out of the communities with which they interact as builders, designers, and creators (Christian Reformed Church 2002). Within this context, faculty and students are called to teach and learn in a community that seeks to educate the whole person. As a community of Christian scholarship, Trinity Christian College is committed to shaping lives and transforming creation.

SOCIAL WORK DEPARTMENT

The mission of the Social Work Department closely complements that of the college. The mission statement focuses on community-centered generalist practice: "Within a community-centered generalist framework, the mission of the social work department is to provide an opportunity for students to fulfill their callings to Christ-like service through the professional application of knowledge, skills, and values." This mission statement emphasizes active community involvement with a variety of community-centered organizations and the fostering of professional relationships that positively impact the broader community. Although the BSW program at Trinity Christian College is a small program with two full-time faculty members and a current enrollment of thirty-five students, community partnerships with a variety of community-centered organizations multiply the impact of the department's work.

EXPERIENTIAL LEARNING IN THE BSW CURRICULUM

Throughout their course of study, social work students are required to participate in courses that involve experiences within the broader community. For example, in the course "Introduction to Social Work," students are given a case scenario and required to research urban employment and day care options relevant to the specific scenario. Students, who are not typically from the Chicago area, travel on public transportation to the employment and day care facilities they have found within the city and reflect on this process when they return to campus. As students consider this experience, they often comment on the challenges they experienced in locating resources, let alone the amount of time consumed in reaching these services on public transportation. Without fail, students verbalize that this experience increases their empathy for families who daily endure similar struggles.

Students also engage in various service projects tied to their coursework, ranging from completing intake interviews for area agencies providing emergency food services to participating in local political rallies on social work issues. Opportunities provided within the curriculum vary according to the needs of area agencies and the ongoing emergence of social policy issues. As students move through the BSW curriculum, they engage in service learning as a component of the total educational experience. The Social Work Department exemplifies the work of Andrew Furco when defining the service-learning approach to education. Furco (1996) describes service learning as a "balanced approach" to education with equal emphasis on service and academics, wherein the community and student benefit reciprocally from the relationship.

An example of service learning in the social work program at Trinity Christian College involves pairing students with older adults residing at a local nursing home. This twenty-hour lab experience occurs during the first social work practice course. In this class, students are matched with nursing home residents who seldom receive other visitors, and they assume the role of "friendly visitor" with their designated partner. As part of the lab experience, each student is required to complete a written journal incorporating reflections on interviewing skills, the opportunities and challenges involved in working with this at-risk elderly population, and a plan for continued development of their interviewing skills. The course instructor also engages the students in discussions during class time, encouraging the class members to reflect with each other on their experiences. This service-learning assignment is an integral component of the initial social work practice class, which emphasizes knowledge and skill building in interviews and assessments with individuals. Students enrolled in the course complete a pre- and posttest instrument to assess their level of achievement of course learning objectives each semester. Over a three-year period, students consistently report positive learning outcomes for learning objectives closely tied to the service-learning experience.

Although the total number of students is small, the data also suggest such outcomes (Social Work Department 2006). Anecdotally, the majority of students report increased confidence in their interviewing abilities and decreased anxiety in working with the elderly after completing this service-learning experience. The nursing home administration eagerly looks forward to the return of a cadre of "friendly visitors" each fall and has begun to request additional partnerships with the college. The range of experiential learning activities social work students complete in the social work core curriculum helps prepare them for the comprehensive service-learning experience they undertake during the final two years of undergraduate study, the social work generalist capstone assessment project, an integral component of the BSW program at Trinity Christian College.

CAPSTONE PROCESS

Although each capstone assessment project at Trinity is unique in terms of project objectives, every generalist capstone assessment project includes goals and objectives congruent with professional BSW learning and builds on the broader general education foundation. The capstone assessment project itself progresses through a series of four semester-long professional seminars coupled with development, implementation, and evaluation of a community-based social action project (figure 11.1).

Building on the social work core curriculum, the generalist capstone assessment project provides students with opportunities to do research, community organizing, team building, assessment, and evaluation within the community context. Unlike the field internship experience, which emphasizes student learning through supervised practice in a social work setting, this cap-

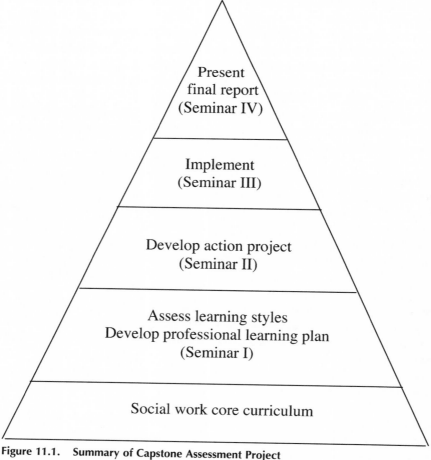

Figure 11.1.   Summary of Capstone Assessment Project

stone experience emphasizes a balanced approach to learning and service. As Furco (1996) explains, service-learning experiences must have some academic context and be structured to ensure that the service enhances the learning and the learning enhances the service. The generalist capstone assessment project works toward achieving this end.

First Professional Seminar

Starting in the junior year of study, social work students participate in the first professional seminar of the capstone series. During this seminar students complete a variety of independent learning projects, including a self-assessment of learning styles, development of an individualized learning plan for professional development, and skill building in selected computer applications. Through these activities, students enhance professional self-awareness and formulate plans for professional development. Students also gain practice in the establishment of goals and objectives while developing their learning plan. The instructor establishes a relationship as a consultant during this initial seminar, mentoring students through the different learning activities. The instructor also gathers information about each student's learning styles to aid with the assignment of student teams for the following semester. Throughout the capstone experience, faculty liaisons remain available as consultants working to foster self-awareness of the skills each student possesses, reflection on the process and content for each project, and awareness of resources (both internal and external) available to student teams for completion of capstone projects.

Second Professional Seminar

During the second professional seminar, students begin the service-learning component of the capstone process. Prior to the spring semester, faculty assign students to teams based on the self-assessment of learning styles that students complete in the first professional seminar. At the start of the second seminar, faculty distribute the assignments, and students are reminded that they will remain in their designated teams for the duration of the capstone assessment project. Student teams then work together for three semesters to develop, implement, and present a community-based social action project. In this second seminar, student teams select the topic for their social action project. To facilitate this process, the faculty liaison for the student team helps match a community partner with each team's chosen topic and helps to establish the initial contact between the community partner and the student team. An initial meeting is scheduled with the community partner, student team, and faculty liaison, at which time the capstone process is reviewed, and the social action project is discussed. During this meeting, an agreement is reached among all partners on the basic elements of the project and ongoing communication processes for completion of the project. At this point, the community partner assumes the role of expert on the chosen project area and primary mentor for the student team. The faculty liaison steps back, remaining a consultant on an as-needed basis. The following is a segment of a project plan submitted by a team that consisted of six social work students:

- *Project title:* Trinity Christian College and Roseland Christian School: A Partnering Approach
- *Purpose statement:* Our purpose is to build upon BSW generalist curricular goals and objectives by working with the after-school program at Roseland Christian School (RCS) and partnering the school with Trinity Christian College (TCC). Our aim is to develop a framework for future use that will give Trinity Christian College students the opportunity for early experience in their major while assisting Roseland Christian School in improving the after-school program.
- *Project goals:* (1) Evaluate existing programs and explore a possible partnership between TCC and RCS that utilizes the strengths of both organizations and will serve to benefit both.
- *Measurable objectives:* (1) Survey Trinity students to discover need and receptiveness to the idea of a program between TCC and RCS.
- *Project tasks/action steps:* (1) Survey Trinity social work and education majors using quantitative means.
- *Evaluation criteria for this task:* Thirty percent response rate

The information presented above shows one goal a student team developed for its capstone project, along with an objective, task, and evaluation criterion established to meet that goal. This student team also proposed two other objectives to address this goal adequately: (1) to interview staff at existing programs that might support such a partnership, and (2) to complete a literature search of similar partnerships that offer support to after-school programs. As each capstone project progresses, all student teams design data-collection tools to help reach their goals. These tools may include written surveys as specified above, structured individual interviews, or focus groups. Evaluation methods for each goal vary and may include responses to a survey, feedback from the community partner, or assessment of relevant literature found for a specific research topic. To assist the community partner in follow-up evaluation of the project, student teams have designed pre- and posttests for program participants and customer-satisfaction surveys for users of resource manuals. For each project task, all student teams are also required to designate responsible persons and set timelines for task completion. In addition, student teams are asked to think ahead and estimate potential project barriers and limitations. Barriers might include personnel availability at the community site, interview space, or computer access.

Instructors encourage students to take ownership of the capstone process from the start and to assume various independent learning roles as active participants in team development, project design, implementation, and evaluation. Instructors provide feedback on the purpose, goals, and objectives for each team's social action project throughout the second professional seminar so that student teams can quickly begin implementation of the social action project when they return in the fall semester. Equally important learning activities during this second seminar provide opportunities for student team reflections on group process, assignment of group member roles, and growth in problem-solving and conflict-resolution skills.

Third Professional Seminar

By the end of the second seminar, each student team has practiced team-building skills within its group, developed an initial relationship with its community partner, and completed a draft of the project plan, which acts as a launching pad for the third professional seminar. In the fall semester, student teams enrolled in the third seminar implement the social action project with the community partner. For the project "Trinity Christian College and Roseland Christian School: A Partnering Approach," the student team acted with a high level of independence during the implementation phase. These students interviewed participants and staff at the after-school program, surveyed Trinity education and social work students to ascertain their interests, completed a thorough literature review, and developed a proposal for future partnership efforts between the college and the Roseland Christian School after-school program. Written progress reports were submitted at regular intervals, demonstrating the team's forward movement on reaching project goals and a high level of group performance. The faculty liaison was asked to review survey materials and the protocol for administering the surveys and structured interviews. The student team grappled with its own group process and worked actively with its community partner.

During that same semester, another student team required additional support negotiating working relationships with the community partner. The faculty liaison worked more closely with that team and community partner, clarifying the intent of the capstone assessment project and helping to define boundaries for the partners. This team also requested support with establishing workload balance among the group members. As a macro practitioner, the faculty liaison anticipates and addresses challenges to project development and implementation and the evaluation of each capstone assessment project. The liaison may assist with issues that include pressure to change project requirements, team conflict, or time-management problems, among other barriers that may negatively impact successful student outcomes. As with any consultation arrangement, the type and extent of involvement varies from project to project. The overall aim remains consistent: support experiences that allow students to practice and develop advanced BSW generalist skills, while community-based agencies receive assistance with projects that will more effectively serve their client populations and act as catalysts for positive community change.

Fourth Professional Seminar

The fourth professional seminar focuses on a final presentation of each student team's community-based social action project. All teams must submit a written narrative incorporating the following elements:

- executive summary
- purpose statement
- project goals
- project tasks
- project barriers
- evaluation plan
- summary of team reflections and lessons learned
- reference list and appendices

Each student team also gives a final oral presentation forty-five minutes to one hour in length to the community partners, faculty liaisons, social work student colleagues, and Social Work Department Advisory Group members using a PowerPoint presentation format. At the close of the oral presentation, students reflect on their journey through the capstone process. A former student commented in the team report, "Unlike most class projects, our capstone project had a purpose and some immediate and long-term implications for an organization. Each person was able to bring varying and vital perspectives to the HIV intervention programs, which was both challenging and enriching. I came away from this project feeling competent, connected and fulfilled" (Lawndale HIV Community Intervention Project 2005, 10). The community partner for the Lawndale HIV Community Intervention Project commented, "This is more than just a class project; the intervention they created was the perfect starting point for my outreach staff" (Lawndale HIV Community Intervention Project 2005, 14).

Overall, students provide exceptionally positive feedback regarding the capstone process, stating that the practice they receive working with community practitioners builds their confidence and gives them an edge when they begin field education placements. Community partners who have served as mentors have found the students' enthusiasm and accountability to be energizing for them in their own practices. Student products have been useful for the community partners in their organizations.

REFLECTION

Throughout the capstone experience, faculty integrate opportunities for reflection into the curriculum. Students have structured time to think, talk, and write about the various learning experiences within and outside of the classroom. For example, during the process of group formation, the students consider the B. Tuckman (1965) model of group development. Student teams submit written group progress reports at scheduled intervals, which reflect on group development using the Tuckman (1965) framework of five predictable stages: forming, storming, norming, performing, and adjourning. Student teams also present conflict-resolution methods for their own teams to the class and share helpful hints with each other so that teams can more effectively grow through the "storming" stage of group development.

As student teams progress through the capstone experience, they prepare written progress reports for the community-based social action project. These reports must include continued reflection on group process and movement toward project goals. Instructors provide students with structured questions to guide their reflection: How is the group negotiating the stresses to accomplish the project purpose? What roles can each member play in the decision-making process to enhance group effectiveness? How are underlying feelings generated during group interactions processed in the group? How are underlying feelings blocking the group process? How does the group as a whole maintain the focus for achieving the project's purpose? and How does the group establish mechanisms to "fight fair"? When students begin to work with the community partner and move toward attainment of project goals, written and verbal reflections include statements about the interaction with the partner and the service environment.

At the time of the oral presentation, the faculty, student team, and community partner all participate in evaluating the community-based social action project. Faculty then summarize the input for the student team and provide a final grade. Excerpts from an evaluation for the project "Trinity Christian

College and Roseland Christian School: A Partnering Approach," are shown in table 11.1 (Social Work Department 2005).

As table 11.1 shows, evaluators assess each element of the team's project using a five-point Likert scale to rate the project from inferior to superior and provide written comments to substantiate their ratings. In addition to this feedback, the Social Work Department collects student self-assessment data that links student learning through the generalist capstone assessment project to each curricular objective. These self-assessments are completed in the initial (pretest) and final (posttest) semester of the capstone experience. Faculty use these results to assess trends on an annual basis, paying close attention to data that reflect a posttest mean score of less than 4.00 (based on a five-point Likert scale) or only minor increases between pre- and posttest scores. Table 11.2 portrays two of the Social Work Department curriculum objectives built on the Education Policy and Accreditation Standards content areas and the mean scores of student self-assessments in these curricular areas. Scores are based on program data from 2003 to 2006 (Social Work Department 2006).

The student self-assessment provides a direct link to assessment of curricular objectives, while the assessment tool for the capstone project itself is not directly linked to these objectives. Results shown in table 11.2 demonstrate a consistent upward trend over the last three years in students' self-assessment of their knowledge and skills associated with curricular objectives. Information provided through both of these mechanisms is instrumental in providing the social work faculty with an opportunity to build on the strengths of the capstone assessment experience and to modify aspects that seem to create undesired challenges for future student teams.

Table 11.1.   BSW Generalist Capstone Assessment Project Evaluation Tool

Project Title: Trinity Christian College and Roseland Christian School: A Partnering Approach

Project Component and Description	Score Inferior --- --- --- Superior 1 --- --- --- 5	Comments
Purpose Statement: Brief and concise; Reflects social work values	5	The statement was well done and thoughtfully presented.
Evaluation Plan: Data collection plan in place; Link to measurable outcomes	5	Very well done! Evaluation measures were specified for each project task.

Table 11.2. Student Self-Assessment of Curriculum Objectives

How confident are you that you can...	Pretest Average	Posttest Average	Academic Year (N = number of students)
	Cannot do at all......Certain can do 1 5		
Model professional use of self by applying critical thinking skills within the context of professional social work knowledge, values, and practice (EPAS 4.6)	3.5	4.4	2003–2004 (N=15)
	2.4	5.0	2004–2005 (N=5)
	3.2	4.5	2005–2006 (N=5)
Understand the value base of the profession while assimilating personal and professional values and ethics, and practice according to the profession's standards and principles (EPAS 4.0)	3.4	4.7	2003–2004 (N=15)
	2.6	4.8	2004–2005 (N=5)
	3.0	4.8	2005–2006 (N=5)

FUTURE DIRECTIONS

Over the last three years, students have worked with an assortment of community-based agencies and completed an array of projects. These partnerships include the following:

- development of an HIV outreach program at a local health center
- design of a foster parent resource manual for a specialized foster care program
- evaluation of a service-learning program in an area high school
- research for an adolescent-pregnancy-prevention video targeted at parents of teens

Both the faculty and student teams exercise flexibility in selecting the topic and agency for the community-based social action project. As B. W. Speck (2001) states, the integration of service learning into the curriculum is "not necessarily tidy" and requires effort on the part of all partners to balance learning and service.

The benefits and challenges of service learning are noteworthy. For social work students, the opportunities to promote social justice in actual social work settings, develop a professional sense of self, and improve academic outcomes are profound (Coles 1993; Heffernan and Saltmarsh 2000; King 2003). The Social Work Department at Trinity Christian College remains committed to providing service-learning opportunities in a variety of contexts. As community partners continue to work with the department, opportunities for additional partnerships also arise. Community partners have become active members of the Social Work Department Advisory Group, class speakers, grant partners, workshop speakers, and field instructors. Graduating students comment that both the extended time working together in teams and "real" opportunities to serve community agencies leave them well positioned to join the professional ranks of social work. The department remains open to student-initiated topics for the social action projects while requiring student teams to offer alternative options should the first choice not prove viable. The Social Work Department continues to refine the evaluation process for the generalist capstone assessment project, working to involve the community partners more actively in the formal assessment process and to link evaluation of the capstone project directly to curricular objectives. The Social Work Department continues to work diligently to fulfill its mission of preparing students to work in a variety of community-centered organizations, while thinking critically and strategically to impact community change positively as developing social work professionals.

REFERENCES

Christian Reformed Church. (2002). *What it means to be Reformed: An identity statement* (2nd ed.). Grand Rapids, MI: Faith Alive Resources.

Coles, R. (1993). *The call of service.* New York: Houghton-Mifflin.

Furco, A. (1996). Service-learning: A balanced approach to experiential education. In B. Taylor (Ed.), *Expanding boundaries: Service and learning* (2–6). Washington, DC: Corporation for National Service.

Heffernan, K., and Saltmarsh, J. (Eds.). (2000). *Introduction to service-learning toolkit: Readings and resources for faculty.* Providence, RI: National Campus Compact.

King, M. E. (2003). Social work education and service learning. *Journal of Baccalaureate Social Work Education, 8*(2), 37–48.

Lawndale HIV Community Intervention Project. (2005). *Multi-level street intervention for the Lawndale communities.* Unpublished manuscript, Palos Heights, IL.

Social Work Department at Trinity Christian College. (2005). *Generalist capstone assessment project handbook.* Unpublished manuscript, Palos Heights, IL.

———. (2006). *Continuous quality improvement data, capstone assessment project.* Raw data, Palos Heights, IL.

Speck, B. W. (2001). Why service learning? *New Directions for Higher Education, 114*, 3–13.

Tuckman, B. (1965). Developmental sequence in small groups. *Psychological Bulletin, 63*, 384–99.

Chapter Twelve

Service Learning for Social Justice: Mandate for Long-Term Evaluation?

Virginia Majewski and Allan D. Turner

> Every experience is a moving force. Its value can be judged only on the ground of what it moves toward and into.
>
> —J. Dewey, *Experience and Education*, 38.

D. E. Giles and J. Eyler (1998) posed ten questions that might constitute a service-learning research agenda. Two of those questions dealt with the impact of service learning on society, on students' future participation and leadership, and "whether this form of education contributes to the long-term development of a social ethic of caring, commitment, and civic engagement" (Giles and Eyler 1998, 69). They called for longitudinal studies that would follow students beyond graduation. To date, the authors of this chapter have not discovered any studies of long-term impacts but have ventured to conduct such a study in spite of not having planned to do so at the time of the service-learning experience. This retrospective, evaluative study had numerous limitations, and for that reason, this chapter is not meant to demonstrate definitive conclusions. However, the authors are compelled to write about the study in order to stimulate discussion about the value of follow-up studies, the kinds of questions educators might pose for evaluating service learning over the long term, and the methodological concerns related to such evaluative efforts.

The service-learning course that prompted the evaluation spanned three years in the mid-1990s with three different groups of students. The location for the on-site experience was an American Indian reservation. The instructors tied course objectives to social work learning objectives in several curriculum areas, including group work practice skills and understanding culturally appropriate responses to social issues. First and foremost, however, the following *Educational Policy and Accreditation Standards* (EPAS) objective related to populations-at-risk, and social and economic justice provided the underpinning for the course: "Students will understand the forms and mechanisms of oppression and discrimination and apply strategies of advocacy and social change that advance social and economic justice" (Council on Social Work Education 2001). The Code of Ethics of the National Association of Social Workers (1.05c) tasks those who educate social workers with the responsibility of providing students with the opportunities to learn and understand the "nature of social diversity and oppression" with respect to a variety of racial and cultural groups. A. R. Roschelle, J. Turpin, and R. Elias (2000) note that without direct interaction, the stereotypes that students hold are rarely challenged. In contrast, with service learning, "individuals whom students previously defined as 'other' become human beings who deserve compassion. Many students then begin developing a strong commitment to social justice that some maintain throughout their adult lives" (Roschelle, Turpin, and Elias 2000, 841–42).

Social justice is a focus in much of the recent literature on service learning (O'Grady 2000; Rosenberger 2000; Wade 2000; Marullo and Edwards 2000; Sachdev 1997; Maybach 1996). C. W. Maybach (1996) stressed the need to look at the impact of service-learning activities on the community and the long-term needs of service recipients as an important factor in designing service-learning curricula. In addition to this, the impact of the experience on students in terms of their recognition of a community's or population's long-term needs and their subsequent activity related to meeting those needs constitutes an important evaluative focus. The purpose of this evaluative study, then, was to determine the long-term impacts of a cross-cultural service-learning experience on participants' concerns for, subsequent involvement with, or work on behalf of oppressed populations and social justice five to seven years after completing the course.

THE IMMERSION EXPERIENCE ON AN AMERICAN INDIAN RESERVATION

This service-learning course was implemented on an American Indian reservation for three years with a total of thirty-five undergraduate students, twenty-nine of whom were social work majors. The course, which engaged students in service activities and provided opportunities for reflection, exposed students to the traditional culture of the Lakota Nation and to a variety of social justice issues that affect American Indian peoples living in reservation communities. In preparation, students participated in a full semester of noncredit preparatory seminars and group projects related to fund-raising and local community service. From the outset, instructors focused on the con-sciousness-raising aspects of the experience with numerous speakers, films, readings, and discussions prior to the trip west.

The course had a somewhat different nature in each of three years, partly due to the instructors' own educational development, but also because of the contacts made in the community. From one year to the next, the immersion experience intensified as the instructors grappled with the questions, Service on whose terms? and Social justice from whose perspective? For example, in the first year, the students' primary service consisted of working in a tribally funded, drug-free summer school program, assisting teachers (most of whom were non–American Indian) in day-to-day activities with children in kinder-garten through sixth grade. The issues that students encountered in their in-teractions with community members included the relative absence of Lakota language spoken by people they met, use of American Indian images as mas-cots, Bureau of Indian Affairs schools and educational opportunities, tourism and economic development, the city council model of tribal government, and "dominant culture" versions of justice and treatment revealed in domestic vi-olence centers or tribal substance-abuse programs. Students also attended a powwow and experienced a sweat lodge ceremony as a recreational activity.

By the second and third years, the instructors had developed acquaintances among more traditional members of the community, and students spent more time outside of the reservation "town" and in close proximity to families nei-ther in the mainstream of the tribal bureaucracy nor recipients of federal aid. Their primary service activities included some involvement in the drug-free summer school program, but they participated in many other services re-quested by community members. These included assisting in an elder feeding program (similar to congregate meals and Meals on Wheels programs), par-ticipating in community cleanup, building a corral and barn, stripping tree trunks for use as tipi poles for a youth immersion camp, and other similar projects. While some of the same issues emerged, students had the opportu-nity to hear the Lakota language spoken, to learn more about the rights of in-dividuals to determine their own lives, to understand and respect traditional values and ways of dealing with problems, and to see the deep connection to spirituality in everyday life. In the second year, they participated in World Peace and Prayer Day in the Black Hills, and in the third year, they helped construct a ceremonial site.

Like the nature of the experience itself, the characteristics of each group of students varied from year to year. Given the course objective to develop group work skills, some key variables included student communication with one another and with the instructors, the propensity toward conflict, the abil-ity to develop shared goals, and commitment to group interests rather than individual interests. In addition to a different mix of younger and more mature students, each group also had varied expectations with respect to the academic side of the course as well as varied ability to address course requirements.

With all of this revealed, the reader is likely to understand at the outset the difficulties with evaluation in the short and long term. Nonetheless, the instructors forged ahead to pose questions about long-term impacts and to attempt to gather some data.

EVALUATION METHODOLOGY

During the three years of implementation of the service-learning project (1995–1997) on the Cheyenne River Lakota Reservation, the instructors entertained the hypothesis that such a hands-on experience would lead to long-term gains in cultural competence, appreciation of diversity, and sensitivity to American Indian issues and social justice. However, they gave no thought to evaluating the long-term impacts of the experience formally. Evaluation at the time was related to individual student performance and was not rigorous in terms of standards for differentiating students by course grade. The success of the program as a whole was assessed largely on an informal basis, using anecdotal data and feedback that the instructors derived from group meetings and student journals.

Several years later, given that there was no pretest or well-documented criteria for a follow-up assessment, the instructors relied primarily on notes and recollections of content in student journals, course papers, group reflection meetings, and their own processing at the time of the experience to structure an evaluation instrument. Both instructors had also assumed different academic positions since the time of the project, resulting in the inevitable dislocation of materials that were collected at the time.

Nonetheless, the instructors felt that an attempt to conduct a long-term evaluation could contribute to the state of the art in program evaluation for service learning and guide future projects in tracking students over time. Indeed, the exercise has led to several conclusions about some necessary steps to support such evaluative efforts, such as giving attention at the outset of the project to a study design that will contribute to effective follow-up research and having evaluators consciously commit to "staying in touch" with participants.

For this study, the instructors decided to start with a mailed survey and asked whether respondents would be willing to do follow-up interviews if necessary. Course records contained contact information; however, the instructors requested updated addresses from three university alumni offices. The total number of mailed surveys believed to reach participants was twenty-four. That is, twenty-four surveys were not returned to the authors due to unknown addresses. The first mailing resulted in four responses, two from the project's first year (1995), one from the second year (1996), and one from the third (1997). A second mailing yielded one additional response from the 1995 group. All the respondents identified themselves. The instructors considered conducting follow-up interviews or a focus group but later decided that time and distance factors constrained such efforts.

Because of the small number of responses ($N = 5$) to the survey, the data were aggregated, and where results were differentiated across the three years of the project, care was taken to protect the identity of the respondent. The instructors idealized that if they could proceed on the evaluative trail, they might create a series of case studies to take into account individual characteristics of participants and the uniqueness of the project during each of the three years. For this report, however, the results remain at a more superficial level of analysis.

Table 12.1 displays the survey questions in an order that attempts to reflect the chronology of the course experience. Because there was no pretest, the instructors asked participants to think back to the period before their participation and then to think about their current situations. Participants then responded to each item on a scale of 1 to 10, with 1 indicating "not at all" and 10 indicating "to a large extent." The qualifier "to a moderate degree" was inserted below the numbers 4 through 7 on the scale.

Related to social justice, the paired questions 3 and 8 and 4 and 9 were meant to give some indication of motivation before the project and years later. Qualitative responses to question 8 (currently involved in activities that promote social justice for American Indian peoples) were perhaps the most revealing for this small group of respondents. Some participated in food and clothing drives or made monetary donations to American Indian organizations. One respondent conducted workshops for school-age children. Another, who scored this item low, indicated that time constraints and a lack of information hindered involvement. Although the scores on the precourse and postcourse items were low, there was an increase, one that instructors would consider a desirable long-term outcome. Involvement in social justice activities with other populations before and years after the experience was somewhat constant, perhaps speaking to the motivation of the individuals to pursue social work or a related career (one respondent was a psychology major).

Items 10 and 11 relate to critical thinking. On average, the respondents reported that they acquired critical-thinking skills with regard to American Indian and social justice issues in general (average score of 7.2 on both items).

Table 12.1. Survey Results

Survey Item	Mean Score 10-point scale 1=low, 10=high (N=5)	Comments
1. My concern about social justice for American Indian Peoples attracted me to the project.	7.4	Concerns from the media related to drugs and alcohol, gambling, unemployment; concern from reading many books
2. Before joining the project, I was aware of social injustices faced by American Indian Peoples in reservation communities.	5.6	Manipulations of U.S. government to eradicate American Indian ideology and social organization
5. Before joining the project, I had some knowledge of American Indian culture and tradition.	4.8	Joined to learn about culture; only a little aware that Indian culture was depressed
6. Before joining the project, I had some knowledge of Lakota culture and tradition.	4.6	
3. Before joining the project, I was involved in activities that promoted social justice for American Indian Peoples.	2.6	Political activist; no activity because of distance from issues
8. I am currently involved in activities that promote social justice for American Indian Peoples.	3.8	Food and clothing drives; workshops for school-age children; time constraints and not knowing how to be involved; monetary donations

4. Before joining the project, I was involved in activities that promoted social justice for a group of people other than American Indian Peoples.	5.4	Rape victims; Americans with disabilities; disabled veterans; mentally ill; none noted on a response of moderate degree; one response of not at all involved
9. I am currently involved in activities that promote social justice for a group of people other than American Indian Peoples.	5.2	Poor, single mothers; economically challenged; help elderly in the community maintain independence and dignity; mentally ill; African Americans; other cultures and drug and alcohol issues
7. Today, I am concerned about social justice for American Indian Peoples.	6.8	
10. During the project, I acquired skills in critically thinking about issues of social justice for American Indian Peoples.	7.2	
11. The project helped me to develop critical thinking skills regarding broader social justice issues.	7.2	
12. During the project, I acquired skills related to culturally competent practice with American Indian Peoples.	7.8	
13. The project helped me to be more culturally competent in my life's work to date.	9.0	
14. During the project, I acquired skills related to working in a group of people with related interests.	8.8	
15. The project helped me to work better in groups of all kinds.	7.4	

Items 12 and 13 asked respondents about cultural competence. The statement, "During the project, I acquired skills related to culturally competent practice with American Indian People," yielded an average score of 7.8, while the item, "The project helped me to be more culturally competent in my life's work to date," elicited an average score of 9.0. These are the positive results social work instructors would hope to achieve, although, again, the authors recognize the limited sample and the characteristics of respondents as a mediating force in drawing definitive conclusions about the impact of the project.

Finally, items 14 and 15 relate to another specific objective of the course, the acquisition of group work skills. Students took a major role in deciding many aspects of course activities and had to work together for positive outcomes. Over the course of the three weeks on-site, they also had to invite members of the local community into their group. Many of the reflection sessions concentrated on how they were "getting along," how they could resolve difficulties and conflicts, how they could be more inclusive in decision making, and how they evaluated outcomes of their actions as a group. Respondents indicated that during the project, they acquired skills for working in groups of people with similar interests (average score = 8.8). They indicated that the project helped them work better in groups of all kinds (average score = 7.4). Because the respondents had all identified themselves, these results were very meaningful to the instructors. Each of the respondents had made his or her own unique contribution to the dynamics of the group during the particular year he or she participated. Each respondent had his or her own positive and negative reactions to the group experience; yet, on average, the results indicate that there was learning and skill development with respect to working in groups.

The following sections provide some insights gained by the authors as a result of carrying out the evaluation.

CONSIDERATIONS FOR
EVALUATION OF SERVICE LEARNING

D. Payne (2000) suggests that naturalistic inquiry provides a dynamic model for the evaluation of service learning. In citing Patton (1987, 7), he notes that a qualitative/naturalistic evaluation would be concerned with

- describing the program or project implementation in detail
- analyzing program or project processes
- describing participants and the nature of their participation

- describing program impact cognitively, affectively, and behaviorally
- analyzing strengths and weaknesses of the program or project based on a variety of data and sources (Payne 2000, 23)

The instructors have done this in previous unpublished analyses of the project and presented their findings at the National Institute for Social Work and Human Services in Rural Areas and the Association of Baccalaureate Social Work Program Directors conference. A long-term naturalistic evaluation would require more in-depth assessment *with* project participants (students and community members), in particular to address the last two points above relating to the program's impact in the many years following its implementation, as well as to address strengths and weaknesses related to long-term impact.

Combining the results of a pre- and posttest instrument with qualitative data from interviews or focus groups would help evaluators triangulate findings to produce some conclusions about the impact of the particular project (Sachdev 1997). When the number of participants is relatively small, treating each respondent as an independent case study may help account for individual characteristics, such as motivation, commitment, and caring. Instructors might then consider an evaluative effort as a series of case studies of the individuals involved. These cases could then be examined to produce a set of common themes that instructors of similar projects might look for in evaluating student outcomes. Or, as T. G. Coste and M. Durker suggest, "The ideal assessment mechanism appears to be creating a portfolio for each service project, one that weaves the voices of the student, the teacher, and the client [*sic*] into a full representation of the effort" (2001, 7). This suggests employing case studies that offer a more comprehensive assessment that takes into account long-term student and community outcomes.

Threats to Validity

Whether an evaluation study is formative, summative, or long-term, it will not stand the test of external validity, or generalizability; nor is that a primary concern (Payne 2000). Using the present study as an illustration, some reasons are obvious: (1) the project spanned three years with variation in service venue and service commitments, (2) preparation for the project varied from year to year, (3) the number of participants overall and in any given year was too small, and (4) evaluation subjects constituted a self-selected sample and were not representative of any predefined student population. With respect to the third and fourth points, the considerable variability in skills, background, values, and expectations of participants makes it impossible to construct necessary controls to yield results that can be generalized even to this particular project at one institution.

The internal validity of a long-term evaluative effort is of more concern. Did the project actually have an influence on the subsequent behaviors, attitudes, and beliefs of the participants relative to stated objectives? If one looks at sources of internal invalidity as explained by Royse (1999), the following factors are operative in assessing the internal validity of our study:

1. *Maturation:* Participants' behaviors, attitudes, and beliefs may change over time due simply to the passage of time and their involvement in the social work profession or advocacy organizations, not as a result of the project.

2. *History:* Other major events may have happened since the experience and influenced participants' behaviors, attitudes, and beliefs. For example, one year after the final project, American Indian activists marked the twenty-fifth anniversary of the occupation of Wounded Knee. If the event reached the awareness of the participants, the effect might have been to increase commitment to action or to dampen enthusiasm for action because of one's feelings about the militaristic rhetoric associated with the 1973 occupation.

3. *Testing:* In this particular study, the testing effects result from participants' being asked years later to indicate what their behaviors, attitudes, and beliefs were before the experience. Participants may have over- or underestimated their pre-experience responses, anticipating what would be an expected outcome of the project. A more deliberate time series design for tracking students, while ideal in many respects, would also result in threats to internal validity, not only from a pretest but from multiple tests over time. Instruments might be designed, however, to account for other threats, such as maturation and history. For this project, there was no comparison group. A comparison group strategy may help reduce testing threats as well.

4. *Instrumentation:* The instructors admit that the wording of items on the survey instrument reflect current thinking related to the Council on Social Work Education's foundation objectives as found in the *Education Policy and Accreditation Standards* (2001) rather than in the stated objectives of the course syllabi as they evolved over the three-year period.

5. *Selection of respondents:* This is a concern because of the self-selection of respondents to the survey. The five respondents opted to identify themselves, and the instructors were not surprised that four of the five were some of the most motivated participants during the experience.

6. *Mortality:* This was perhaps the greatest threat to internal validity because of the number of participants who could not be tracked down five, six, and

seven years after the experience. Assuming the subjects' addresses were valid, it appears that some opted not to respond.

RECOMMENDATIONS FOR LONG-TERM EVALUATION

In spite of the many threats to validity, instructors of social work service-learning courses might ponder some key long-term evaluative questions related to the profession's commitment to social justice. For example,

- If service learning can be considered an intervention, what are the effects on the community? Are there long-term structural improvements in the community? Have the voices of service recipients been heard (Harkavy and Benson 1998; Weah, Simmons, and Hall 2000)?
- Have all participants (students and community partners) learned to think in collaborative and culturally appropriate ways about local and global issues (Weigert 1998)?
- Have students made a long-term commitment to cultural diversity by continuing to engage in interactions with diverse others (Rhoads 1998; Weah, Simmons, and Hall 2000)?
- Have students made a long-term commitment to social justice through their engagement in activities that continue to benefit the community and vulnerable groups (Wallace 2000)?

Long-term studies might not necessarily ask how the service links theory and practice (a short-term outcome, in most cases), but rather how the behavior resulting from the theory-practice link is carried forward through the participant's life or career. Do we expect that students will continue to process their learning from the experience and apply it to their lives as citizens of the nation and the world?

Instructors should also consider that assessment of this nature must be planned in advance of the project. This includes reaching agreement with participants that they will be contacted later or even that they will continue to keep journals related to prominent course themes.

As academic units and institutions are increasingly under pressure to deliver more "bang for the buck" from tuition and tax dollars, long-term outcomes assessment of service learning may prove beneficial and support the high level of investment in time and resources. Educators want to believe that the long-term impact of these experiences includes greater understanding across diverse populations, different ways of viewing the world, and the creation of a more just society. It is one thing to believe, however, and another to offer evidence.

The authors recommend that if service learning in the name of social justice is to be more than just a craze, attention to documenting and assessing long-term outcomes should be a critical concern.

REFERENCES

Coste, T. G., and Durker, M. (2001). Assessing the effects of incorporating service in learning: The search for a comprehensive process of service learning evaluation. *Academic Exchange Quarterly, 5*(1), 10. Retrieved September 5, 2001, from http://web5.infotrac-college.com/wadsworth/session/717/847/15309429/7!fullart.

Council on Social Work Education. (2001). *Educational policy and accreditation standards.* Alexandria, VA: Author.

Dewey, J. (1938). *Experience and education.* New York: Touchstone.

Giles, D. E., Jr., and Eyler, J. (1998). A service learning research agenda for the next five years. *New directions for teaching and learning*, No. 73. San Francisco, CA: Jossey-Bass.

Harkavy, I., and Benson, L. (1998). Theoretical bases for academic service-learning. In R. A. Rhoads and J. P. F. Howard (Eds.), *Academic service learning: A pedagogy of action and reflection* (11–20). San Francisco, CA: Jossey-Bass.

Marullo, S., and Edwards, B. (2000). From charity to justice. *American Behavioral Scientist 43*(5), 895–912.

Maybach, C. W. (1996). Investigating urban community needs: Service learning from a social justice perspective. *Education and Urban Society, 28*(2), 224–36.

O'Grady, C. (2000). *Integrating service learning and multicultural education in colleges and universities.* Mahwah, NJ: Lawrence Erlbaum Associates.

Patton, M. Q. (1987). *Creative evaluation* (2nd ed.). Thousand Oaks, CA: Sage.

Payne, D. (2000). *Evaluating service-learning activities and programs.* Lanham, MD: Scarecrow Press.

Rhoads, R. A. (1998). Critical multiculturalism and service learning. In R. A. Rhoads and J. P. F. Howard (Eds.), *Academic service learning: A pedagogy of action and reflection* (39–46). San Francisco, CA: Jossey-Bass.

Roschelle, A. R., Turpin, J., and Elias, R. (2000). Who learns from service learning? *American Behavioral Scientist, 43*(5), 839–47.

Rosenberger, C. (2000). Beyond empathy: Developing critical consciousness through service learning. In C. O'Grady (Ed.), *Integrating service learning and multicultural education in colleges and universities* (23–43). Mahwah, NJ: Lawrence Erlbaum Associates.

Royse, D. (1999). *Research methods in social work.* Chicago: Nelson-Hall.

Sachdev, P. (1997). Cultural sensitivity training through experiential learning: A participatory demonstration field education project. *International Social Work, 40*(1), 7–25.

Wade, R. C. (2000). Beyond charity: Service learning for social justice. *Social Studies and the Young Learner,* (March/April), 6–9.

Wallace, J. (2000). The problem of time: Enabling students to make long-term commitments to community-based learning. *Michigan Journal of Community Service Learning,* (Fall), 133–42.

Weah, W., Simmons, V. C., and Hall, M. (2000). Service-learning and multicultural/multiethnic perspectives. *Phi Delta Kappan*, (May), 673–75.

Weigert, K. M. (1998). Academic service learning: Its meaning and relevance. In R. A. Rhoads and J. P. F. Howard (Eds.), *Academic service learning: A pedagogy of action and reflection* (3–9). San Francisco, CA: Jossey-Bass.

Chapter Thirteen

Service Learning in Social Work: A Curricular and Evaluative Model

Marilyn Sullivan-Cosetti

Learning is the process whereby knowledge is created through the transformation of experience.

—David A. Kolb, as cited in M. Troppe,
Connecting Cognition and Action, 1.

Growing interest in and support for service learning appears to spring from two opposite political perspectives. Liberals, anxious to retrieve the kind of idealism and concern for the public good that fed efforts such as the civil rights movement and the Peace Corps, see service learning as instilling these values in students today. Conservatives, who worry about the decline of individual responsibility and virtue in public life, find service congenial to orienting students toward lives of volunteerism that might lessen the need for formal government to address social needs. To some degree, these two impulses have shaped a consensus around the virtues of service learning for higher education today.

Service learning may be defined as a community-service activity that relates directly to, and strengthens, the academic component of a specific area of study. *Community service* is defined as involvement in community issues with the purpose of achieving a public good (Morton 1993; Rein 1995). Service learning has three distinct components:

1. preparation that involves both understanding the organization's goals and objectives and acquiring the necessary skills for the service learning to be performed
2. participation that involves the actual work performed at the organization
3. reflection that involves critical analysis of the experience through journal writing, class discussion, and/or a formal essay

195

As A. Strage notes, "It should not be surprising that this instructional method is effective. Rooted in Deweyan principles of experiential education (1938), academic service learning contains three essential elements: students learn course content as they serve their community; and reflect on the connections between explicit course content and their experiences in the field" (2004, 1). This experience enables students to "gain further understanding of course content, a broader appreciation of the discipline and an enhanced sense of civic responsibility" (Brindle and Hatcher 1996, 222).

The goals of service learning include the following:

- improving student learning (Giles and Eyler 1998; Tai-Seale 2001; Cameron et al. 2001)
- exploring moral and ethical positions, both personally and professionally (Giles and Eyler 1998)
- enhancing personal development (Eyler and Giles 1996, 1999; Kendrick 1996; Rhoads 1997)
- promoting democracy and citizenship (Giles and Eyler 1998; Eyler and Giles 1996; Markus, Howard, and King 1993; Kendrick 1996)

These multiple goals include the concepts of enhancing participatory democracy, social justice, and voluntary service. The underlying assumption is that formal education is the best vehicle for an informed citizenry.

Service learning enhances the academic experience because performance of the service is directly linked to the didactic material. It illuminates, enhances, and makes concrete the theories, concepts, and methods described in class. The pedagogical benefits of service learning include inspiring inquiry, empowering students, and moving from concrete experiences to abstract thinking. Service learning relates directly to social work because the service activities selected by the instructor and the students are within the purview of professional social work activities.

SOCIAL WORK PROGRAM OF STUDY

Service learning is imbedded in the social work curriculum of an undergraduate social work program at a small (1,800 students), coeducational, faith-based university in the East. The program has a sixty-credit undergraduate social work major accredited by the Council on Social Work Education. In each of the three years of study prior to the senior year field practicum course, students complete service-learning courses. The following courses include service-learning activities that occur prior to the field practicum, which is taken in the first semester of the senior year as a five-hundred-hour block placement:

- "Introduction to the Profession of Social Work"—first semester, first year
- "Generalist Practice I: Individuals"—second semester, second year
- "Generalist Practice II: Families and Groups"—first semester, third year
- "Generalist Practice III: Organizations and Communities"—second semester, third year

The service learning aspect of each course will be briefly explained.

In the first social work course, the service-learning activities involve the instructor's introducing students to a variety of community services. Visits to, and participation in, activities at a day care center, a food distribution warehouse, a food pantry, and a residential senior citizen center for elderly religious women, as well as a trip to the state prison, help students understand how vulnerable populations are served in this geographic area. Social workers practicing in child-protective services, health care, mental health, education, and gerontology are guest speakers. All of these speakers augment learning about the fields of practice in social work, while the textbook emphasizes methods of generalist social work practice. Additionally, students are encouraged to join and participate in the activities of the social work club, which include service evenings at the local youth shelter and a men's homeless shelter, fund-raising, listening to graduate school speakers, and participating in co-curricular school and community-wide events. In this course, students receive 5 percent extra academic credit for participation in the social work club. This is useful as an incentive to introduce students to the social work club. The academic credit is for participation in the club's activities; it does not include attending meetings. This does not occur in any other social work course.

In the first professional practice course, entitled "Generalist Practice I: Individuals," the service-learning activities are performed by the students under the guidance of the instructor. Human service agencies providing services to individuals are selected so that students are exposed to all aspects of social work practice with individuals. Activities include interviews with agency staff, job shadowing, attendance at case conferences, and accompanying staff on home visits where permitted. Students are encouraged to select human service agencies focusing on populations-at-risk for their service-learning activities.

In the second professional practice course, "Generalist Practice II: Families and Groups," the focus is on observation, job shadowing and assistance, where appropriate, with organizations focusing on dependent and delinquent youth and with organizations that provide wraparound services for emotionally disturbed youth and their families. The instructor must approve all service-learning activities before they are undertaken. Social work with families is done through (1) a family-therapy clinic operated by the university; (2) other human service agencies dealing with families, including adoption services; and (3) various forms of health care, including hospice services. Each student is expected to perform service-learning activities with both groups and families.

In the third professional practice course, "Generalist Practice III: Organizations and Communities," the instructor again accompanies social work students on many service-learning activities. An emphasis is placed on activities that include both an urban and rural focus, including

- a tour of an urban inner-city neighborhood accompanied by the local community organizer
- a visit and tour of a small-town human services center that operates like a one-stop human services mall
- participation in a lobby day at the state capitol sponsored by the National Association of Social Workers, PA Chapter

Additionally, the students pick a topical area of interest (e.g., health, housing, early childhood education) and work with a local organization providing that service. In this fashion, both the experiences of working in neighborhoods and with formal organizations are covered.

The service-learning experiences are uniquely tailored to match the didactic material in each of the four courses. However, there are common components to the experience as follows:

- twenty-five hours of service learning in each course
- class discussion and oral reflection on the experience, both with and without the instructor present
- a common service-learning journal-entry reflection form that is used in all courses, including the field practicum

The service-learning journal-entry form (called a service-learning log) is a one-page form that asks for the student's name, site information, and the date and hours of the service-learning experience. It also requests cumulative hours on each form. After this information is described, there are three parts to the form:

- summary of the experiences (What did you do?)
- cognitive analysis (What did you learn? Please relate learning to theory, principles, concepts, and research, as appropriate.)
- affective responses (What did you feel? Please note reactions to and feelings about the experience.)

Students are asked to sign and date the form and complete one form for each service-learning activity. Faculty evaluate the journal entries in the first two categories only. The experience is evaluated only to the extent that the student describes it as a learning experience for him- or herself. The second category, cognitive analysis, is evaluated according to the student's description of the application of service activities to the academic material. The third section is read by the instructor but not evaluated. All journals are confidential and are read only by the instructor.

By the first semester of their senior year, students have selected, in conjunction with the field coordinator, an organization in which to perform their five-hundred-hour-block field placement, where the student will be supervised by a staff member possessing a master's degree in social work and two years' postmasters experience. The field coordinator visits the agency three times during the practicum. The five hundred clock hours in the organization are accompanied by a weekly, two-hour, in-class field seminar that integrates theory and practice. The learning team consists of the student, the field supervisor, and the field coordinator. There are formal, written evaluations of the student, the field placement site, and the field practicum experience. The faculty believe that the service-learning activities of the previous four courses, spanning the first three years of study, are an excellent preparation for the field practicum experience.

EVALUATION METHODOLOGY

While there are many ways to evaluate service learning in the academic setting, including faculty satisfaction, faculty-observed learning, student satisfaction, student self-reported learning, and outcomes assessment, this ongoing research project decided to focus on student satisfaction and student self-reported learning. The method used was a pretest, posttest analysis within each service-learning course over a five-year period. Of particular interest to this project is the historical series of research studies that focused on similar questions but employed an experimental or quasi-experimental design (Markus, Howard, King 1993; Miller 1994; Cohen and Kinsey 1994;

Kendrick 1996). Each of these studies was a comparative course section study in which some sections incorporated a community-service component, while others did not. Each of these studies administered pretests and posttests to both groups in an attempt to assess empirically the impact of the service-learning component on student learning and/or the development of student values and attitudes. While these studies suggest that service learning can increase student learning and influence value and belief development, the results were mixed. Since the social work program at this school is small, with one section of each course, the professors used the survey method of a pretest and posttest questionnaire for each course.

RESULTS

The service-learning results for all four courses were tallied together for the terms from fall 1999 through spring 2004 ($N = 104$). Following the initial demographic data, name and date, and course-related information, which included the course name and identification number and the student's year at the university, the pretest form comprised four open-ended questions.

Pre-Service-Learning Analysis

The first question asked about students' expectations for service learning in this course. In terms of student expectations, the responses, in order of frequency, were as follows:

- Students wanted to gain knowledge from hands-on experiences — 40 percent
- They wanted a variety of field experiences — 30 percent
- They wanted more experience in the community — 15 percent
- Students gave other responses — 15 percent
- Total — 100 percent

The second question queried students about what connections they saw between the core concepts in the course and the service-learning experience. They responded as follows:

- Students hoped to put theory into practice — 40 percent
- Students wanted to explore different content in courses — 22 percent
- Students wanted to become more caring and honest — 3 percent

- Students wanted to learn about community needs and how   2.5 percent
  to respond to them
- Students wanted to understand that social work is about   2.5 percent
  generalized practice
- Students responded "don't know"   30 percent
- Total   100 percent

The third question asked, "What questions or concerns do you have as you begin the service-learning experience?" Students responded as follows:

- They said they had no concerns   45 percent
- They said they were uncertain   18 percent
- They wondered whether they would learn from the   12 percent
  community contacts
- They responded "don't know"   25 percent
- Total   100 percent

The final question was, "What previous experience, if any, have you had in community service or volunteer work?" Students responded as follows:

- They had one experience   35 percent
- They had two to five experiences   52 percent
- They had six to ten experiences   3 percent
- They reported no experience   10 percent
- Total   100 percent

Students were asked to write any additional comments they had about beginning the service-learning experience. Their comments portrayed anxiety, nervousness, fear, and concern about their ability to perform the service. A representative sample of student comments includes the following:

- "My only concern would be that members of the organization be open to my observing them."
- "I would want to be able to have enough time to become familiar with both school and medical practice."
- "Will the organization really include us in the process or will we just observe?"
- "Will I have the time to do it?"
- "Will I find an organization which I can work with."
- "Where can we do our service learning? What are some recommendations?"

Post-Service-Learning Analysis

The post-service-learning questionnaire had more questions than the pre-service-learning questionnaire. After the demographic and course-related data were collected, there was a Likert-type seven-point scale with responses ranging from very dissatisfied (1) to very satisfied (7). The scale was calculated as follows:

- Responses 1, 2, and 3 were rated as very dissatisfied.
- Response 4 was rated as dissatisfied to satisfied.
- Responses 5, 6, and 7 were rated as very satisfied.

The responses to each of the following four questions on the scale were positive:

1. Apply concepts I learned in class to the service-learning experiences:
   - 86.5 percent were very satisfied   ($N = 90$)
   - 8.7 percent were dissatisfied to satisfied   ($N = 9$)
   - 4.8 percent were very dissatisfied   ($N = 5$)
   - Total = 100 percent   ($N = 104$)
2. Better understand the concepts presented in the course:
   - 94.2 percent were very satisfied   ($N = 98$)
   - 2.9 percent were dissatisfied to satisfied   ($N = 3$)
   - 2.9 percent were very dissatisfied   ($N = 3$)
   - Total = 100 percent   ($N = 104$)
3. Class preparation for service learning was adequate:
   - 76.9 percent were very satisfied   ($N = 80$)
   - 15.4 percent were dissatisfied to satisfied   ($N = 16$)
   - 5.8 percent were very dissatisfied   ($N = 6$)
   - Total = 98.1 percent   ($N = 102$)

   Totals do not equal 100 percent because there are two missing data points.
4. Course strengthened learning:
   - 87.5 percent were very satisfied   ($N = 91$)
   - 9.6 percent were dissatisfied to satisfied   ($N = 10$)
   - 1.9 percent were very dissatisfied   ($N = 2$)
   - Total = 99.0 percent   ($N = 103$)

Totals do not equal 100 percent because there is one missing data point.

The responses to two additional questions were also positive; namely,

1. The service learning was challenging to the student.
2. The contributions of fellow students were satisfactory.

Both of these questions had large amounts of missing data, so their numeric results are not reported.

Another method of analysis for these scalar responses was to calculate a mean score for each item. This analysis was performed, and the results are shown in table 13.1. All of these data are in the positive direction, namely, in the satisfied or very satisfied category. Clearly, students reported that service learning strengthened the learning experience in these courses.

Table 13.1. Mean Scores on Post-Service-Learning Questionnaires

Items	Mean Score
1. Better able to understand concepts	5.82
2. Better able to apply concepts	5.63
3. Class preparation time was adequate	5.46
4. Contribution of other students was adequate	5.13
5. Strengthened the learning experience in this course	5.73

Note: Scale scores ranged from 1 - very dissatisfied to 7 - very satisfied.

Part II of the questionnaire asked students to select a series of responses to the question, "What did you learn as a result of your service-learning experiences?" Each of the items was analyzed as a yes or no response. The results are, in general, positive, although these data do suggest that more work needs to be completed in the area of connecting theory to practice through service-learning activities. In addition, the goal of collaborative teamwork, where important, is not being realized according to the students' responses. In each category, 10.6 percent of these data were missing. Table 13.2 shows the responses in each category. The last answer suggests that most students, because of their busy schedules, perform their out-of-class service-learning hours by themselves.

Another area evaluated involved problems that students experienced performing the service-learning activities. In each category, 10.6 percent of these data were missing. Table 13.3 presents the responses to these items.

Table 13.2. Student Responses to the Question, What Did You Learn as a Result of Your Service-Learning Experiences?

	Yes (%)	No (%)
Service learning puts theory into practice	43.3	46.2
Service learning teaches hands-on learning	66.8	22.6
Service learning enhances the lectures	46.2	43.3
Service learning gives us an opportunity to practice	50.0	39.4
Service learning makes new connections between the academic material and the real world	53.4	36.1
Service learning helps me benefit from collaborative teamwork	32.7	56.7

Table 13.3.   Student Responses to the Question, What Problems Did You Experience Doing Service-Learning Activities?

	Yes (%)	No (%)
I experienced personal time/scheduling conflicts	25.0	64.4
I experienced time/scheduling conflicts with the site of my service learning	30.8	58.7
I started my service learning too late in the semester	23.1	66.3
Any other problems you experienced?	11.5	77.9

Clearly the no responses are in the majority, indicating that students reported that the service-learning experience did not cause them problems. These findings are important in light of the busy schedules that current students manage.

Lastly, a summative question was asked: "Do you think the service learning in this course should be changed or remain the same?" The students responded overwhelmingly that the service learning should not be changed. Excluding the 10.6 percent missing data, the results were

- Yes, change   26.9 percent
- No, do not change   73.1 percent

CONCLUSION

In summary, the service-learning experiences across the four courses appear to be positive for a majority of students. These data on student satisfaction and student self-reported learning are corroborated in exit interviews with graduating seniors, who often explain to the program director that while the service-learning experiences were often difficult to perform, looking back, they were very useful.

Areas needing improvement include

- better translation of theory into practice
- clearer connection between the service-learning activities and the course material
- possible time/scheduling conflicts with the site

Faculty continue to be involved in weekly discussions regarding these issues, their satisfaction with the service-learning experiences, and their observations of student learning. Faculty agree that students become more active learners through the service-learning process and that the power differential in the classroom between faculty and students is reduced through service-learning activities. Faculty also remark on the positive relationship-building experiences for students performing off-campus service-learning activities.

Future research plans include separation of the data to find similarities and differences among the four service-learning courses. Additionally, outcomes assessment for service-learning activities is planned for the 2007–2008 academic year with the introduction of two widely used, reliable, and valid instruments:

- Rutgers University Civic Attachments and Public Life Scale
- The Tennessee Self Concept Scale

The plan is to assess students' scores on these two instruments at the beginning and end of the social work program. With the addition of these two instruments, the program will be able to assess outcomes in the areas of personal and professional growth and civic values development, which will contribute to assessment of the four goals for service learning. However, much work remains to be completed, particularly in the area of whether the benefits of service learning last (Strage 2004). As Strage (2004) reminds us, S. Billig and A. Furco noted the dearth of longitudinal studies and lamented, "Too little is known about how service-learning experiences can be designed to have longer-term effects and indeed what the longer-term effects are on dispositions, attitudes and behaviors" (2002, 222). This continuing assessment hopes to contribute new evidence to answer these questions.

REFERENCES

Billig, S., and Furco, A. (2002). Supporting a strategic service-learning research plan. In S. Billig and A. Furco (Eds.), *Service learning through a multidisciplinary lens* (217–30). Greenwich, CT: Information Age.

Brindle, R., and Hatcher, J. (1996). Implementing service learning in higher education. *Journal of Higher Education, 67*, 221–39.

Cameron, M., Forsyth, A., Green, W., Lu, H., McGirr, P., Owens, P., and Stolz, R. (2001). Learning through service: The community design studio. *College Teaching, 49*, 105–13.

Cohen, J., and Kinsey, D. (1994). Doing good and scholarship: A service-learning study. *Journalism Educator, 48*, 4–14.

Dewey, J. (1938). *Experience and education.* New York: Macmillan.

Eyler, J., and Giles, D. E. (1996). The impact of service learning program characteristics on student outcomes. Paper presented at the National Society for Experiential Education Conference, Snowbird, UT, 1996.

———. (1999). Where is the learning in service-learning? San Francisco: Jossey-Bass.

Giles, D. E., and Eyler, J. (1998). A service learning research agenda for the next five years. In R. A. Rhoads and J. P. F. Howard (Eds.), *Academic service learning: A pedagogy of action and reflection* (65–72). San Francisco, CA: Jossey-Bass.

Kendrick, J. (1996). Outcomes of service-learning in an introduction to sociology course. *Michigan Journal of Community Service Learning, 3*, 72–81.

Markus, G. B., Howard, J. P. E., and King, D. C. (1993). Integrating community service and classroom instruction enhances learning: Results from an experiment. *Educational Evaluation and Policy Analysis, 15*, 410–19.

Miller, J. (1994). Linking traditional and service-learning courses: Outcomes evaluations utilizing two pedagogically distinct models. *Michigan Journal of Community Service Learning, 1*, 29–36.

Morton, K. (1993). Models of service and civic education. An occasional paper of the project on integrating service and academic study. *PA Campus Compact*, 1–9.

Rein, G. (1995). *An examination of service learning.* New York: Simon and Schuster.

Rhoads, R. A. (1997). *Community service and higher learning: Explorations of the caring self.* Albany: SUNY.

Strage, A. (2004). Long-term benefits of service learning: When and where do they manifest themselves? *College Student Journal, 38*(2), 257–61.

Tai-Seale, T. (2001). Liberating service learning and applying the new practice. *College Teaching Journal, 49*, 14–18.

Troppe, M. (1995). *Connecting cognition and action: Evaluation of student performance in service learning courses.* Denver, CO: Educational Commission of the States/Campus Compact.

Part IV

THE BIGGER PICTURE:
CIVIC ENGAGEMENT ON CAMPUS

Chapter Fourteen

The Bigger Picture: Social Work Educators' Role in Civic Engagement

Mary Campbell and Nancy Bragg

CONCEPTUAL BACKGROUND OF SERVICE LEARNING

Service learning was named in the 1960s by Bill Ramsey and Robert Sigmon, community coordinators of research internships addressing Southern regional problems, to describe the reflective approach they used with their community-development interns. Their interns' experiential education consisted of using the service experience as a setting for learning. Service to others was an expression of values, and the needs of the community determined the nature of the service provided. The goals of service and learning were mutually interdependent, and the power of the approach came from integrating service with learning (Stanton 1999).

Although higher education has historically focused on the central task of developing the character of the student, encompassing specifically the value of moving from self-interest to larger-than-self-interest, many institutions gradually drifted from their mission of educating for civic responsibility (Newman 1985, 57). By the mid-1980s, the public began to see higher education more as an individual, private benefit than a common, public good. The media portrayed college students as self-centered and materialistic. In 1984, students who were actively involved in their communities responded to the public image of student apathy by creating the Campus Outreach Opportunity League (COOL), a national nonprofit that helps college students start, strengthen, and expand their community-service programs.

Frank Newman, president of the Education Commission of the States, asserted that, "If there is a crisis in education in the United States today, it is less that test scores have declined than it is that we have failed to provide the education for citizenship that is still the most significant responsibility of the nation's schools and colleges" (1985, 31). He joined together with presidents from Brown, Georgetown, and Stanford universities with the belief that more students would become involved in community service if higher education provided them with the encouragement and supportive structures to do so. In 1985, these four men founded Campus Compact: The Project for Public and Community Service, a coalition of public and private two- and four-year higher education institutions. These founders committed to providing leadership on their campuses to develop students into educated and active citizens. Initially, most of this activity occurred through community-service work centered on student volunteer service.

In the 1980s, experiential education was becoming increasingly more prevalent in American higher education. Students at many institutions had opportunities for fieldwork, cooperative education, and internships. At the October 1987 annual meeting of the National Society for Internships and Experiential Education, Tim Stanton of Stanford University connected the complementary traditions of public service and liberal arts education with experiential learning in a paper commissioned by the Kettering Foundation (Kendall 1999). Service learning was recognized as a form of experiential learning.

Campus Compact took an active role in support of federal legislative initiatives resulting in the National and Community Service Act of 1990. It became apparent that if service to the community was to be institutionalized, it had to be integrated into the work of the faculty. Community service became the umbrella term for faculty-driven service learning, which involved connecting learning with community service through structured reflection, as well as the more familiar volunteer service.

Both Campus Compact and the Corporation for National Service stimulated rapid growth in the number of campuses offering service-learning courses. In 1991 Campus Compact launched training and funding initiatives under the name Integrating Service with Academic Study. Campus teams of faculty members from across the country attended these multiple-day work sessions, where teams integrated learning and service with intentional links to the academic and student-development missions of their institutions.

Like other service-learning pioneers with a social change orientation, Sigmon, the creator of the term *service learning*, adhered to the conceptualization of service learning, which prioritized service over learning. He realized that other emerging practitioners related and emphasized service and learning in different ways, so he created the following nonhierarchical conceptual typology to show the varying emphases (the capitals for emphasis and hyphens for linkage appeared in the original):

- SERVICE-learning: The focus is on service as primary with learning secondary.

- Service-LEARNING: The focus is on learning goals with service secondary.
- service learning: The service and learning goals are separate and important, but not linked.
- SERVICE-LEARNING: The service and learning goals are equal and reciprocal for all involved (Sigmon 1994).

As faculty from different disciplines reflect on service and learning and the relationships between the two, they come up with diverse perspectives on service learning that are most relevant to their disciplinary purposes and approaches. Sigmon's service-LEARNING orientation is somewhat similar to that of social work education in that service-LEARNING emphasizes learning built on an academic/curricular foundation of knowledge, reinforced by the use of service, to produce professionals committed to working actively for a more socially just world. Within the curriculum, students in a community-organizing course might work with grassroots organizers in addressing a community concern, or students in a policy course might visit and lobby legislators. These curricular experiences are built on the academic foundation of working toward a better world. Social work educators and the profession as a whole have historically seen service as a component of our discipline, as well as the means through which learning best occurs.

Some learning-centered service-learning advocates define service learning as course based with purely academic outcomes (Bringle and Hatcher 1996). Reflection on the experience connected with the learning objectives is a key component of quality service learning. Other service-learning definitions include student development outcomes (Jacoby and Associates 1996), which can also be legitimate if students reflect on their experience to achieve educational development outcomes.

Student learning and development outcomes from service learning generally fall into six educational development areas: (1) academic/disciplinary outcomes connected to the content of the course; (2) personal/individual outcomes, such as courage to try new things; (3) social/societal outcomes, such as a better idea of how our society's health care system impacts real people; (4) civic/cultural outcomes, such as a greater sense of civic responsibility to contribute to the community; (5) ethical/moral outcomes, such as a moral obligation to value the inherent worth and dignity of all people; and (6) career/professional outcomes, such as affirmation of a career decision to become a social worker (Furco 1997; Bragg 2000). Social/societal, ethical/moral, and civic/cultural developments all contain an important intellectual core. The responsibility for developing these outcomes often falls to the general education or liberal arts curriculum and can be addressed through service learning. The promotion of strong critical-thinking and problem-solving

skills essential for active involvement in our democratic society can also occur through service learning within discipline-based majors.

Cocurricular service learning, such as a social work club visit to a prison
drug-rehabilitation program with reflection during travel time in the van or
faculty-sponsored alternative spring break trips with structured reflection
time together every evening, reinforce the values stressed within the curriculum with the emphasis on SERVICE-learning. Many extracurricular community-service options cannot be considered service learning because they do
not address *intentional* learning objectives through structured reflection. Although volunteer service experiences, such as carrying boxes during fresh-
man move-in, collecting funds for a telethon, or raking leaves for elderly
neighbors, do not have planned learning outcomes, *incidental* learning often
occurs.

INCORPORATING SERVICE
LEARNING INTO FACULTY WORK

Thousands of faculty members have embraced service learning and have
driven the service-learning movement by incorporating it into the faculty
workload of teaching, research, and service. Faculty service-learning work
has been made public in the series of discipline-based service-learning monographs published by the American Association for Higher Education, in the
peer-reviewed *Michigan Journal of Community Service Learning,* in books,
and in professional higher education, disciplinary, and service-learning conference proceedings and publications. Much of the scholarship on service
learning can be considered *scholarship of engagement*, a term created by
Ernest Boyer (1990) in his work commissioned by the Carnegie Foundation
for the Advancement of Teaching examining the meaning of scholarship.
Boyer defined scholarship of engagement as "connecting the rich resources
of the university to our most pressing social, civic and ethical problems, to
our children, to our schools, to our teachers and to our cities" (1996, 19–20).

SERVICE LEARNING IN THE
CONTEXT OF CIVIC ENGAGEMENT

During the mid-1990s, when service learning was expanding, educational institutions began to see developing graduates committed to their role as engaged, responsible citizens as a renewed priority in a world with increasingly
complex problems. The "engaged campus" (Holland and Gelmon 1998)

emerged, promoting the "university as citizen" (Bringle, Games, and Malloy 1999) with community engagement at the institutional level as a priority. As this larger institutional agenda became better defined, "civic engagement" gained widespread acceptance as the encompassing conceptual framework (Saltmarsh 2005). Civic engagement has broad appeal, promoting two-way partnerships between America's colleges and universities and the publics they serve. Civic engagement advocate Thomas Ehrlich and his colleagues defined civic engagement as "working to make a difference in the civic life of our communities and developing the combination of knowledge, skills, values and motivation to make that difference. It means promoting the quality of life in a community, through both political and non-political processes" (2000, vi).

Civic engagement has become part of the agenda of many national education associations, including the American Association of State Colleges and Universities, which initiated the American Democracy Project. This unfunded project consists of over two hundred state institutions that commit to finding ways within their curricula to prepare students to engage in meaningful civic actions as a way to contribute to a more energized democracy. Service learning is one means by which American Democracy Project faculty members can move their students toward civic engagement.

DIRECTING FUTURE SERVICE LEARNING TOWARD POLITICAL AND COMMUNITY ENGAGEMENT

In a recent piece on the Carnegie Foundation for the Advancement of Teaching website, T. Ehrlich (2006) maintains that preparation for active citizenship includes not only service-learning experiences that promote an individual sense of civic responsibility but also those that support more systemic political or policy-related engagement and understanding at the local, state, national, and international levels. The Carnegie Foundation for the Advancement of Teaching is taking the lead by initiating the recent Political Engagement Project. This new political role for service learning is a daunting undertaking, but for social work educators who strive to assist students in becoming aware of macro-level activity, this new direction for the field of service learning is completely compatible with the historical roots of the profession. For example, frequently spearheaded by students and faculty in policy courses in cooperation with their statewide National Association of Social Workers (NASW) chapter, social work students in numerous institutions participate in what some call "lobby day" or "social work day at the legislature." They travel to their state capitals, learn about current legislation sponsored by their professional organization, and meet directly with legislators from their home districts.

The Carnegie Foundation for the Advancement of Teaching's new elective classification called "Community Engagement" constitutes another direction for service learning. Community Engagement "describes the collaboration between institutions of higher education and their larger communities (local, regional/state, national, global) for the mutually beneficial exchange of knowledge and resources in a context of partnership and reciprocity" (Driscoll 2006).

SOCIAL WORK'S CIVIC ENGAGEMENT VALUES

The moral and civic values associated with civic engagement mirror the values and philosophy of social work educators and the Council on Social Work Education. Ehrlich notes that a "morally and civically responsible individual recognizes himself or herself as a member of a larger social fabric and therefore considers social problems to be partly his or her own; such an individual is willing to see the moral and civic dimensions of issues, to make and justify informed moral and civic judgments and to take action when appropriate" (2006, xxvi).

The renewed emphasis on integrating civic engagement experiences into what was traditionally "straight" academic learning will result in a more involved student body. Students will have their values challenged and will experience the effect of their involvement in improving the quality of lives around them while still students. In reality, many of the students in our courses, especially at the graduate level, are adult learners who bring with them an abundance of service-related experiences and are already committed to making a difference in their communities. Curriculum-driven service learning, in order to enrich the experiences of adult learners, must take into account ways to accommodate their current involvements.

By expanding the viewpoints of students across campus from personal to local, from local to national, and from national to global, institutions of higher education lay a foundation for the more educated and active citizens of the future. Graduates will be able to contribute both personally and professionally to their home communities as informed and involved board members for local United Way agencies, as mentors at Boys and Girls Clubs, or as individuals who actively express their views to their political representatives or perhaps run for political office themselves.

As one looks to the National Association of Social Workers Code of Ethics, it is clear that the six core values driving the profession of social work could contribute to meaningful conversations with others across campus. Social workers are well experienced in translating these core values into principled actions:

- *Service*: to help people in need and to address social problems
- *Social justice*: to challenge social injustice
- *Dignity and worth of the person*: to respect the inherent dignity and worth of all persons
- *Importance of human relationships*: to engage people as partners in the helping process
- *Integrity*: to act in a trustworthy manner in alignment with the profession's values
- *Competence*: to develop and enhance cultural understanding and professional expertise (NASW 1999)

Instructors of traditional academic courses can teach students about the value of cultural diversity and the need to become more culturally aware, but it is the exposure to diversity through experiential learning that allows students to understand and appreciate more fully the contributions that result from a diverse society. Transformation takes place through exposure to new knowledge, application of core values, and active involvement in experiential learning and reflection.

The NASW Ethical Standard 6.01, Social Workers' Ethical Responsibilities to the Broader Society, sets forth our role to "promote social, economic, political, and cultural values and institutions that are compatible with the realization of social justice" (NASW 1999, 27). This standard could provide guidance to the American Democracy Project as it continues to evolve the value base of that national movement.

SOCIAL WORK EDUCATORS' CONTRIBUTIONS

Faculty members naturally adopt perspectives on service learning that are most relevant to their disciplinary approaches. In chapter 1, Amy Phillips suggested a relevant social justice orientation to service learning for social work educators. The theme of becoming a responsible citizen with the skills needed to pursue and promote positive social change runs through all social work courses. As faculty who have been teaching and designing service and experientially based curricula for decades, we are ideally situated to assist our colleagues across campus with integrating service learning into their own particular curricula. Social work educators have historically developed strong networks in communities and could connect campus colleagues to a variety of organizations, agencies, school settings, and government programs. Colleagues could also benefit from social work educators' partnerships, networking, and supervision skills. For example, on the authors' campus, a business class on leadership recently partnered with a social work class to produce a campuswide resource by collecting information on service-LEARNING projects from throughout the community to post on the university's American Democracy Project website.

Social work educators could help develop service-LEARNING workshops to bring faculty together for professional development and to learn how to integrate service learning into their curricula. Serving as consultants to faculty in other departments, social work educators could assist them in finding ways to achieve their course goals through service-learning experiences. Clearly, it is essential that the service activities be meaningful and relevant to the students and that they enhance their academic learning. Through the use of an integrated learning model such as that shown in figure 14.1, social work educators could assist other faculty in developing meaningful assignments.

An example utilizing the Integrated Learning Model can be seen in the partnership experience between a faculty member in the business-leadership class and a faculty member in the social work program teaching a graduate-level human behavior course. Collaboratively, the students designed a university Web page to display potential service-learning projects at local social service agencies. The business students provided the expertise to develop and design the university Web page, and the social work students served as consultants to the business students and provided linkages to the agencies. The social work faculty member began with the conceptual knowledge phase of the Integrated

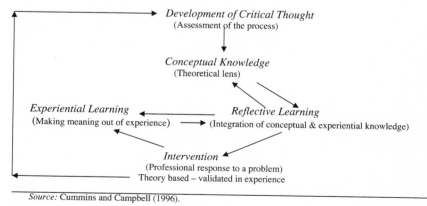

Source: Cummins and Campbell (1996).

Figure 14.1.   Integrated Learning Model

Learning Model. Through presentations, she integrated *theoretical content* about organizations, using examples from the students' experiences of attempting to work with agencies. These classroom discussions allowed the social work students to *conceptualize the knowledge* about organizations and *reflect on and integrate the conceptual and experiential knowledge* throughout the semester. Faculty members from both disciplines were able to guide the students' learning experiences through their *discipline-based conceptual knowledge* and develop the ability of their students to *think critically* through their *strategies of intervention*. When problems arose, the social work students relied upon their theory-based knowledge to design strategies for use by the business students. The advice provided by the social work students was validated when the business students were able to use *their* theory-based responses successfully. The critical thinking that resulted from this service-learning experience was invaluable to students from both disciplines and will enable them to develop higher-level critical-thinking skills that can be applied later to any situation. According to the Integrated Learning Model, the process is not carried out in steps or in a series but rather as a system that flows in many directions and is tested throughout the learning process.

Social work educators have the skills necessary to spearhead discussions of the value of service-LEARNING among faculty from diverse disciplines. These conversations could play a significant role in transforming the civic engagement culture of their campuses. Collaboration on interdisciplinary service-learning project teams could produce positive outcomes, bringing together like-minded faculty from across campus.

Historically, social work education has been grounded in experiential education, in developing social workers to improve communities and to take action based on the core values of the profession. What better opportunity for social work educators to further that goal than as leaders within the civic engagement movement on their campuses, leading the charge, setting standards, generating ideas, encouraging the novices in service learning, and integrating the values of the profession into campuswide initiatives.

REFERENCES

Boyer, E. (1990). *Scholarship reconsidered: Priorities of the professoriate*. Menlo Park, CA: Carnegie Foundation for the Advancement of Teaching.
———. (1996). The scholarship of engagement. *Journal of Public Outreach, 1*(1), 11–20.
Boyte, H., and Hollander, E. (2000). *Wingspread declaration on the civic responsibilities of research universities*. Retrieved February 1, 2006, from the Campus Compact website at www.campuscompact.org/resources/detail.php?id=62.

Bragg, N. (2000). *Faculty engagement in service learning*. Unpublished doctoral dissertation, Normal, Illinois State University.

Bringle, R. B., Games, R., and Malloy, E. A. (1999). *Colleges and universities as citizens*. Needham Heights, MA: Viacom.

Bringle, R. B., and Hatcher, J. A. (1996). Implementing service learning in higher education. *Journal of Higher Education, 67*(2), 221–39.

Cummins, L., and Campbell, M. (1996). *Walking our talk: The connection between integrated learning and integrated social work practice*. Paper presented at the Council on Social Work Education Annual Program Meeting, Iowa City, IA, 1996.

Driscoll, A. (2006). *Community engagement elective classification*. Retrieved August 31, 2006, from the Carnegie Foundation for the Advancement of Teaching website at www.carnegiefoundation.org/classifications/index.asp?key=1213.

Ehrlich, T. (Ed.). (2000). *Civic responsibility and higher education*. Phoenix, AZ: Orynx Press.

———. (2006). *Service-learning in undergraduate education: Where is it going?* Retrieved August 31, 2006, from the Carnegie Foundation for the Advancement of Teaching website at www.carnegiefoundation.org/perspectives/sub.asp?key=245&subkey=1251.

Furco, A. (1997). *School-sponsored service programs and the educational development of high school students*. Unpublished doctoral dissertation, University of California at Berkeley.

Holland, B. A., and Gelmon, S. (1998). The state of the "engaged campus." *AAHE Bulletin, 51*(2), 3–6.

Jacoby, B., and Associates. (1996). *Service-learning in higher education: Concepts and practices*. San Francisco, CA: Jossey-Bass.

Kendall, J. C., et al. (1990). *Combining service and learning: A resource book for community and public service*. Raleigh, NC: National Society for Internships and Experiential Education.

Mehaffy, G. L. (2005). The story of the American democracy project. *Change, 37*(5), 67–74.

National Association of Social Workers (NASW). (1999). *Code of ethics*. Washington, DC: Author.

Newman, F. (1985). *Higher education and the American resurgence*. Princeton, NJ: Carnegie Foundation for the Advancement of Teaching.

Saltmarsh, J. (2005). The civic promise of service learning. *Liberal Education, 91*(2), 50–55.

Sigmon, R. L. (1994). *Serving to learn, learning to serve: Linking service with learning*. Washington, DC: Council for Independent Colleges Report.

Stanton, T. K., Giles, D. E., Jr., and Cruz, N. I. (1999). *Service-learning: A movement's pioneers reflect on its origins, practice, and future*. San Francisco, CA: Jossey-Bass.

Index

AAHE. *See* American Association for Higher Education

abuse, 24, 138

academic content: integration of civic engagement into, 214; service learning v., 27, 47, 196

academic coursework: at Camp Viva, 141–42; community service integration with, 22; traditional, 215

academic practice, 26

Accreditation Standard 8, 161

accreditation standards, xiii, 8, 41, 50, 81, 93, 144, 176, 181, 190

activism, 121

Addams, Jane, 85

adolescence, 85

African American community, 98

agencies. *See* community partners

aging, 117, 118

alcoholism, 110

Allen, Robin, xiii, 54

Alvarez, A., 99

ambiguity, tolerance of, 103

American Association for Higher Education (AAHE), xii, 121, 131n2, 212

American Association of State Colleges and Universities, 213

American Behavioral Scientist, 11

American Democracy Project, 213, 215, 216

American Indian reservations, 45, 181

Ames, Natalie, xiii, 55

Amizade Global Service Learning, 45

analysis: method of, 203; pretest and posttest, 199–204

Anderson, D. K., 63

appearance, of students, 111

Arts and Science Curriculum Committee, 141

assessment: at American Indian reservation, 184; students' self, 171, 176; tools, 205

Association of Baccalaureate Social Work Program Directors (BPD), xii, 189

attitude, change of, 89

awareness: GLBT, 123; social work and, self, 86–87, 171; students', 31, 88, 158, 171, 214

baccalaureate social work (BSW), 63, 80, 93, 96, 167, 168, 172, 174

Bacon, Francis, 46

Bailey, D., 93

Batchelder, T. H., 95

219

behavior, 51, 86
beliefs, change of, 89
Benson, L., 46
Billig, S., 205
biology, 110–11
Blackboard, 45, 151, 153; Discussion
  Board of, 161
Boise State University, 147, 162
Bolaños, Patricia, xiii, 55
boundaries, 112
Boyer, Ernest L., 4, 212
BPD. *See* Association of Baccalaureate
  Social Work Program Directors
Bragg, Nancy, xiv
Brascia, Kara, xiii, 54
Bringle, R., 21
BSW. *See* baccalaureate social work
Bureau of Indian Affairs, 183
Bush, George, 9
Butin, D. W., 27, 28
Butler, S. S., 63
Butterfield, A. K. Johnson, 6–7

CAAF. *See* Children Affected by AIDS
  Foundation
Campbell, Mary, xiv
campus, xiv, 3, 4, 121, 125, 210;
  engaged, 212; service-learning
  activities on, 49
Campus Compact, xiv, 3, 4, 121, 210
Campus Outreach Opportunity League
  (COOL), 3, 209
Camp Viva, 133, 135–37, 144;
  academic component of, 141–42;
  Campus Ministries Center,
  connection between, 144; Family
  Time at, 143; field placement v., 143;
  orientation of, 139–40; outcomes of,
  142–45; paper, 141; schedule of,
  140; screening process, 139; social
  work values of, 138; staff members,
  136–37; students' connection to
  campers at, 143; students'
  responsibilities at, 140; volunteers
  for, 137, 144

"The Camp Viva Experience," 137–38,
  139, 143, 144, 145
"Can You Guess the Straight Person?"
  126
capstone process, at Trinity Christian
  College, 169–77
career, choosing, 87–88
Carlson, Patricia, xi, xiii, 55
Carnegie Foundation for the
  Advancement of Teaching, 212, 213,
  214
Cedar Crest College, 61, 69, 72
Cedar Crest Democratic Academy, 61
Cedar Crest Political Engagement
  Module, 67
"change versus charity," 9, 47
Charlesworth, Leanne, xiii, 54
Checkoway, Barry, 6
Cheyenne River Lakota Reservation,
  184
Chicago Awareness Center, 98
children: differences of professional
  opinions about, 88; poverty rate of,
  78; preparation of, 79
Children Affected by AIDS Foundation
  (CAAF), 135
Christianity, 167
citizens, 210; active, 214; graduates as
  responsible, 212; oppressed, 11;
  responsible, 215
citizenship, 62; preparation for active,
  213
civic engagement, 4–5, 61, 162, 217;
  service learning and, 6–9, 212–13;
  social work's values of, 214–15
civic responsibility, 29, 209, 213, 214
civil rights movement, 195
classroom, 155; in community, 160;
  democratic, approach, 67–68;
  discussions, 113–14, 217;
  engagement, 61, 62; field placement
  issues and, 8; integration of
  experience with learning from, 113,
  127; learning, 29, 32; learning,
  application of, 77, 96, 107; learning

Just Practice Framework (Finn and
 Jacobson), 13n4

Kahne, Joseph, 9, 47
Kasper, B., 93–94
Kendall, J. C., 142
Kettering Foundation, 210
King, M., 135
King, M. E., 54
Kinsey, D., 28
Knee, Ryan Tolleson, 11
knowledge: application of, 4, 25–26, 29,
 77, 107, 130–31, 148; integrating
 two elements of, 41
Koney, K., 93
Koob, J. J., 135
Kropf, N., 7, 8

Lakota Nation, 182–83
language, absence of Lakota, 183
Lawndale HIV Community Intervention
 Project, 174
leadership, 43, 216
learning. *See* classroom; education
Lee, C. R., 108
Lee, J. A. B., 25
legislation, 213–14
liberals, 195
lifespan development theory, 110–11
Likert scale, 71, 176
longitudinal studies, 205; on impact of
 service learning, 181
Lovell-Troy, Larry, 10

macro dimension, 83–84, 93–94, 96,
 98
Majewski, Virginia, xiii, xiv
"Making GLBT Issues Visible on a
 Rural, Catholic Midwestern
 Campus," 125
Malinowski, Rose, xiii, 55
Marullo, S., 11, 48
master of social work (MSW), 63, 137,
 145, 199

matching. *See* partnering process
maturation, 190
"mature service," 10
Maybach, C. W., 182
"Meaning of Difference," 124, 126
media: portrayal of college students,
 209; students required to view, 159
meetings, 65; face-to-face, 71;
 precourse, 73
Michalski, J., 134–35
*Michigan Journal of Community Service
 Learning*, 4, 212
micro practice courses, 34–36
middle class, 122
Midwestern Deans and Directors
 Forum, 93
Miley, K. K., 24
Mills, C. Wright, 10
Minnesota Human Rights, 122
Mishna, F., 134, 135
morals, 214
mortality, 190–91
Morton, K., 9
Mosca, J. L., 94
MSW. *See* master of social work
multisite shotgun model, 155–56,
 157–58

Nadel, Meryl, xiii, 45, 56
naïve thinking, 53
Nasstrom, K. L., 108
NASW. *See* National Association of
 Social Workers
National Association of Social Workers
 (NASW), 74, 198, 213; Code of
 Ethics, 214–15; Ethical Standard
 6.01, 215
National Coming-Out Week, 125
National Community Service Act, 26,
 28, 210
National Institute for Social Work and
 Human Services in Rural Areas, 189
national legislation, in support of
 service learning, 3

About the Authors

Robin Allen, MSW, PhD, is an associate professor and director of the BSW program in the School of Social Work at Boise State University in Boise, Idaho. Her research interests include service learning, school social work, and understanding the impact of gender on violence. Dr. Allen may be contacted at rallen@boisestate.edu.

Natalie Ames, MSW, EdD, is an assistant professor in the Department of Social Work at North Carolina State University in Raleigh. Her research interests include the scholarship of teaching and learning, health literacy, access to health care, and health disparities. Dr. Ames can be contacted at nrames @social.chass.ncsu.edu.

Patricia Bolaños, PhD, is an associate professor of Spanish in the Hispanic Studies Department at St. John's University and the College of Saint Benedict in St. Joseph, Minnesota. She is a faculty member of the Gender and Women's Studies Department, where she teaches on a regular basis. She may be contacted at pbolanos@csbsju.edu.

Nancy Bragg, MS in Ed, EdD, is an instructional assistant professor in the Educational Administration and Foundations and the Curriculum and Instruction departments at Illinois State University in Normal. Along with service learning, she is interested in reflection, theory to practice, professional learning communities, teaching who we are, and enhancing student development. Dr. Bragg may be contacted at njbragg@ilstu.edu.

Kara Brascia, MS, is the director of service learning at Boise State University in Boise, Idaho. She has twelve years of experience building campus-community partnerships among faculty, students, and community agencies. Her research focuses on public information campaigns and volunteer management. She may be reached at karabrascia@boisestate.edu.

Mary Campbell, MSW, is an associate professor in the School of Social Work at Illinois State University in Normal. Her interests lie in the areas of community development, the impact of international adoption, service learning, and homelessness. She can be contacted at mecampb@ilstu.edu.

Patricia Carlson, MSW, is an instructor at the School of Social Work at the University of Nebraska at Omaha. She incorporates service learning into her macro courses and is involved in community development efforts. She also chairs the Admissions Committee and may be contacted at pcarlson@mail.unomaha.edu.

Leanne Charlesworth, MSW, PhD, is an assistant professor in the Department of Social Work at Nazareth College in Rochester, New York. In addition to pedagogy, her areas of interest include poverty, child maltreatment, and child and family well-being. Dr. Charlesworth may be reached at LCharle8@naz.edu.

Stephene A. Diepstra, MSW, PhD, has teaching experience at both the undergraduate and graduate levels. Her research interests include foster care and adoption, as well as the incorporation of service learning into social work courses. She may be contacted at diepstra@sbcglobal.net.

David C. Droppa, PhD, is an associate professor of social work and field coordinator at Seton Hill University, Greensburg, Pennsylvania. He also maintains a private clinical and consultation practice. His research interests include service learning in policy practice, families, outcome evaluation, and collaboration among human service organizations. Dr. Droppa may be contacted at droppa@setonhill.edu.

Sharlene Furuto, MSW, EdD, is a professor in and chairperson of the Social Work Department at Brigham Young University, Hawaii, in Laie, Oahu. Besides service learning, she is interested in cross-cultural research with an emphasis on Asian and Pacific Islander Americans and the indigenous and formal social welfare systems in Oceanic and Asian Rim countries. She encourages global collaboration and may be contacted at Furutos@byuh.edu.

Annemarie V. House, MSW, is an associate professor of social work, director of undergraduate field education, and director of the Office for Students with Disabilities at Nazareth College in Rochester, New York. As a licensed clinical social worker, her practice areas include field instruction, child welfare, and gerontology. She can be contacted at ahouse7@naz.edu.

Virginia Majewski, MSW, PhD, is an associate professor in and chairperson of the Division of Social Work at West Virginia University in Morgantown. In addition to service learning as a pedagogical approach for social justice, her research and teaching interests include hunger and food insecurity, rural community organizing, and American Indian issues. Dr. Majewski may be contacted at Vimajewski@mail.wvu.edu.

Rose Malinowski, MSW, DrPH, is an associate professor and director of field education in the Social Work Department at Trinity Christian College in Palos Heights, Illinois. In addition to service learning, her research interests include family violence and spirituality and social work practice. Dr. Malinowski may be contacted at rose.malinowski@trnty.edu.

Meryl Nadel, MSW, DSW, is an associate professor in and director of the Center for Social Research in the Social Work Department at Iona College, New Rochelle, New York. In addition to service learning, her research interests include social work and social welfare history, prevention, qualitative methods, and social work involvement in the summer camp movement. She may be contacted at mnadel@iona.edu.

Amy Phillips, MSSW, MDiv, PhD, is an associate professor of social work at Minnesota State University, Moorhead. Her professional interests focus on antiracism, cultural competence, and service learning. Dr. Phillips may be contacted at ap@mnstate.edu.

William Rainford, MSW, PhD, is an assistant professor in the School of Social Work at Boise State University in Boise, Idaho, where he teaches at both the BSW and MSW levels. His areas of expertise in both the classroom and as a researcher are social policy, government welfare programs, homelessness, and paternalistic regulation of women in society. Dr. Rainford can be reached at willrainford@boisestate.edu.

Roy Rodenhiser, MSW, EdD, is an associate professor in and director of the Boise State University School of Social Work in Boise, Idaho. In addition to service learning, his research interests include assessment of social work education and assessment of organizations. Dr. Rodenhiser may be contacted at royrodenhiser@boisestate.edu.

Paul Sather, MSW, is the director of the Service Learning Academy at the University of Nebraska at Omaha (UNO). He served as the associate director of the UNO School of Social Work from 1998 to 2004. He may be reached at psather@mail.unomaha.edu.

Marilyn Sullivan-Cosetti, MSW, PhD, is an associate professor in and director of the Seton Hill University Social Work Program in Greensburg, Pennsylvania. Her research interests include service learning in the academy, juvenile female violent offenders, and community organization practice. Dr. Sullivan-Cosetti may be reached at Cosetti@setonhill.edu.

Allan Turner, MSW, PhD, is an assistant professor in and director of the MSW program at Edinboro University of Pennsylvania in Edinboro. In addition to service learning, his professional and research interests focus on mental health service provision to individuals with severe and persistent mental illness.

Dr. Marie L. Watkins is the director of the Weider Center for Service Learning and associate professor in the Department of Social Work at Nazareth College in Rochester, New York. Dr. Watkins's areas of research interest include gender equity, after-school programs, community youth development, and macro social work practice. She can be reached at mwatkin2@naz.edu.

Barbara Weitz, MPA, MSW, taught undergraduate social work courses at the University of Nebraska at Omaha, from 1989 to 2005. Service learning was integrated into her social work research and women's issues courses. Her current research is focused on women and leadership. She can be reached at bweitz@mail.unomaha.edu.

John R. Yoakam, MDiv, PhD, is an associate professor in and chair of the Social Work Department at the College of St. Benedict/St. John's University in St. Joseph, Minnesota. In addition to service learning, his research interests include gay, lesbian, bisexual, and transgender studies; gerontology; social welfare history; and HIV/AIDS. Dr. Yoakam may be contacted at jyoakam@csbsju.edu.